LONDON
AND THE
Georgian Navy

LONDON
AND THE
Georgian Navy

PHILIP MacDOUGALL

The
History
Press

Front cover illustrations. Top: Somerset House from the south or riverside, *c.* 1820; *below:* The naval dockyard at Deptford in 1810.

First published 2013

The History Press
The Mill, Brimscombe Port
Stroud, Gloucestershire, GL5 2QG
www.thehistorypress.co.uk

British Library Cataloguing in Publication Data.
A catalogue record for this book is available from the British Library.

ISBN 978 0 7524 7485 4

Typesetting and origination by The History Press
Printed in Great Britain

Contents

Introduction

While many books have been published on the history of London, none have concentrated on the metropolis and its associations with the Royal Navy. Yet, as I demonstrate in this book, there were few areas of the capital that were not, in some way, either connected with the Navy or dependent upon it for survival and growth.

The most obvious connection was that London was the centre where all decisions relating to the Navy were taken and then actioned. Here, the Palace of Westminster and Downing Street were important players in the decisions taken as to levels of funding and how the fleet would be deployed. In addition, the Admiralty possessed a number of administrative buildings strung across London, together with supply and manufacturing bases that turned a government desire into actuality.

As for the City, London's original business zone, this was no less connected with the Navy. During the Georgian period the City was dominated by expanding mercantile companies together with the banks. Indeed, it was entirely dependent upon the sea service for its very existence. Without the Royal Navy there would have been few possibilities for growth, given that the City's financial expansion was very much dependent on overseas trade. Fundamentally, the Navy ensured the existence of safe sea lanes that permitted extensive numbers of London-based companies to embark upon overseas trade in the first place. Of equal importance was a strong and powerful Navy able to support overseas military expeditions of conquest that also created trading monopolies controlled by the larger City trading enterprises. And this goes without even mentioning the Navy's own insatiable desire for materials, much of them met by London-based merchants operating through the city markets. In fact, the Navy was as dependent on the City, as the City was upon the Navy. While the latter provided security for overseas trade, the City ensured that the infrastructure (including credit facilities) was available for the Navy to expand in unison with trade.

Another important connection with the Navy existed to the east of the City and in many of those outlying parishes that were part of the great urban conglomeration. Administratively separate from London they might have been, technically falling into the counties of Essex, Kent and Middlesex, but physically they were either indistinct or, in the case of Kentish London, rapidly becoming indistinct by way of geography and common pursuit from the city. Here existed the Navy's industrial base: various dockyards, both private and government owned, that built and repaired many of the Navy's ships while also housing the artisans who carried out this skilled work. Nor did it stop there, for on the east side of London were various centres for the processing and storage of food as required by the crews of these same warships together with storage areas for various items of ships' equipment including ordnance.

And the connection still does not end. A sizeable proportion of any crew that manned the Navy's warships would also be drawn from London. Many ships had 30 per cent or more of their crew drawn from the London area. This particularly applied to the lower deck, the seamen who carried out the labour-intensive tasks of moving the sails and manning the guns. For the most part they also came from the east side of the metropolis, an area dominated by the shipping world and so spawning trained seamen in great number. In total contrast, the more affluent areas to the west were home to many officers of the quarterdeck, not necessarily born and bred in London, but living there because of its proximity to the Admiralty.

Prologue: Death of a Hero

Georgian London and the Royal Navy were a completely intertwined entity. Each and every sector of the great metropolis was connected in some way with the sea service. The most palpable of these links was direct employment, with thousands of Londoners at various times having either served on board a ship of war or contributed to the work that kept the Navy at sea. Far less obvious was the connection that most others in London also had with the Navy, through the fact of London's wealth being dependent on the ability of the Navy to protect overseas trade. London was entirely reliant on this trade, being a great commercial city that had been created to sustain the merchant and the financial profits he generated. Everyone who lived in London benefited in some way from the Navy. It was a symbiotic connection but, because of its partial invisibility, many were quite oblivious of this uncontracted bond.

How could it be otherwise? The near-destitute crossing sweeper or marginally better off waterman might make few connections between the possession of an income, however minimal, and the wealth that supported the complex infrastructure of which they were a part. But recognition of the Navy as special was something they did share with those who, through being more closely connected with commerce, were more aware of how the naval and commercial world were mutually dependent.

Of course, there were down sides to this close association, and these affected Londoners in different ways. Most obvious was the expense of maintaining such a force: this was borne by those with any sort of income. And even if you could not afford to pay for the Navy, you might end up serving in it. The press gang was only one way that the Navy recruited men to its service. But any resulting concerns were seemingly put aside when the capital was mourning a naval loss or celebrating a triumph. Sea battles, in particular, would result in adulatory crowds, celebratory banquets and gifts galore poured upon those who had orchestrated such a masterful stroke. Similarly, anyone perceived to have failed or to have acted against the immemorial traditions of the service, would find a London mob stoning the windows of their town houses or having an effigy of their likeness publicly burnt.

The Battle of Trafalgar, resulting in the destruction of a combined French and Spanish fleet, was one of the most decisive naval engagements ever fought. It brought London's adulation of the Navy to new heights. Yet the tone of the celebrations was tempered by the loss of the city's favourite admiral, the often controversial Lord Nelson. As one London newspaper, *The Times* editorialised:

> That the triumph, great and glorious as it is, has been dearly bought, and that such was the general opinion, was powerfully evinced in the deep and universal affliction with which the news of Lord Nelson's death was received. (*The Times*, 7 November 1805)

Suggestive, indeed, of a widely held viewpoint was the notion, also pursued by *The Times*, that:

> There was not a man who did not think that the life of the Hero of the Nile was too great a price for the capture and destruction of twenty sail of French and Spanish men of war. (*The Times*, 7 November 1805)

The Morning Post, another widely read London newspaper, put a different spin on the event, but still regarded the loss of Nelson as a tragedy:

> But while we mourn at the fate of Britain's darling son, we have the consolation to reflect that he has closed his career of glory by a work that will place his name so high on the tablet of immortality, that succeeding patriots can only gaze with enthusiasm, scarcely hope to reach the envied elevation, whilst a nation's tears, to the latest period of time, will drop like so many bright gems upon the page of history that recalls the fall of the great hero. (*The Morning Post*, 7 November 1805)

Although the battle itself had taken place on 21 October 1805, the news was not confirmed until a dispatch from Admiral Collingwood arrived at the Admiralty in Whitehall during the early hours of Thursday 6 November. This told of 'a complete and glorious victory' but one tainted by the loss of him 'whose name will be immortal and his memory ever dear to his country'. First Lord of the Admiralty, Charles Middleton, 1st Baron Barham, having been awoken at 1.30 a.m., immediately set about ensuring that the news was taken to the King, then at Windsor Castle, and various ministers of state. Among the latter was Prime Minister William Pitt; an Admiralty messenger took the news to nearby Downing Street. Pitt was awoken from his sleep, something to which he was not unaccustomed, although on this occasion he was unable to return to his repose, continually reflecting on the image of the 'immortal Admiral' whom he had so recently spoken to in that very house.

News of Trafalgar now began to spread by word of mouth, helped by the publication of an 'extraordinary' edition of the government-authorised *London Gazette* together with a second, late morning edition of some of the London newspapers. For those who, by mid-morning, were still not in the know, a hint of something unusual having taken place was given by the firing of an accolade of guns in Hyde Park and on the Tower. Yet, through the loss of Nelson, feelings towards the victory were mixed, resulting in a confused response. While guns may have been blazing away in the morning, many of the owners of larger houses around the city, who would normally have bathed their mansions in a blaze of light, merely showed a few plain lamps in the windows, these soon to be joined by wreaths that bore the telling motto, 'Nelson and Victory'. The theatres of London also reflected this ambiguity. The Theatre Royal, Covent Garden, in an impromptu addition to the evening performance, had on stage statuesque naval heroes and a half-length portrait of Nelson that carried the epigram 'Horatio Nelson OB 21st Oct'.

It was not until the following day, Thursday 7 November, that full details of the battle really became available. The morning editions of all the London papers carried the unedited copy of Collingwood's dispatch that had appeared in the *London Gazette Extraordinary*.

By now, others had considered how they would treat the event. In particular the larger business institutions of the City, in contrast to the muted lighting to be found elsewhere, elected to emphasise their indebtedness to Nelson and the Royal Navy by heavily decorating the exterior of a number of key buildings. The Guildhall, with a bust of Nelson as a centrepiece, was emblazoned with a crown and anchor over the front of the building, while India House, the home of the East India Company, was decorated with lamps that were offset by a huge anchor motif to the front and stars on each side of the building. So impressive was this particular display that 'it was hardly possible to move along the street' due to the illuminations having 'attracted such a crowd of people' (*The Morning Chronicle*, 8 November 1805). At the Theatre Royal in Covent Garden, music was now added to the original impromptu display while at Drury Lane, performances were ending with a rousing chorus of *Rule, Britannia!*

The behaviour of those from the seamier underside of the metropolis, otherwise known as the London mob, was also strange. Normally, the mob could turn any piece of sensational news into several nights of lawlessness, but it too was muted, for not 'a single pane of glass was broken from one end of the town to the other', with the knowing correspondent of *The Morning Chronicle* explaining that while 'the voice of the mob is in general more imperative' on this occasion its views were exercised in 'moderation' (*The Morning Chronicle*, 8 November 1805).

As the weekend approached, so did one of London's grandest annual events: the banquet at Mansion House that honoured the newly elected Lord Mayor, on this occasion, Sir James Shaw. Attended by the elite of the City and those in London that the City most wished to impress, the guests included royalty, high-ranking ministers of state (including the Prime Minister) and leading merchants. Among those also invited were the Russian, Prussian and Turkish ambassadors. Inevitably, therefore, every effort was made to emphasise both the importance of the recent victory and the capital's commitment to the on-going war against Napoleon's France. To this end, Nelson became a useful point of focus, with the The Times on the morning of the banquet reporting:

> The preparations made for the dinner on this day are on a very grand scale. The inside of Guildhall is adorned with different devices. The whole length portrait of Lord Nelson is removed out of the council chamber, and placed over the seat of the Lord Mayor, with a prodigious number of lamps, and the flags of the different nations he has conquered. At the Sheriff's table is placed a bust, in marble, with the brow of the conqueror of the Nile adorned with oak and laurel leaves. (The Times, 11 November 1805)

Lloyd's, through its particular connections with maritime trade, was another London institution heavily indebted to the Navy. At that time housed in the Royal Exchange, Lloyd's showed its gratitude through establishing in July 1803 the Patriotic Fund that provided grants for those wounded while in the service of the Crown. Trafalgar, although a British victory, had resulted in a considerable number of British seamen suffering death or injury. At a special meeting of the fund management committee, held on 14 November, it was agreed that a further appeal should be sent to both existing and possible new subscribers, with pledged sums accepted by all branch banks within the greater metropolis and also at the bar of Lloyd's Coffee House. By mid-December, over £23,000 had been received, with Lloyd's and its subscribers contributing the greatest amount but with additional sums also received from collections made in churches. This was made easier by the King declaring Thursday 5 December as a day of General Thanksgiving to Almighty God. Temple Church and Lincoln's Inn Chapel, which were frequented by the legal fraternity, raised £321 and £181 respectively.

For most Londoners, the desire to celebrate the victory at Trafalgar was impeded by an equal need to mourn the loss of the hero. Giving generously to church collections on the day of remembrance was, in itself, a significant act that helped resolve the problem while helping reinforce the clear line that stood between celebrating the victory and grieving for the dead. In placing notes and coins into the collection plates, many were heard to mention the name of Nelson with a sigh. Of even greater importance, and further assuaging London's desire to memorialise the man who had led the fleet, was that Nelson was soon to be honoured with a state funeral. Admittedly, in his will, Nelson had requested that he be buried alongside his reverend father in the churchyard of Burnham Thorpe, but he had then conveniently added 'unless his majesty should be graciously pleased to direct other ways'. Almost certainly, if Nelson had not provided the necessary codicil, the request in his will would have been ignored, since it had become an essential national requirement that St Paul's Cathedral should be his final resting place.

The planned funeral procession, which would pass from the Admiralty in Whitehall, into the Strand and then along Fleet Street, would have the advantage of providing a suitably extended route that would allow thousands of Londoners to line the streets and be part of the final act. Previous to this, the general populace was also to be given the chance of paying its respects to the body lying in state at the Seamen's Hospital in Greenwich.

It was on board *Victory*, the flagship at Trafalgar, that Nelson was returned to England, secured in a complex arrangement of coffins that saw the body directly placed in one of elm, the timber for this previously taken from *L'Orient*, a French ship destroyed at the Battle of the Nile. In turn, this elm coffin had been placed into a completely sealed lead coffin, before the two were placed in a much larger one also made out of elm. With *Victory* anchoring off Sheerness on Sunday 21 December, the body was then transferred on the following day to the Seamen's Hospital at Greenwich, carried up river by the naval yacht *Chatham*. Arriving just after 1 p.m., the triple coffin arrangement was taken off at dusk and carried by some of the crew of *Victory* to King William Court and the vast Painted Hall.

However, the coffin viewed by the general public on the three days of lying in state was outwardly different from the one that was brought from the Mediterranean. Instead of the plain elm exterior, something much more magnificent had been added. Designed by a number of leading London craftsmen, the publicly seen coffin was of mahogany and decorated with a series of panels representing national symbols or Nelson's past deeds. Included, for instance, was a lion holding the union flag and a crocodile that represented the victory at Aboukir Bay.

During Nelson's lying in state, the Painted Hall was hung with black cloth and brilliantly lit by fifty-six candles in silver holders. Placed at the upper, raised end of the hall was the decorated mahogany coffin, covered by black drape with only the foot uncovered. Set around the coffin were various flags, including ten placed a few steps back and emblazoned with the single emotive word: Trafalgar.

This was the opportunity for which much of London had waited: the chance to directly pay respect. With Sunday 5 January set aside as the first day, the township of Greenwich was thrown into total confusion. All regular stagecoaches travelling to Greenwich were packed, with the passengers they disgorged into the town joined by hundreds more who had travelled by hackney carriage. Accidents by the score were reported to litter the roads around Greenwich, and a number of carriages overturned in their haste to reach the sought destination. Adding to the confusion were many thousand pedestrians thronging the roads out of London, all making their way to the gates of the hospital. Chaos reigned supreme! Matters were not helped when an official announcement that the hospital would open at 9 a.m. was later countermanded by an instruction that, due to a service taking place in the Painted Hall, the gates of the hospital would remain closed until 11 a.m. This ensured that by mid-morning a great and eager multitude had assembled. Upon the gates being opened, and despite attempts to limit entry, the crowd simply pressed forward:

> The scene now became very alarming. The most fearful female shrieks assailed the ear on every side. Several persons were trodden underfoot and greatly hurt. One man had his eye literally torn out by coming into contact with one of the entrance gateposts. Vast numbers of ladies and gentlemen lost their shoes, hats, shawls and the ladies fainted in every direction. (*The Morning Chronicle*, 2 January 1806)

Fortunately, on approaching the Painted Hall and the steps that provided access, matters were better organised and a large contingency of the Greenwich Volunteers ensured a single-file entry and exit.

On the following day, through the arrival of the King's Life Guards, accidents were much reduced. Of events on the third day, *The Times* provided a graphic description:

> The steps leading up to the entrance of the Great Hall was the principal scene of contest; and curiosity, the ruling passion of the fair sex, rising superior to all of the suggestions of feminine timidity, many ladies pushed into the crowd, and were so severely squeezed, that many of them fainted away, and were carried off apparently senseless to the colonnade; we were however highly gratified that they were rather frightened than hurt and that no injury occurred more serious than a degree of pressure not altogether so great as could be wished. (*The Times*, 8 January 1806)

Elsewhere in London, plans were going ahead for the organisation of the actual funeral, with considerable responsibility placed into the hands of the Royal Heralds and the College of Arms. Traditionally responsible to the Sovereign for all matters connected with heraldry, it also had a general responsibility for the organisation of large state occasions. It was this body that announced that the public would be admitted to the hospital at 9 a.m. each morning, so helping create the chaos that descended upon Greenwich on the Sunday. It was the College of Arms that would establish orders of precedence, requiring that nobility, clergy and gentry who wished to join the public funeral procession from the Admiralty to St Paul's Cathedral should supply their title, names and addresses. With this information they would be 'ranked in the procession according to their several degrees, dignities and qualities'. It was also laid down that dress was to be mourning, with any servants in attendance to be similarly attired.

It is at this point that another hero of the age, albeit the fictional creation of C.S. Forester, enters the story. This is Horatio Hornblower, then a newly appointed captain in the Royal Navy and charged with overseeing the transfer of Nelson's body from the Seamen's Hospital to Whitehall Steps. As with the funeral procession itself, this was to be a highly formal occasion, with the College of Arms once again playing a leading role. For this reason, Hornblower has to meet with Henry Pallender, described as the Blue Mantle Pursuivant at Arms at the College of Heralds. Undoubtedly, Hornblower was referring to the Bluemantle Pursuivant of Arms in Ordinary, a junior officer of the College of Arms, a post at that time held not by Henry Pallender but by a certain Francis Martin. At the meeting Hornblower receives details of the task ahead of him:

> Along the processional route apparently there were fifteen points at which minute guns were to be fired, and His Majesty would be listening to see that they were properly timed. Hornblower covered more paper with notes. There would be thirty-eight boats and barges in the procession, to be assembled in the tricky tideway at Greenwich, marshaled in order, brought up to Whitehall Steps, and dispersed again after delivering over the body to a naval guard of honour assembled there which would escort it to the Admiralty to lie there for the night before the final procession to St. Paul's. (C.S. Forester, *Hornblower and the Atropos*, 1953, Ch. 1)

Although in the book Hornblower encountered a problem with the funeral barge he commanded, when it sprang a serious leak and nearly sank, no such difficulty was encountered in reality. On Wednesday 8 January, Nelson's coffin was carried out of the Painted Hall to the northern gates of the hospital that led to the river. Proceeded by 500 Greenwich Pensioners together with a royal band of fifes and drums playing the *Dead March* from *Saul*, it was followed in turn by Sir Peter Parker, Admiral of the Fleet and chief mourner, together with his supporters and assistants. Also in attendance were numerous naval officers including six lieutenants from *Victory*:

> The body being placed on board the state barge, the several members of the procession took their place on board their appointed barges, when the Lord Mayor of London Corporation, proceeded from the Painted Chamber, uncovered, to the river side, and went on board their respective barges, appropriately decorated for the solemn occasion, the great bell over the south-east colonnade chiming a funeral peal the whole time. (*The Times*, 9 January 1806)

The barge, rowed by sailors from *Victory*, carried Nelson's coffin along the Thames towards the City. A flood tide flowed in its favour, but there was a strong wind blowing against the barge.

Along the banks from Greenwich to Westminster Bridge, an immense concourse formed, while to witness the carriage of the coffin from Whitehall Stairs to the Admiralty, the overlooking windows and streets were crowded with spectators.

With Hornblower much relieved that his charge did not sink below the waters of the Thames, and with the coffin safely secured within the Admiralty, the final act was now about to commence. This was the ceremonial carriage of the coffin to St Paul's Cathedral and the service of interment. Everything now hinged on the Court of Arms having thoroughly prepared for that day. With the eyes of the nation and hundreds of thousands of Londoners wishing to play their part, nothing could be permitted to go wrong. Among the best prepared were the owners of buildings that stretched along the Strand and Fleet Street, many of them having advertised the availability of their windows to those who might be interested. In various London newspapers, adverts, including this one in *The Times*, appeared in the days leading up to the funeral:

LORD NELSON'S FUNERAL. – LADIES and GENTLEMEN may be accommodated with SEATS to see the Grand PROCESSION, on the First Floor, having a commodious bow window, commanding an expansive view of St Dunstan's Church nearly to the Old Bailey. Enquire at No. 184 Fleet Street. Please ring the bell.

A vast number of labourers were fully occupied during the night that preceded the funeral, cleaning and laying gravel along the length of Whitehall, the Strand and Fleet Street. Just as the labourers completed their work, and with morning beginning to break, volunteer units, such as the East London Militia, the Royal York Marylebone Volunteers and the East India Regiment, began to take up position along the now cleansed length of the three thoroughfares. At Hyde Park too, mounted Life Guards were also present at this unusual hour. They were responsible, under instruction from the College of Arms, for assembling the arriving carriages that would be joining the procession before leading them across Piccadilly, into St James's Park and through Horse Guards to the Admiralty. A failure to ensure that the officers were fully versed with their task was to create problems later in the day, when it was discovered that not everyone had been correctly placed by rank, quality and status, requiring an impromptu reorganisation outside the cathedral and thus causing one unnecessary delay.

At half past ten, the procession set out from the Admiralty, led by the Duke of York at the head of several regiments. Following immediately behind were twelve marines and forty-eight seamen who had served under Nelson. They were playing a particularly important role in the day's events and drew a firm connection between the battle and those who had suffered. The College of Arms had also bestowed upon itself a particularly important position within the procession, with messengers of the College, the Blue Mantle Pursuivant and the Rouge Dragon Pursuivant of Arms, all in separate carriages, among the front rank. As for the nobility, still not in order of status, they were immediately in front of the coffin that had been placed on a funeral car designed to take on the appearance of *Victory* through having been given a stern carved in naval fashion.

At St Paul's Cathedral, several tiers of seating had been set aside for the public, with these fully occupied by 7 a.m. To prevent the remaining reserved seats being similarly taken, 200 members of the London Regiment of Militia had been ordered on guard. Fortunately, for the dignity of the College of Arms, they were completely successful in carrying out this arduous use of their military training. As for the funeral procession, this did not even begin to arrive at the cathedral until well past midday, with a two-hour service not to commence until around 4 p.m. As such, one has to marvel at the dedication of those members of the public who had to remain in position for over nine hours, since the slightest attempt to move would almost certainly have resulted in the loss of that precious seat.

Much now went as might be expected: those who formed the funeral procession having arrived and entered, anthems were sung, orations given and the coffin finally brought to its assigned area beneath the great dome. Here, the stone floor had been cut away, allowing the coffin to be lowered directly into the crypt. First though, the dean of the cathedral read the remainder of the funeral service, with a herald from the College of Arms proclaiming the style and title of the deceased and concluding with a full description of the merits of Lord Nelson. Now the ceremony of lowering the body began, continuing for about ten minutes, during which time the building was in total silence. Breaking into the planned arrangement, however, were the actions of the crew of *Victory* who had escorted the coffin. At the end of the ceremony it had been intended that they should carefully furl the scarred battle flags that *Victory* had flown at Trafalgar and which covered the coffin. However, instead of following their instructions, the crew tore the flag in strips, each taking a piece as a memento of the commander they so admired.

Two notable absentees were the Prime Minister, William Pitt, and the King. For his part, Pitt had the perfect excuse. Terminally ill, he had less than two weeks of life ahead of him and was at the time of the funeral convalescing in the spa resort of Bath. As for the King, such an event was probably viewed as beneath his dignity. But much more important, in the case of Nelson, the King was one of the few people in the country who despised the man, disapproving of the way Nelson had discarded his wife and embarked on a very public relationship with Emma Hamilton. Invited to a levee at the Palace of St James shortly after the Battle of the Nile, the King, aware as he was of the relationship with Emma Hamilton, had asked of Nelson a question but then pointedly turned away before the answer was given. Nor did Nelson's success at Trafalgar temper this lack of regard, for on receiving the news at Windsor the King certainly expressed his regret but went on to dictate a letter that bestowed all of his praise upon Nelson's second-in-command, Lord Collingwood.

With London having now laid to rest the man who had masterminded the great triumph, attention could be given to how best to maintain and make use of this acquired seaborne supremacy. Much of Nelson's legacy was to be in the hands of London's merchants and traders, who now had a further assurance that vessels sent out would be even safer while at sea. For this reason, ever-greater numbers of ships began to leave the wharves and newly built docks along the banks of the Thames. The decisive victory at Trafalgar and the continued employment of Royal Navy warships throughout the world's oceans ensured that London (if it did not already) had surely reached the point where it as good as ruled the world.

THE ADMINISTRATIVE HUB

Introduction

London was the administrative hub of the Georgian Navy and, as such, the home of a massive bureaucratic infrastructure. Here were to be found the men who ultimately controlled the destiny of the nation, manipulating the world's largest seagoing fleet to ensure the continuance and growth of London's dominance over much of the world. While a few of the individuals in the upper echelons of naval administration also appear in the wider annals of history, the vast majority, even if they were generally known at the time, have been lost to subsequently written history. But, known or unknown, they ensured the global presence of the Navy, giving it the ability to defend Britain's commercial interests wherever they might be threatened. By the end of the Napoleonic Wars, this administrative hub was responsible for the building of warships, the repair and maintenance of over 900 ships in service, the recruitment, provisioning and medical needs of 130,000 seamen, and the delivery of stores to meet Navy and Army needs throughout the world.

Central to this task was the Admiralty, housed on the west side of Whitehall, in a building purpose built to provide office space and residential accommodation. This building primarily served the needs of the Board of Admiralty, an overarching body that took responsibility for all matters relating to the Navy other than that of strategy. Strategy was the responsibility of the Cabinet, of which the senior member of the Board, the First Lord, was always a member. It was his task to advise members of the Cabinet as to the value of any adopted strategy, with the Admiralty, once an order had been confirmed in writing, issuing the necessary instructions for the mobilisation and disposition of both individual warships and assembled fleets. A printed report of December 1787, addressed to George III, described the work of the Admiralty in the following terms:

The business of the board of Admiralty is to consider and determine upon all matters relative to Your Majesty's Navy and Departments thereunto belonging; to give direction for the performance of all services, all orders necessary for carrying their direction into execution; and generally to superintend and direct the whole Naval and Marine establishment of Great Britain. (Fees Commission, 5th Report, 1)

Not all the members of the Board had naval experience. It was certainly not a requirement of the First Lord, with a number of holders of this post being civilians appointed as much for their loyalty to the party in government as for their experience in the management of a government department. However, this was more likely during the later Georgian period than in the earlier years, with a number of noted seagoing officers achieving this senior naval position in the years leading up to the Napoleonic Wars. Ensuring that naval expertise was always available to the Board, irrespective of any such knowledge held by the First Lord, was that at least one junior commissioner was always a naval officer.

Housed within the Admiralty were the various offices required by Board members, with other rooms set aside for secretaries and clerks. In addition, the building also housed the Marine Office (the headquarters of the Royal Marines) and the Hydrographer (responsible for cataloguing and assembling navigational charts with Alexander Dalrymple, appointed in 1795, the first holder of this office).

For the performance of duties relating to the material side of the Navy and the overseeing of an extensive civilian workforce that included clerics, artisans and labourers, the Admiralty was dependent on a number of civilian boards. Each had its own area of expertise, with none of them housed in the Admiralty. Instead, and up until the 1780s, each of the boards had offices that were on the east side of London and within the shadow of the Tower. Of these, that of the Navy Board was particularly significant, having had a continuous existence since 1660, when it was responsible for overseeing all activities associated with the upkeep of the fleet and those who served in it. However, as warships grew in size and quantity, the Admiralty had concluded that it would be better if a number of specialised boards were created, leaving the Navy Board to concentrate on the material condition of the fleet and control of naval expenditure. The former was undertaken through the Board's direct management of the government-owned royal dockyards and the issuing of contracts for the building and repair of ships in private yards, while control of expenditure primarily involved the scrutiny of accounts and payments made together with preparing the annual naval estimates and approving payment of seamen and workmen employed in the dockyards.

Among the various boards to be subsequently created were the Victualling, Sick and Hurt, and Transport boards. As for the specialisms that each undertook, the

Victualling Board was responsible for meeting the food and liquid needs of British seamen in whichever ships and on whichever seas they served. To undertake this task, the clerical staff employed under the Victualling Board arranged contracts for the supply of provisions while directly administering a number of victualling yards that stored provisions in bulk while undertaking manufacturing and food processing activities. In addition, the Victualling Board also performed a range of similar duties for the Army, arranging bulk supplies for the Army store premises at St Catherine's Dock, which stood close to the Tower, and establishing contractor-run depot ships for garrison towns abroad. As for the Sick and Hurt Board, this took responsibility for the supply of medicines to warships and all naval facilities, together with the appointment of surgeons and the overseeing of naval hospitals. Finally, the Transport Board was responsible for the hire of ships for the transport of troops and stores and, given that it only existed in wartime, liaising with the Admiralty to ensure that ships being thus utilised were adequately protected from an enemy attack by naval escort ships.

In addition to the offices of the various boards operating under the instructions of the Admiralty, there were two other bodies linked to the administrative needs of the Navy. Also located on the east side of the capital, they were the Navy Pay Office and the offices of the Ordnance Board. The former served much as if it were the Navy's private bank, receiving and disbursing all cash sums on behalf of the civilian boards. Whether it was seamen's wages, officers' pensions or cash demands by contractors, all payments were handled by the cashier and clerks of the Navy Pay Office. As for the various ledgers that recorded these payments, they were eventually forwarded to the relevant branches within the Navy and Victualling offices where they were audited and filed. The Ordnance Board on the other hand was much more distantly associated with the Admiralty, being technically outside the Admiralty's domain. Responsible for the supply of guns and other weapons to the Navy, its duties were considerably more diverse as it was also responsible for artillery, engineers, fortifications, military supplies, transport and field hospitals. While not falling directly under the hierarchy of the Army, the most senior member of the Ordnance Board, the Master General of the Ordnance, would always be drawn from the senior ranks of the Army and would, accordingly, sympathise with the needs of the land forces rather than the Navy.

This splintering of naval bureaucracy, combined with a tendency for each of these bodies to claim varying degrees of independence, resulted in the Admiralty not always being in a position to fully implement the orders and instructions it had issued. The Boards, seeing themselves as professional experts, would challenge the Admiralty, questioning the correctness of an Admiralty requirement, especially when influenced by the need to overcome technical or logistical difficulties. These might be unseen by members of the superior board whose concerns were those of seagoing fleets rather than the difficulties of building and designing ships or ensuring that essential quantities of stores could be suitably gathered. In the case of the Ordnance Board, a further range of difficulties emerged, with a natural desire on the part of that Board to prioritise the needs of the Army with this resulting in less attention to naval ordnance.

2

The Admiralty

The Admiralty's location was dictated by the land in Whitehall upon which it stands becoming available for development. This was in 1694 when an earlier property, Wallingford House, the family home of the Villiers, had been razed to the ground. Coincidentally, Wallingford House was already connected with the Navy through George Villiers, 1st Duke of Buckingham (1592–1628), having been First Lord of the Admiralty and using the house to conduct the business of the Navy. Furthermore, the Lords of the Admiralty continued to meet here until 1634. Upon its demolition the Lords of the Admiralty were able to strike a deal with the leaseholders and trustees of the site for construction of 'a new house for an Admiralty office' (TNA ADM2/174, f.455). Construction was soon under way and the building was completed by June 1694. However, this was not to be the building occupied by those who administered the Navy during the Georgian era. For, although the new office was a sizeable building that had been constructed of 'well-burnt brick and substantial timber', it was of a poor standard (*Survey of London*: Vol. 16, pp. 45–70). Leastways, within thirty years, the Admiralty required the building to be replaced by an entirely new structure on the same site.

It is to the Admiralty, still referred to at this time as Wallingford House, that greater attention now needs to be given. It was in February 1723 that the Lords of the Admiralty determined to move forward on the construction of this building, placing before the King in council a memorial that outlined the poor state of the office and the proposal that 'the same shall be taken down and others erected in their room' (TNA ADM3/34, 2 February 1723). In giving its approval to this request, the council also agreed to the estimated cost of £22,400. This had been the figure submitted by the Office of Royal Works, with Thomas Ripley the Admiralty's chosen architect for the project. Previously, Ripley had been employed on the Customs House, a building that, in common with the new Admiralty offices, dramatically failed to keep within the given estimate.

Having gained approval for a new office building, progress was rapid. Within weeks the clerks of the Admiralty had been removed to temporary premises in St James's Square with the old building completely demolished by the end of

May 1723. To facilitate the erection of the offices, the Ordnance Board was induced to remove a small facility they possessed in St James's Park, as 'otherwise the said buildings cannot be carried on in the manner directed by his Majesty's Order in Council'. Although ready for occupation in September 1725, the new Admiralty Office was not completely finished for a further twelve months.

The addition of a later stone screen that was placed in front of the building in 1759 resulted from a request made by the Westminster Bridge commissioners to acquire part of the land that fronted the offices for the purpose of widening the road that ran between Westminster and Charing Cross. In return for the Admiralty's agreement, which at first was not forthcoming, the Bridge commissioners agreed to pay £650 in compensation and also to provide the Admiralty with an unused parcel of land (24ft by 25ft) left over from the widening programme. To facilitate construction of the road, the Admiralty was also required to demolish an existing wall and 'to Cause a new stone-wall with one large gate and two doors to the same and other conveniences to be erected ... for fencing ... so much of the said Admiralty Court-Yard as shall remain after the said Street shall be widened'. The demolition of the old wall and the erection of the new screen was entrusted to Robert Adam, whose accepted estimate of the cost was £1,293 11s. At around this time, use was also made of the additional land acquired from the Bridge commissioners, to the north of the offices and providing space for a porters' lodge (*Survey of London*: Vol. 16, pp. 45–70).

The screen represents Adam's first major work in the capital, with the architect subsequently working on a number of town houses in London. Generally regarded as an architectural masterpiece, the building nevertheless has its critics. According to one early twentieth-century writer, Adam's 140ft screen together with the Admiralty building 'harmonise as badly as could be expected of a bluff old sea-dog and a genteel *dilettante*' (Hussey, 1923). The screen, not inappropriately, has a naval theme, with engravings of sea horses and prows of a Roman galley and a naval frigate. The latter possesses particular interest, being of the eighteenth century and having its gun ports open and projecting cannons.

One advantage of the screen, apart from it hiding the ill-proportioned Admiralty building with its unnecessarily massive colonnaded entrance porch, is that it protected the building and its occupants from over-enthusiastic Londoners. The screen came into its own in February 1779, when it stood as a barrier to a crowd determined upon laying siege to the building. They were supporters of Admiral Keppel and following his acquittal in a politically charged and motivated court martial were attempting to wreak their vengeance on Vice-Admiral Hugh Palliser, the man who had laid charges against Keppel. At that time Palliser held office as a junior naval lord and the building represented the most obvious symbol of Keppel's opponent.

A further alteration to the Admiralty complex of Wallingford House was undertaken during the eighteenth century, with construction of an official residence for the First Lord, known as Admiralty House. Before this building was built, the First Lord had been accommodated in Wallingford House (nowadays more commonly referred to as the Ripley Building), thus intruding on space that was under pressure due to a need for more offices. However, it was the lack of privacy resulting from the First Lord having to share his living quarters with the junior lords of the admiralty and the clerks who often worked late into the night that led one holder of the office, Richard Viscount Howe, to request of the Prime Minister in 1783 'a few small rooms of my own where [I] might dwell in greater privacy'. Following a discussion in Parliament the proposal, together with a building estimate of £13,000, was agreed. In preparing the site, which immediately connected to the building designed by Ripley, it had become necessary to purchase adjoining land on which stood two houses 'called Little Wallingford House and Pickering House'. Then owned by Sir Robert Taylor, the purchase was finalised on 16 December 1785 at a cost of £3,200. These houses were pulled down in the course of the following year, with a three-storey building of thirty rooms designed in a simplified form of the Palladian tradition blended onto Wallingford House. Approached from Whitehall, the main front is of brickwork with stone dressing but attracts little attention through it being partially hidden by the Adam screen. Even from St James's Park, where more of the building was once visible, there was little hint of its true size, appearing only as a square Georgian block with a small, railed garden from which there was (and continues to be) no point of entry (*Survey of London*: Vol. 16, pp. 45–70; Cilcennin, 1960, p. 9).

Not unnaturally Wallingford House and Admiralty House became familiar to naval officers of the period as it was here that they reported when seeking a new post or being praised on a service performed. Having passed through the porticoed main entrance that gained entry to both buildings, a clerk would make a note of their name, before requesting they sign the First Lord's Visitors' Book, to the right of the door. Having carried out these formalities, they would be ushered into the Captains' Waiting Room, immediately to the left of the entrance. Here they would remain for a varying length of time before being directed into the library of Admiralty House for a meeting with the First Lord.

All this provides a useful starting point for a more detailed examination of the Admiralty complex as it existed upon the completion of Admiralty House in 1788. The hall that stood immediately beyond the porticoed entrance had walls adorned with Doric pilasters supporting a frieze and cornice, while from the ceiling, suspended by a chain with a royal crown, was a lamp of late eighteenth-century workmanship. Also in this entrance hall were a number of leather chairs provided for the porter and doorman. Excessively large for a hallway, it was warmed by a large, open fire with a grey marble surround. The Captains' Room, although adjacent to the hallway, was entered from a doorway from a corridor to the left. Despite its performance of a fairly mundane task, it was entered through a heavy, oak door with a pediment surround, while the room itself had panelled walls and a vaulted ceiling.

Assuming that the awaiting officer was directed to the library, which was used by the First Lord as a reception room and office, he would cross the entrance hall and continue through a doorway pierced in the old south wall of Wallingford House that gave access to Admiralty House. This brought him to the inner hall, another room designed to impress through it having been given a wagon-vaulted ceiling which immediately catches the eye. A further feature of this room was a cast-iron stove designed as a copy of the rostral column in Rome that had been erected to celebrate a naval war. Again, chairs were in evidence, the ones in this room bearing the Admiralty shield and dating to *c.* 1722. Ordered at the time when the Ripley-designed building was under construction, they had been made from mahogany specially imported from Jamaica.

From the inner hallway an oak, panelled door leads to the drawing room and from there to the music and dining rooms. To reach the library it was necessary to ascend the great staircase leading off the inner hall, this staircase having iron balustrades designed by Samuel Pepys Cockerell and the work of John Mackel. The library itself, on the second floor, was reached by way of an ornate doorway surrounded by two magnificent Grecian-style columns and a decorated tympanum archway. On entering, the expectant officer was confronted by a brightly lit room with a superb view of St James's Park. Facing the window on the far side was an open fire with a marble surround. This was one of eight chimney pieces which, at the time of construction and to economise on costs, had been taken from other properties. While the exact provenance of each piece cannot be confirmed, it is known that four came from Wricklemarsh House in Blackheath, then on the verge of demolition, with three pieces coming from York House in Twickenham and one from Egremont House in Piccadilly. Undoubtedly the most impressive item of furnishing within the library was a long case clock by Thomas Tompion (1639–1713), who worked in Fleet Street and was known as the father of English clockmaking. It was presented to Queen Anne during her appointment as Lord High Admiral in 1708 and had remained in the library ever since. Having a moulded mahogany case with panelled plinth and arched trunk door, the clock face itself has a twenty-four-hour graduated, silvered dial chapter (now coded as MOD10/6121/1, the clock is currently part of the Ministry of Defence horology collection). On the same floor as the library is the state bedroom of the First Lord with a further reception room and dressing room together with a bridge that connects at this level to Wallingford House. Above, on the second floor, were a further six bedrooms and a vestibule.

Returning to Wallingford House, much of the accommodation on the ground floor was given over to offices, while the second floor had residential accommodation for a number of the junior lords. Of particular note is the Board Room on the first floor where the Lords of the Admiralty held their daily meetings; these were attended by the Board Secretary, who later transcribed notes made at the meeting into a formal minute book. Here, intelligence was gathered and discussed, decisions taken as to who should command, which ships should be put to sea, the number of vessels to be built and how economies should be made upon war being concluded. The focal point of the room was a bay at the far end containing a globe and, above that, the famous wind dial controlled by a vane on the roof. This indicated current wind direction, so allowing a more informed decision to be taken as to which ships had sailed or could be ordered to sea. A marble fireplace with a fireback bearing the arms of Charles II had above it a collection of pull-down maps that helped inform Board members when taking decisions on fleet movements or on the known whereabouts of enemy vessels. The room itself was lined with oak while a deeply coved ceiling, reconstructed in 1786, had a surface ornamented by white roses picked out in white and gilt. Elaborate carvings executed in pear wood that include representations of a range of nautical instruments, attributed to Grinling Gibbons, festoon the south wall immediately behind the chair occupied by the First Lord.

A long mahogany table occupied much of the length of the room. It was around this table that members of the Board gathered for their daily meetings, with important items read out by a clerk of the office. The First Lord, when present, chaired the meetings, with decisions taken having to be approved by the majority of the Board. While the naval lords had the role of providing advice on technical matters, no board member was given any formal responsibilities until the adoption of a scheme put forward by Charles Barham, who held the post of First Lord at the time of Trafalgar. With so many demands at that time placed on the Admiralty, he felt it essential that a clear distribution of business be introduced to ensure greater efficiency. For himself, he reserved 'the general superintendence and arrangement of the whole' business while the three professional (naval) lords were each given a formalised role. Of these, the 'senior or first professional lord' was, in the absence of the First Lord, to undertake the duties assigned to the First Lord. His more particular responsibility was for the naval ports and with the approbation of the First Lord, to 'dispose of the movement of all ships on Home and Foreign stations' together with the 'direction of seamen and marines' and 'the arming of ships'. He was also to give out instructions to naval officers while ensuring there were no irregularities in promotions.

The second professional lord was tasked with all matters relating to the inferior boards, keeping up 'an intercourse with the heads of such Boards when information or explanation [was] necessary'. Finally, the third professional lord was to superintend the appointment of all commission and warrant officers but only 'under the inspection of the First Lord'. As for the 'civil lords' for which

Barham clearly had little time, he merely assigned them the duty of signing documents and papers 'daily issued from the office' for the purpose of keeping 'the professional lords uninterrupted in the various important duties committed to their charge' (TNA ADM3/256, May 1805).

While each of the junior lords was assigned an office, the Board Room was often used by the First Lord as his own office. Leastways, this was the situation, prior to the building of Admiralty House when the library of that building was adapted to this use. It was through the use of the Board Room by John Montagu, 4th Earl of Sandwich, who held the office of First Lord on no less than three occasions, that a significant new word entered the English language. As he used to demand, when working late into the night, that for purposes of sustenance, he be brought slices of cold meat tucked between two pieces of bread, others took to ordering 'the same as Sandwich'; thus the word sandwich entered the English language. An alternative origin has been suggested, it being said that Lord Sandwich was fond of this form of food because it allowed him to continue playing cards, particularly cribbage, without getting his cards greasy from eating meat with his bare hands.

It was in the Board Room that Sandwich, while at work into the night, received the devastating news on 7 April 1779 that his mistress, Martha Ray, had been shot while leaving a performance at the Covent Garden opera house. Since returning to the Admiralty in 1771 Sandwich, although married, had been living openly with Miss Ray, with whom he was very much in love. Martha Ray was murdered by James Hackman, a deranged former Army officer, who had also fallen in love with Sandwich's mistress. The news came as a terrible blow to the First Lord; on receiving the news, as recorded by Joseph Craddock, a close friend:

> His Lordship stood, as it were, petrified; till suddenly seizing a candle, he ran upstairs, and threw himself on the bed, and in an agony exclaimed, leave me for a while to myself – I could have borne anything but this. (Craddock, re-quoted Rodger, 1979, p. 124)

A hastily written note in Sandwich's hand was rushed the following morning to the Hon Robert Boyle, a naval captain and a further close friend:

> For God's sake come to me immediately, in this moment I have much want of comfort of a real friend; poor Miss Ray was inhumanely murdered last night as she was stepping into her coach at the playhouse door. (Rodger, *The Admiralty*, p. 124)

Not unnaturally, given the current popularity of naval fiction that draws inspiration from the Georgian period, the Admiralty, but especially the Captains' Waiting Room, Library and Board Room have often featured in books. Patrick

O'Brian in several of his Jack Aubrey novels makes use of the Admiralty as a backdrop, with a particular passage in one book hinting at the anxiety felt by officers when called to meet with the First Lord and of the subsequent disaster that might fall upon the less favoured. It is Dr Maturin, espionage agent, friend and confidant of Captain Jack Aubrey who has been called to the Admiralty on this occasion:

> The plunge into the Admiralty courtyard; the waiting room, with half a dozen acquaintances – disconnected gossip, his mind and theirs being elsewhere; the staircase to the First Lord's room, and there, half way up, a fat officer leaning against the rail, silent weeping, his slab, pale cheeks all wet with tears. A silent marine watched from the landing, two porters from the hall aghast. (Patrick O'Brian, *Post Captain*, 1972, p. 174)

Lord Ramage, the fictional creation of Dudley Pope, was also summoned to the Admiralty in the early part of 1797, arriving in a carriage that had approached the building from Charing Cross:

> Telling the coachman to wait, Ramage walked up the steps into the spacious entrance hall where a large six-sided glass lantern hung from the ceiling and his footsteps echoed on the marble floor. On his left the large fireplace was still full of ashes from the night porter's fire and on each side of it were the curious hooded black armchairs which always reminded him of a widow's bonnet. (Dudley Pope, *Ramage and the Freebooter*, 1977, p. 8)

A subsequent meeting with Lord Spencer takes place not in the library but the Board Room:

> Right or wrong, it was here in this room that the decisions were made that governed the activities of more than six hundred of the King's ships whether they were cruising the coast of India or the Spanish main, blockading Cádiz or acting as guardships at Plymouth. If the ships were the fighting body of the Navy, he [Ramage] reflected, here was its brain, working in a long room which had three tall windows along one wall and was panelled with the same oak to build the ships. (Pope, *Ramage and the Freebooter*, p. 10)

Pope, himself a noted naval historian with a number of carefully researched books to his name, uses this knowledge to provide a useful description of the Board Room from the perspective of the captain who had just been brought to that room:

And Ramage saw it was an impressive room which had absorbed something of the drama and greatness of the decisions their lordships had made within these walls during the last five score years or more, sitting at the long, highly polished table occupying the middle of the room. (Pope, *Ramage and the Freebooter*, p. 11)

To this Pope adds:

Ramage intrigued by several long cylinders looking like rolled-up white blinds and fitted on to a large panel over the fireplace, walked over and pulled down one of the tassels. It was a chart of the North Sea. A convenient way of stowing them. Then he noticed the whole panel was surrounded by a frieze of very light wood covered with carvings of medical and nautical instruments and symbols of the sea. (Pope, *Ramage and the Freebooter*, p. 11)

Horatio Hornblower, possibly the most famous of those fictional naval heroes, made an appearance at the Admiralty sometime during 1805, although he did not meet with the First Lord but with the Second Secretary, William Marsden. The latter, a very real person, who held the post from 1804–07, was able to get Hornblower to agree to a clandestine operation that would eventually lead to the Battle of Trafalgar. Having passed into the hall of Wallingford House:

The doorkeeper led Hornblower into a waiting room and bustled off with the note and the letter [that Hornblower had given him]; in the waiting room there were several officers sitting in attitudes of expectancy or impatience or resignation, and Hornblower exchanged formal 'good morning' with them before sitting down in a corner of a room. It was a wooden chair; unfriendly to his tormented sitting parts, but it had a high back with wings against which it was comfortable to lean. (Forester, *Hornblower and the Crisis*, pp. 77–8)

A digression into fiction has allowed a glimpse into the nature of these rooms that those who were actually required to attend rarely chose to provide, although occasionally it does sneak through into a first-hand account. Frustration in having to await endlessly in the Captains' Waiting Room resulted in one summoned officer, if a Cruickshank cartoon is to be taken at face value, applying these words to the chimney piece:

In sore affliction, tried by God's commands
For pestilence Job a great exemplar stands;
But in these days a trial more severe
Had been Job's lot, if God had sent him here.
(Cilcennin, *Admiralty House*, p. 9)

Going beyond the Waiting Room to the library, consider this summary of an actual meeting between Lord Cochrane (1775–1860) with First Lord, Earl St Vincent. At the time Cochrane, a future admiral, was relatively low on the captain's list but was recognised as one of the Navy's most audacious commanders. In modern times, some have suggested Cochrane was the inspiration for Hornblower and a number of other fictional naval heroes. Yet Cochrane had many enemies, having outspokenly accused some of his superior officers of incompetence, cruelty, corruption and laziness. Among those enemies was John Jervis, Earl of St Vincent, First Lord of the Admiralty, who stood in the way of his advancement. In a meeting in the library of Admiralty House, held upon the renewal of war with France in 1803, Cochrane sought a new command. This account is provided by Cochrane and, if reading between the lines is permitted, is suggestive of both parties to this discussion using highly colourful language that could possibly be heard, should a window have been open, in nearby St James's Park. Cochrane's formal request was immediately met by the First Lord categorically stating that no vessels were available. However, Cochrane had done his homework:

> I began to enumerate several, all of which his lordship assured me were promised to others. On mentioning the name of some in a less forward state, an objection was raised by his lordship that they were too large. This was met by a fresh list, but these his lordship said were not in progress. In short, it became clear that the British Navy contained no ship of war for me. I frankly told his lordship as much, remarking that as 'the Board was evidently of opinion that my services were not required, it would be better for me to go back to the College of Edinburgh [where he had recently been in attendance] and pursue my studies, with a view to occupying myself in some other employment'. His lordship eyed me keenly, to see whether I really meant what I said, and observing no signs of flinching – for beyond doubt my countenance showed signs of disgust at such unmerited treatment – he said, 'Well you shall have a ship. Go down to Plymouth, and there await the orders of the Admiralty'. (Thomas Cochrane, *Memoirs of a Fighting Captain*, 2004, p. 61)

Perhaps the missing harsh words are provided by O'Brian when his own Jack Aubrey confronts St Vincent in the same room when asking that he be given command of a sloop. St Vincent is disinclined to allow this and makes his feelings clear; to Aubrey he angrily declares:

> You fling your money about – ducks and drakes – you talk about marriage, although you know, or ought to know, that it is death to a sea-officer's career, at least until he is made post – you lead drunken parties at a Tory by-election – you come here and say you *must* have a ship.

When Aubrey offers a defence to his claim and reminds St Vincent of a recent successful action, the First Lord further explodes:

> What the fucking hell is this language to me, sir? Do you know who you are talking to, sir? Do you know where you are?

The argument continues for a short while before reaching an abrupt end:

> A door opened and closed, and the people in the corridor saw Captain Aubrey stride past, hurry down the stairs and vanish into the courtyard. (O'Brian, *Post Captain*, p. 65)

Charles Lord Barham, First Lord at the time of Trafalgar, was soundly asleep in his bedroom at Admiralty House when the news of the great victory was brought to him. It had been brought by Lieutenant John Richards Lapenotière, commander of the naval sloop *Pickle*. Lapenotière had brought his vessel from the scene of the battle into Falmouth Bay, having been instructed to convey to the Admiralty without delay various dispatches relating to the battle. Arriving at Wallingford House during the early morning of 6 November he was immediately taken to Marsden who took the decision to rouse the First Lord from his slumbers. It was not a difficult decision to take as, only a few months previously, Barham had showed great annoyance on not being woken when a piece of urgent news had arrived. In Marsden's words:

> Drawing aside his curtain, with a candle in my hand, I awoke the old peer … from a sound slumber; and to the credit of his nerves be it mentioned, that he showed no symptom of alarm or surprise, but calmly asked: 'What news, Mr. M?' We then discussed, in a few words, what was immediately to be done, and I sat up the remainder of the night, with such of the clerks as I could collect, in order to make the necessary communications at an early hour to the King, the Prince of Wales, the Duke of York, the Minister, and other members of the Cabinet, and to the Lord Mayor, who communicates the intelligence to the shipping interest at Lloyd's Coffee-house. (William Marsden, *A Brief Memoir of the Life and Writings of the Late William Marsden*, 1838, p. 116)

Other areas of the house that figure in naval history are the dining and drawing rooms. These are part of the official residence of the First Lord and it became the practice of the 2nd Earl Spencer, while First Lord, to invite all officers of the rank of captain and above to attend for dinner before they sailed to take up a new command. In the earlier description of the house, both rooms were glossed over but here it might usefully be added that both were, in keeping with the rest of the house, show pieces designed to reflect the importance of the First Lord. Heavily decorated with statuary marble, both mantle pieces were probably removed from York House, the panels of the one in the dining room depicting Hercules Rejecting Pleasure and Choosing Virtue. A further feature of the dining room was a large three-light window divided by an Ionic column. As for the dining table itself, it is possible that this was created from the Jamaican mahogany ordered at the time of constructing the third Wallingford House.

Lord Nelson was twice invited to dinner by Earl Spencer, accompanied both times by his wife, Lady Frances Nelson. On the first visit, held in 1798 before Nelson sailed on board *Vanguard* for the Mediterranean and ultimately Aboukir Bay, he could not have been a more doting husband, upsetting the seating arrangement by insisting that he be seated next to his wife so 'that he would not voluntarily lose an instant of her company'. At least this was the view taken by Lady Spencer, the hostess on both occasions. Referring to the second dinner party that took place on 11 November 1800, by which time Nelson had embarked on his famous affair with Emma Hamilton, Lady Spencer in a gossipy letter written to Lady Shelley, noted Nelson to be clearly less enamoured by his wife. In this letter she told of how he treated Frances Nelson with nothing less than 'contempt'. After dinner, according to Lady Spencer, Nelson's wife, 'perhaps unadvisedly but with good intention peeled some walnuts and offered them to him in a glass. As she handed it across the table, Nelson pushed it away so roughly, that the glass broke against one of the dishes.'

Between May 1827 and September 1828 Admiralty House was not occupied by the First Lord but the Lord High Admiral. This was the result of an intriguing political experiment that saw the Duke of Clarence (later King William IV) given a post with those who then made up the Board having their commissions revoked. In a biography of William IV, historian Tom Pocock explained:

The following month [February 1827], the Prime Minister, Lord Liverpool died and a new administration was formed by the former foreign secretary, George Canning. In the political upheaval that this brought, one of those who refused to serve in the cabinet was Lord Melville and a replacement as First Lord of the Admiralty had to be found. Canning and the King, casting about for a successor, seemed to have passed over the long standing claim of the Duke of Clarence on the grounds that he was not suitable as a cabinet minister. Then they had second thoughts. An idea struck them, which Canning knew would appeal to the King's love of mock-historical pageantry and the Duke's longing for recognition, and would also dispose of any attempted return to office by Melville. The archaic and extinct title of Lord High Admiral would be revived. (Pocock, 1991, p. 188)

It was assumed that the Duke would be setting himself up as a mere figurehead and that he would accept the advice of a specially created council with Sir George Cockburn, a much respected naval officer and gunnery expert, at its head. In the event, the Duke adopted a less than passive role, introducing a number of worthwhile reforms but failing to consider their financial implications. Furthermore, he did not always believe in consultation, clashing with Cockburn over the setting up of a gunnery committee. In an angry exchange of letters, Clarence demanded Cockburn's resignation with the matter brought to the attention of the Duke of Wellington, Prime Minister since the beginning of 1828. Wellington, in turn, referred it to George IV, indicating that it should be Clarence who should resign. In supporting Wellington, the King wrote to Clarence, pointing out a few essential facts relating to the position of Cockburn:

> … it is with a feeling of deepest regret that I observe the embarrassing situation in which you have placed yourself. You are in error from beginning to end. You must not forget, my dear William, that Sir George Cockburn is the King's Privy Councillor, and so made by the King, to advise the Lord High Admiral.
>
> What become of Sir George's oath, his duty towards me, his sovereign, if he fails to offer such advice as he thinks necessary to the Lord High Admiral? Am I, then, to be called upon to dismiss the most useful, perhaps the most important naval officer in my service for conscientiously acting to the letter and spirit of his oath and his duty? The thing is impossible … (Pack, 1987, p. 266)

Whether it was a First Lord and a number of junior lords or the Lord High Admiral and an advisory council that headed the Admiralty, all were dependent on the numerous clerks and secretaries that were employed in Wallingford House, with their offices mostly situated on the ground floor. Most important were the offices of the First and Second Secretaries who served as the direct link between the Board and its clerical staff, responsible for the efficient functioning of the office. All incoming letters were addressed to the secretaries and normally included the phrase 'be pleased to inform their lordships'. Outgoing letters, always signed by one or other of the secretaries would begin 'I am commanded by their Lordships'. While no clear distinction at one time existed between the tasks they performed, it gradually came to be accepted that the First Secretary had a more political role, with the Second Secretary overseeing all clerical work.

At first this had no impact upon the secretaries' tenure of office, with both serving under numerous First Lords irrespective of changing governing administrations. This security of employment becomes idiosyncratic when it is also mentioned that it was not unusual for the secretaries to be members of the House of Commons and expected to use their vote in support of the government in office. In time, however, a more intense political refinement was introduced when second secretaries were removed on party loyalty grounds in both 1804 and 1806. This was at a time of intense political rivalry, with the Whig St Vincent, on the first occasion, appointing Benjamin Tucker, formerly his private secretary, to the office of Second Secretary. Upon the Tories regaining power, Tucker was quickly removed and replaced by Barrow, with the latter removed from office upon a further change of government in 1806 and being replaced by Tucker, with Barrow reappointed in April 1807. Of his dismissal in 1806, Barrow was later to write:

> I was fully aware of what was to be my fate, and had it speedily announced to me by a message from [the incoming First Lord] the Right Hon. Charles Grey, through Mr Marsden. (John Barrow, *An Auto-Biographical Memoir of Sir John Barrow, Bart, Late of the Admiralty* …, 1847, p. 291)

More significantly, Grey had gone on to say that under different circumstances he would have been quite happy to have retained the services of Barrow, if it had not been for the previous ousting of Tucker, 'the faithful, confidential, and attached secretary of the Earl of St Vincent' who had given up a commissionership on the Navy Board 'to follow his old master' (Barrow, p. 291). This undoubtedly was true, for Barrow, upon his re-appointment, was to continue as secretary for a further forty-two years, even serving under a Whig administration with Grey holding office as Prime Minister. As for the First Secretary's post being of a more political nature, this was a product of that period of musical chairs, with it being deemed that it should be this post that altered upon the change of administrations and the Second Secretary remaining in office to secure continuity.

While the clerks who the two secretaries supervised began their careers on the lowest steps of the office ladder, the secretaries were brought in from outside. As much as anything they were head hunted for their efficiency and zealousness. Barrow, for instance, had served as private secretary to Lord Macartney while Marsden had held a senior East India Company appointment. Tucker, of course, had been St Vincent's private secretary, while earlier Admiralty secretaries had often served on the Navy Board. However, being a good administrator was not the single most important factor leading to an appointment; falling under the favour and subsequent patronage of an existing First Lord was of equal significance. Thus, Tucker was under the patronage of St Vincent with Grey feeling sufficiently indebted to St Vincent as to make Tucker one whom he also favoured. Further demonstrating the importance of the office was the high level of remuneration which each received, the salaries paid being greater than that given to the junior lords. For the First Secretary the annual salary was fixed in 1800 at £3,000 per annum, while that for the Second Secretary was £1,500.

In addition, and in common with the junior lords, the First Secretary was also provided with accommodation at Wallingford House, so explaining why Marsden was present that November night when Captain Lapenotière brought the news of Trafalgar.

The number of clerks varied from the forty or so employed in the 1770s to a peak figure of sixty-five in 1815. The greater part of their duties consisted of writing neat copies of letters leaving the Admiralty with a separate hand-written copy for retention. This, of course, was an age when neither carbon paper nor mechanical copying devices existed, each letter having to be separately written. A number of clerks, however, did have more specialised duties with a third- and second-class clerk employed as readers to the Board at their meetings, while a further clerk was retained as a translator. In addition, a clerk of the first class was provided with an enhanced salary to live in close proximity to the Admiralty so that he might attend any urgent overnight business. For most of the clerks, the hours of employment were from 11 a.m. through to 4 p.m., with alternate clerks working on the early morning post or late into the evening on correspondence being sent out. In addition, a small number of clerks were attached to the Marine Office and Marine Pay Office, with the latter directly supervised by the Paymaster of Marines, an office that had been created in 1755 and which continued until 1831.

Once correspondence had left the hands of the clerks it had to be delivered to the intended recipient. On occasions it might be imperative for instructions to be quickly passed to ships lying in the various fleet anchorages. Initially this was achieved through hastily written letters taken either by dispatch rider or one of several coaches that regularly plied between London and the naval ports. At the very least, a lapse of many hours had to be accepted, with it being impossible to get a message to Portsmouth in less than twelve hours while for the instruction of ships of the Western Squadron and lying in Plymouth Harbour, it would take considerably in excess of a full day. However, all this changed during the 1790s with the construction of a series of signalling stations that eventually linked Wallingford House to the naval outports. While this did not diminish the need for lengthier communications to be sent either by coach or dispatch rider, it did mean brief urgent instructions would arrive in hours, not days.

The first chain of signalling stations was an experimental line of fifteen signalling stations that linked London to Deal (for communicating messages to ships lying in the Downs) with branches to Chatham and Sheerness (the latter for ships anchored in the Thames). Making use of a series of opening and closing shutters contained within a 20ft-high frame, the line and its signalling stations were constructed over a period of twelve months. On the roof of Wallingford House, from where Admiralty messages were sent, a hut for the signallers was constructed together with a shutter device. For the relaying of messages out of

London, the next station to Wallingford House was on the roof of a house in Lambeth, now 36 West Square (a distance of 1.25 miles), with a second located on Plow Garlic Hill in Nunhead (4.25 miles), where a weather boarded, timber-framed hut was erected. For the further relaying of messages, including those at the terminal points at Chatham, Sheerness and Deal, a total of fourteen stations were constructed.

The success of this line, which was able to pass a simple message between Deal and London in less than ten minutes, led to the subsequent addition of further lines to Portsmouth, Yarmouth and eventually Plymouth. To facilitate these lines, additional stations in London for the route to Portsmouth were constructed on the roof of the east wing of the Chelsea Royal Hospital together with a two-room hut quickly built in Putney. This latter was placed on land owned by the former First Lord, 2nd Earl Spencer, for which he charged an annual rent of 5s. As for the relaying of messages to Yarmouth, a shutter above a weather boarded hut was established on Hampstead Heath (Telegraph Hill).

Using a series of six opening and closing shutters, with some being held open and others closed in varying sequences, a total of sixty-three differing patterns (or changes) could be produced, each representing either a letter of the alphabet or a commonly used phrase. These shutters, which were grouped in two vertical rows and placed on the roof of each signalling station, were of such size that they could be observed on clear days over a distance of 10 miles by any observer using a standard issue naval telescope. While the operation of each station was normally placed in the hands of a midshipman and two assistants, the one sited on the roof of Wallingford House was commanded by a lieutenant. While the assistants were responsible for operating the ropes that operated the shutter boards and observing the two neighbouring stations at West Square and Chelsea it was the task of the lieutenant to write down the message and ensure it was passed to either a senior clerk or secretary. Lapenotière, who brought the news of the victory of Trafalgar to Lord Barham, had been unable to use the signalling system that could have conveyed a message from Plymouth as he was carrying a number of lengthy dispatches that needed to be conveyed direct by hand. Despite Lapenotière taking fresh horses on nineteen occasions, it still took him thirty-seven hours to cover the distance from Falmouth to Wallingford House.

A cost-cutting exercise following the defeat of Napoleon in 1814 resulted in the abandonment of the shutter lines; this was soon recognised to be a serious mistake. The outcome was the re-opening of the line to Chatham, using a new system for conveying messages and with a realigned route through London. These changes were in response to some of the problems thrown up by the earlier system. Particularly irksome had been the frequent necessity of having to delay sending messages from Wallingford House due to poor visibility brought about by pollution, even though the London stations had been deliberately sited much closer to one another than those outside the metropolis. When visibility was poor, an Admiralty messenger was employed to physically take a written message to the first of the stations operating in clear visibility. If there was an incoming message, and should there be fog in the Thames valley, messages received at the Putney station were taken to Chelsea by the gardener of a nearby house, for which service he was paid 1s.

A second problem related to the cumbersome nature of the shutter telegraph. Each board measured approximately 6ft by 5ft and was manually operated by pull ropes to register a change, resulting in the communication of anything beyond a simple instruction proving a drawn-out affair. On the line to Chatham it had been estimated that it would take as long as one hour to transmit thirty-three words from one station to the next. On the other hand, a single change, such as the one used midday for the synchronisation of time, could be passed the entire length of the line in only two minutes.

The new system of signalling was devised by Admiral Sir Home Popham (1762–1820). Much simpler in concept, it involved a single, fixed, vertical 30ft pole, with two movable 8ft arms attached to the pole by horizontal pivots at their ends, one arm at the top of the pole, and the other arm at the middle of the pole. Furthermore, the signals of the Popham semaphore were found to be much more visible than those of the earlier shutter system. Using both the original West Square and Nunhead stations, the new semaphore system was rolled out across Kent, the necessary mechanism constructed by the Henry Maudslay engineering company at their works in Pimlico. It was in May 1816 that the changes were brought to Wallingford House and *The Times* alerted its readers to what would be required:

> The telegraph frames at the top of the Admiralty are to be removed and the improved semaphore consisting of a hollow mast from whence two arms project in various directions will be erected in their stead. The utility of this invention is to be tried, by way of experiment, in a few days, from London to Sheerness, and the number of stations, it is said will not exceed nine, several are erected. (*The Times*, 9 May 1816)

Despite the subsequent success of the experiment, with the semaphore stations frequently able to convey messages when the shutter telegraph would have been unusable, the line to Chatham was only to remain until 1822. Instead, and still in a very cost-conscious mood, the Admiralty decided that its resources would be better concentrated on reopening the line to Portsmouth through the adoption of the new system and the transfer of the semaphore machinery to the signalling stations of the Portsmouth line, with an order for a necessary additional seven semaphore devices placed with Henry Maudslay.

Work on developing the line to Portsmouth began in 1818 with a survey of the old Portsmouth shutter line resulting in a few minor locational changes. In London, and as the first relay station on the redesigned line to Portsmouth, a semaphore and hut were placed on the roof of the Royal Military Asylum in Chelsea. This more convenient location had simply not been available before as the location of a shutter, since it was not built until 1801. From there, messages were relayed to Putney Heath, where a purpose-built three-storey brick building was constructed. Sited close to the hut of the earlier shutter line, it had the semaphore device stepped on a heavy beam placed on the floor of an upper room. The next stage in the routing of messages out of London saw the erection of further purposes-built structures on Kingston Hill and Cooper's Hill (Claygate) amongst others before terminating at a station constructed on the top of the sail and rigging loft in the dockyard at Portsmouth.

The transfer of machinery from the Chatham line to the Portsmouth line was undertaken during April and May 1822, with the line coming into use shortly afterwards. A possible branch, breaking away from the Portsmouth line at Chatley Heath (Cobham) was considered, with construction of several stations undertaken. However, this line was never completed, partly due to cost but more especially because of the development in the 1830s of the electric telegraph that could relay long-distance messages, irrespective of visibility in a matter of minutes. As for the Portsmouth line, already completed and in full use, this continued in operation until December 1847, when it was completely abandoned.

For matters connected to the material side of the Navy, ship construction, the issuing and ordering of supplies and the well-being of seamen, an equally regular stream of correspondence passed between Wallingford House and the offices of the civilian departments initially clustered in the area of the Tower. These messages and instructions would be hand delivered, taken across London by one of several Admiralty messengers, of which there were never more than six including a head messenger.

Let us, as an example, follow one of these messages across London. It was possibly taken by William Cooke, who served as Chief Messenger from 1768 until 1781 (having himself formerly been a messenger). By foot, it would need at least forty-five minutes and requires a walk along the entire length of the Strand, passing Somerset House (the future home of the Navy's civilian departments) before entering Fleet Street. From here, passing to the south of St Paul's Cathedral, we enter the financial quarter of the City, with the messenger now possibly going along Canon Street gaining, as he did so, a distant view of Mansion House and passing the Bell and Bear pub on Rat Alley (where sustenance might have been taken), before entering Great and Little East Cheap, and on to Tower Street from which all of the civilian offices of the Navy could, at this time, be easily reached.

THE BOARD OF ADMIRALTY AND THE DETERMINATION OF LONGITUDE AT SEA

It was at Wallingford House, adjacent to Whitehall, that the commissioners for the 'Discovery of the Longitude at Sea' would meet, their task being to encourage research into a 'practical and useful' means to determine longitude while at sea. For a nation that was setting out on the road to global seaborne domination, this was an essential pre-requisite, the accurate determination of longitude permitting vessels on an east–west ocean voyage to be more perfectly navigated, so ensuring shorter ocean voyages and a greater chance of avoiding charted natural hazards. Usually referred to as the Board of Longitude, and headed by the First Lord of the Admiralty, the commissioners were originally appointed by an Act of Parliament that received royal assent on 20 June 1714, some twelve days prior to the accession of George I. While naming an initial twenty-three commissioners, it was not intended that they should all meet as a board but that they should be available as knowledgeable individuals who could be consulted by those who wished to bring forward an idea for the determination of longitude at sea.

At the time the Act was passed, and for the greater part of the eighteenth century, oceanic navigation was fraught with difficulty. While it was relatively easy to assess the latitude of a ship, working out the longitude was much more complex, requiring time-consuming observations and calculations. Often it came down to a simple guestimate that could result in the position of a ship on an easterly or westerly voyage of several days having a recorded position that was inaccurate by 50 or more miles.

In October 1707, Admiral Sir Cloudesley Shovell, while returning to England as commander of the Mediterranean Fleet, lost four ships when they were swept on to the hazardous Gilstone Ledges close to the Scilly Isles. The wreck resulted from an inability to accurately calculate longitude, Shovell believing his fleet to be further to the east. It was this disaster, claiming in excess of 1,500 lives, including that of the admiral, which directly led to the establishment of the 'Board of Longitude'.

It was not until 30 June 1737 that the Board, chaired on that occasion by First Lord Sir Charles Wager, met for the first time, following a successful trial at sea of a time piece designed by John Harrison which permitted for a reasonably accurate calculation of longitude. At that time, it was not necessarily expected that a solution to measuring longitude would be based on accurate time keeping, many believing that the solution lay in the careful measurement of the moon in relation to the sun. However, a solution through the use of astronomy was rejected by Harrison who worked on the development of a sea clock that, through its use of accurate time keeping, would make the calculation of longitude relatively simple.

The principle Harrison employed is that for every 15 degrees travelled east, local time moves forward one hour. Having gauged local time (most commonly through the use of a sextant that will show when the sun has reached its local apparent noon) this is then compared with the time at a previous reference point. Following this, a simple calculation based on the time difference will result in the longitude of the ship being known. To do this, a clock previously set to 'home time' must remain accurate for a meaningful calculation to be made; it was this that John Harrison achieved, for no previous time piece taken to sea had the same degree of accuracy.

That first meeting of the Board confirmed the progress being made by Harrison, with a grant of £500 given to him 'for enabling him to make experiment of a machine invented by him in the nature of a clock work to keep time at sea and make another of the same'. In the meantime, alternatives continued to be explored, with the Board beginning to meet more regularly.

Initially it is to be supposed that a junior clerk of the Admiralty was called upon to undertake many of the clerical duties, with this being formally recognised in 1762 with the appointment of John Ibbotson, one of the junior clerks, as secretary to the Board at a salary of £40 per year. In the meantime, Harrison continued to develop accurate seagoing time pieces for a further three decades, eventually producing a chronometer that, among others, was verified by George III, as accurate to within one-third of a second per day. For his work, Harrison received a monetary award from Parliament that amounted to £8,750, a sum that he was only able to enjoy for the remaining three years of his life. As for the Board of Longitude, this was finally wound up in 1828, having its last meeting at Wallingford House on 15 July of that year, under the chairmanship of Second Secretary John Barrow. From encouraging research into the discovery of longitude, the Board had by that time taken on a slightly wider remit, including navigational matters in general while continuing to involve itself in the further development of marine chronometers.

3

The Civilian Boards

The offices with which the Board of Admiralty at Wallingford House were in such frequent contact were those that housed the commissioners or principal officers of the Navy, the Victualling, and Sick and Hurt boards. Within these buildings, deliberation was made as to how requests from the Board of Admiralty might be fulfilled, with instructions then issued to the appropriate outstations, be it a dock or victualling yard, a naval hospital, an employed agent or a private contractor for the actual undertaking of the work that was involved.

The commissioners of the Navy Board were housed, together with sixty or more clerks, in the Navy Office. Until 1789 and a move to Somerset House, this was located in a building some 200 yards north-west of the Tower on the south side of Crutched Friars, with a further entrance leading off Seething Lane. Designed by Sir Christopher Wren and completed in 1683, it replaced an earlier building occupied by the Navy commissioners that had been destroyed by fire. The fire in question was not the Great Fire (1666), which the building narrowly escaped, but a lesser conflagration in January 1673 that nevertheless destroyed thirty neighbouring properties. The building had previously been converted from a large house into the Navy Office in 1654 at a cost of £2,400. Its destruction necessitated the construction of purpose-built offices that also included more expansive living quarters for the commissioners, each of whom was expected to be resident.

While the 1683 Navy Office no longer survives, an impression of its appearance can be gained from a contemporary engraving by Benjamin Cole (reproduced in Maitland, 1784, p. 385) and an anonymously written description dating to the mid-1740s (Anon 1746). The engraving, executed by Benjamin Cole sometime around 1760, is particularly useful as it provides a ground-level view of the Navy Office as seen from the main entrance that leads off Crutched Friars. It seems likely that the area was protected by a surrounding wall with access gained through a gateway that then led on to a paved courtyard. Confronting the visitor at this point was a seven-bayed (2-3-2) brick building flanked by two detached wings. The central building, which provided the primary working space for the commissioners and the senior clerics of the office, was entered through an ornate doorway with an open-scrolled pediment supported by columns. This gave access to a spacious entrance lobby dominated by a wide staircase that led to the Board Room and the offices of the clerks who worked most closely with the commissioners. On the ground floor were a number of additional offices reserved for the commissioners themselves.

To the rear of the building, as noted in the written account, there existed a 'handsome little paved square and looks like an eminent Mathematician with all his apparatus about him'. The courtyard was further described as being surrounded by buildings on all sides, these being the two detached wings together with a further structure to the rear. This last building contained the offices of the Sick and Hurt Board and had a separate entrance from Tower Hill. As for the detached wings that flanked the courtyard and the central office building, these were approached through an open corridor that ran each side of the main building and entered through pedimented but otherwise unadorned doorways. They gave a rather oppressive feel to the complex, appearing overly close to the main building. Both wings were of twelve bays and three floors in height with an additional attic storey. Providing office space, one of the wings also accommodated the ticket office, which was a branch of the Navy Office where tickets for the wages of disabled, discharged or deceased seamen were examined. A further function of these wings was to provide the commissioners with accommodation, stables and outhouses.

The number of appointed commissioners to the Navy Board never fell below six, with the Comptroller, surveyor and secretary (formerly Clerk of the Acts) of particular significance. It was the Comptroller who chaired meetings, sitting at the head of the table around which the Board met. While it was generally recognised that he was the pre-eminent member of the Board, superintending the various branches of the Navy Office and attending meetings with the First Lord and other members of the Cabinet, he was officially of equal standing to that of all other commissioners.

Seated to one side of the Comptroller during meetings of the full board was the Navy surveyor, the principal officer responsible for the design of warships and the running of the dockyards; he headed a separate branch of the Navy Office. However, his authority was severely limited as he was an equal member of the Board and unable to take decisions without the agreement of others. Nevertheless, he was the Board's expert on shipbuilding and repair, since the surveyor was always a Master Shipwright of a royal dockyard. However, even if the surveyor wanted to visit a dockyard to inspect efficiency or the progress of work, he could not do so without 'the concurrence and by the direction of the Board at large' (J.M. Collinge, *Navy Board Officials 1660–1832*, 1978, p. 22).

Seated on the other side of the Comptroller and responsible for the day-to-day running of business was the Clerk of the Acts. In plain terms, this was the Navy Board's clerical officer and a position once held by Samuel Pepys. In 1796, the title was abolished, with the post now given the more accurate appellation of secretary. Whether as Clerk of the Acts or secretary, the post holder was expected to take responsibility for correspondence, the general running of the Navy Office and the keeping of minutes. The major difference was that the secretary was no longer a voting member of the Board, so he could no longer share in the decision-making process. In fact, and as made clear by Pepys in his diaries, the Clerk of the Acts had had the potential for being a very active member of the Board, with Pepys himself visiting the dockyards on several occasions, where he uncovered a number of abuses. Nevertheless, and following the alteration of 1796, the secretary was still permitted to head this particular branch of business on the same basis as those directly headed by a principal officer, rather than themselves now being overseen by a voting member of the Board. As for the existing Clerk of the Acts, George Marsh, he was reappointed to an alternative post on the Board, so allowing him to continue as a commissioner rather than becoming a servant of the Board, while the assistant Clerk of the Acts was re-designated secretary.

The remaining commissioners were either extra commissioners brought in to support the work of the Board during times of extreme pressure or they headed various branches that oversaw financial expenditure. Among the latter were the Deputy Comptroller (responsible for contracts), the Controller of Victualling Accounts (responsible for examining the financial accounts of the Victualling Board while agreeing payments) and the Controller of Storekeepers' Accounts (responsible for directing and distributing stores and the related accounts). Each, when seated around the Board table, took up positions in strict order of the perceived importance of the branches that they oversaw and by which order they also signed official documents.

George Marsh shared with Samuel Pepys not only the office of Clerk of the Acts but the habit of keeping a diary. Admittedly, Pepys's diary is considerably more detailed, but nevertheless Marsh does make a few interesting remarks about his labours at the Navy Office, together with the Victualling Office where he was also employed as a commissioner between 1763 and 1772.

Of particular interest is the means by which Marsh acquired his first appointment to the Victualling Board. This came about through the offices of the Earl of Egmont who, at that time, was First Lord of the Admiralty. Marsh, a few years earlier, had undertaken some important clerical work for Egmont with this resulting in a promise that he would provide favours in return. This was the normal means of acquiring most government sinecures, those having the power to make such appointments granting office to those who either owed them a favour or to those who might be able to offer some future advantage. On taking office as First Lord, Egmont had appointed Marsh his private secretary, while hinting that Marsh would be offered a more important government post when a suitable one became available. This became a reality in October 1763, but not without Marsh first undertaking a somewhat dubious course of action, aware that Egmont might not be in office for any great length of time. In a diary entry dated 20 October 1763, Marsh wrote:

> Knowing Mr Rule one of the Commissioners of the Victualling had been long ill, I wrote him an anonymous letter signifying that I would give him £1000 and insure him superannuation too if he was inclined thereto. As soon as he received the letter had answered it and wished to see me [sic]. Whereupon I took a hackney coach and went to his house the same night [and Rule] on seeing me, and being quite satisfied of my interest, applied the next day for superannuation. (Diary, 20 October 1763)

In other words, Marsh had manipulated the situation to ensure that the vacancy existed prior to Egmont ceasing to be First Lord.

From the Victualling Board, and as a result of experiences gained, Marsh was later moved to the Navy Board as Controller of Victualling Accounts. Having made a success of this office, he was appointed Clerk of the Acts in July 1773. It was not a position that he had sought, bringing with it several distinct disadvantages:

> This branch is attended with no increase of income, and in the branch I had before as Comptroller of the Victualling Account of the Navy, I might or not, attend the Board every day, just as suits my will or convenience. (Diary, 26 June 1773)

Marsh, possibly through his own contentiousness, something he admits to in his diary, was not a particularly well-regarded member of the Board, with his own clerk, Robert Gregson, in a communication to Lord Shelburne, accusing Marsh of being 'a man totally unfit for the employment, as he can neither read, spell nor write'. These, however, are somewhat difficult claims to substantiate, given that Marsh, in his diaries, writes with ability. Indeed, Gregson would have been well advised not to make an enemy of Marsh, for he had friends in high places (being on speaking terms with the King and many leading politicians of the day) and he was not averse to using these contacts to favour his own advancement.

The diary kept by George Marsh also demonstrates the security of office that was possessed by those appointed to the Navy Board. Marsh himself was to continue in office until his death in October 1800 at the age of 78. However, knowing there were some who might be anxious to remove him as he approached his eighth decade he attempted to trade on this to squeeze some further advantage for himself. Writing to Earl Spencer at the time he was First Lord, Marsh promised to resign if he should be offered a baronetcy. The letter was couched in the following terms:

> I must rely on your Lordship's benevolence and candour to excuse my troubling you upon the subject of my own situation, but having been near sixty one years in His Majesty's Service, thirty two of which a Commissioner of the Victualling and Navy, and twenty two thereof in the branch of the latter, termed Clerk of the Acts of the Navy, and have always executed my Duty with the utmost fidelity and attention, I trust and hope it may not be thought improper or unreasonable in mentioning the mortifications I have felt in seeing Baronetcies conferred on many of my brethren, who comparatively, have been but a short time in office, whilst I have been overlooked.
>
> My Lord I consider your administration from the liberality and attention have shown to all the ranks as a favourable opportunity for me to solicit your Lordship's influence to provide me a similar mark of His Majesty's Royal favour, in addition to such a pension as I should hope from my very long services, and my period of life (seventy three) your Lordship will think me worthy of. Under such circumstances I should be inclined to resign. I have the honour to be with the greatest respect, My Lord your Lordships most obedient and most humble servant. (Diary, 21 August 1795)

Spencer refused to countenance this request but did subsequently offer him a knighthood should he choose to resign. Marsh refused, in the belief that his health was strong enough to continue in office for several more years.

A coincidental and fortuitous arrangement was the Victualling Office being only a few hundred yards from the Navy Office, so helping easy communication and contact between the two boards. It had not been an arrangement specifically designed from the outset as the Victualling Office site on Little Tower Hill had emerged out of its initial use as a yard for the storage of victuals and proximity to the Thames. Formerly the site of a Cistercian abbey that had been acquired by the government during the Reformation, its earliest use as a victualling yard had occasionally been performed under contract. This was certainly the case during the years immediately following the Restoration (1660) with the named contractor, Denis Gauden, agreeing to provide victuals at the rate of 6d per man for ships in harbour and 9d for ships at sea. It was a completely privatised operation and government involvement was limited; the Navy Office simply had to examine the accounts and ensure payment. However, it proved none too successful an experiment, with myriad complaints relating to the quality and quantity of supplies resulting in the Admiralty imposing a system of direct management.

It was through the creation of a Victualling Board in 1683, initially consisting of seven commissioners, each receiving a salary of £400 per annum, that the Admiralty resolved the issue of how future management of naval victualling supplies should be handled. In terminating the arrangement of supply by contract, the Tower Hill site automatically reverted back to the government, with the new Board making use of the various buildings on that site, some dating back to the days of the Cistercian monks, with others having been added during the early and mid-seventeenth century.

To administer the facilities in London and the other victualling yards established at Portsmouth, Plymouth and Rochester, an already existing house that stood close to the original gatehouse of the monastery was provided with additional office space, accommodation for some of the commissioners and a meeting room. However, this was only a stopgap measure, the house being quite unsuited to the needs of a government enterprise that would eventually develop tentacles reaching to every continent.

The house was demolished in the 1720s and replaced by a new building known as the Grand Office. No longer in existence, it is fortunate that a painting of the Grand Office survives together with a general outline plan. While the former is a watercolour dating to about 1800 (shortly before the Grand Office was demolished) the outline plan is discernible from a map of the victualling establishment drawn in 1776 (BL Crace Collection, portfolio viii, 46). The painting shows the Grand Office to have been a substantial nine-bayed (3-3-3) brick building that, in some respects, had an outward appearance not dissimilar to the main Navy Office building. From a pedimented middle bay, access to the building was gained from a relatively unadorned doorway at first floor level and approached by an exterior stairway. The 1776 map shows that the entry door gave access to offices and other rooms leading away from the hall. The Grand Office would also have contained a boardroom, probably on the first floor, with the upper floors providing accommodation for the junior commissioners. As for the First Commissioner, the senior member and chair of the Board, he was provided with a much more palatial residence at the rear of the Grand Office.

A further office of significance close to the Tower was the Navy Treasury which, since 1664, had been situated in Old Broad Street but prior to that had been in Leadenhall Street. Also known as the Navy Pay Office, the office itself was on the west side of Broad Street and created out of three terraced town houses seemingly constructed during the early seventeenth century. None of these were remarkable in design, with each retaining its original porticoed entrance leading straight out onto a paved street. Within the building, offices had been established for the various clerks as well as an official residence for the Treasurer of the Navy.

Although when originally established as an office of state, the Treasurer of the Navy had very real duties, these had slowly been discarded. In fact, by the end of the eighteenth century, the post was considered little more than a sinecure, with the former duties of the Treasurer undertaken by a senior clerk of the office carrying the title Paymaster of the Navy. On occasions, the Treasurer might confer with the Paymaster, but little else was now expected of him. For this reason, and for the fact that the Treasurer of the Navy was drawing, by the end of the eighteenth century, an annual salary of £4,000, it was a much sought-after post.

Yet sinecure or not, a serious problem did arise for Henry Dundas, 1st Viscount Melville, who held the post from 1783 to 1801. He was accused, shortly after leaving office and while holding the office of First Lord, of failing to curb a series of questionable transactions carried out by Alexander Trotter, the Navy Paymaster, resulting in Melville having to defend himself against impeachment in the House of Commons. An inquiry had revealed that the Paymaster, who had connections with Coutts Bank, had opened a series of accounts in his own name, placing large sums of money into these accounts and profiting from the accrued interest. While the Navy had not suffered a loss, such speculation was deemed unacceptable. That Henry Dundas, as Treasurer of the Navy, was drawn into the controversy resulted from the possibility of him being aware of the transactions. Furthermore, the fact that Dundas had borrowed money from Trotter, money that might well have been drawn from public funds, did little to strengthen his position. With the opposition in Parliament baying for his blood, he was forced to resign as First Lord, although the attempted impeachment failed through his being acquitted.

The Tower of London, within whose shadows many of the early offices of the civil departments of the Navy had been established, was the home of the Ordnance Board. An independent administrative authority that could trace its origins back to the fourteenth century and the Wardrobe of Arms, it was responsible for the supply of guns and other weapons to the Navy. Furthermore, and here it is useful to borrow a few sentences from a select committee on finance that scrutinised the activities of the Board towards the end of the eighteenth century, the Board defrayed 'the Expense of the Artillery, Corps of Engineers and other military Corps attached to the Ordnance Service; and also the charge of repairing and building Fortifications, at Home and Abroad; excepting Field Works Abroad'. To this should be added a later acquired responsibility for the upkeep of Army barracks and for the supply of stores to convict establishments in the various penal colonies. In view of these significant non-naval responsibilities, all that needs to be noted of the offices of the Ordnance Board in London is that it formed the most active department within the Tower, possessing a number of offices on the south side. In 1774, as a result of a considerable fire, a number of buildings occupied by its administrative staff were destroyed leading to construction of a new administrative office completed in 1780. In turn, however, in 1788, this was devastated by a second fire leading to the construction of enlarged offices with new, purpose-built storehouses.

In 1789, the various offices of the three civilian boards of the Navy were relocated *en masse* to a newly constructed, purpose-built government office complex: Somerset House. It had also been proposed that the Ordnance Board was to move to Somerset House. However, opposition from the War Office, combined with the recent building of new offices within the area of the Tower, saw the abandonment of this idea, with the Ordnance Board remaining *in situ*. For the principal officers and the clerical staff of the Navy's civil departments this must have been a truly monumental event but it was surprisingly downplayed by George Marsh, then Clerk of the Acts, in the diary he kept of passing events, with the entry relating to 29 August:

> We finished business at the Navy Office in Crutched Fryers [*sic*] and removed all the books and papers to that at Somerset place in the Strand, and took possession thereof this day.

Situated alongside the Strand, Somerset House brought the inferior boards appreciably closer to the Admiralty, but the distance was still significant and one that precluded regular daily liaison. Perhaps the greatest advantage, apart from providing a greatly increased working area for departments that had outgrown their existing offices, was bringing about greater cooperation between the various civilian boards. Furthermore, it also permitted the eventual amalgamation of the civil departments, something that would not have been possible if the earlier offices had been retained.

The project to build Somerset House resulted from the availability of an extensive area of land previously occupied by a Tudor palace that had outlived its usefulness and fallen into considerable decay. As such, it passed out of royal hands, with demolition of the building creating a huge tranche of land in a very central location. It was this that prompted the scheme to build a sufficiency of office space to allow the moving of numerous government departments and the sale of the buildings that they had previously occupied. In the case of the Navy Office, the vacated site was to net £11,500 while the former site of the Victualling Office and attendant buildings, once cleared, was earmarked for the building of an equally important government establishment, a new Royal Mint.

Somerset House, a vast quadrangular building facing the Strand on its north side and the Thames to the south, was designed by William Chambers, then

Comptroller of the Board of Works and a co-founder of the Royal Academy. While the Strand frontage was reserved for use by a number of learned societies, including the Royal Academy and the Society of Antiquarians, much of the rest of the building was given over to the Navy and other government offices. Under construction by 1780, with the north block already completed by that date, Chambers provided Parliament with a report on the general progress of construction work:

> The building which faces the Strand extends in front 135ft, is 61ft deep, and has two wings, each 46ft wide and 42ft in depth, the whole being seven storeys high; it is faced with Portland stone, built with hard grey stock bricks, Russian timber, and the best materials of all kinds. All the fronts of this structure are decorated with a rustic arcade basement, a Corinthian order of columns and pilasters, enriched windows, balustrades, statues, masks, medallions, and various other ornamental works necessary to distinguish this principal and most conspicuous part of the design.

To this he added:

> The work just described forms the upper part (or north side) of a large quadrangular court, being in width 210ft and in depth 296ft, which is to be surrounded with buildings 54ft deep and six storeys high.

As to the progress of works:

> All these buildings surrounding the said court are now raised two storeys high (excepting at one corner where the old palace yet standing has prevented it); they have two floors laid on and the third storey carried up to a considerable height on all, the which forms the bottom of the court, and at the same time makes a considerable portion of the great river front, which when finished is, according to the general design, to extend in length 600ft.

A massive undertaking, the complex was not to be completed until at least 1801, by which time building costs had spiralled to £462,323, a sum well in excess of Chambers' original estimate that it would 'certainly not exceed the sum of £250,000'. In the meantime, as each block surrounding the central courtyard was completed, they were made available for occupation. As with the buildings previously occupied, those entitled to accommodation were suitably provided for, with rooms having been set aside on the upper levels of the two blocks.

Two notable rooms in Somerset House, both occupied by the commissioners of the Navy, were the Board Room and a model room. The former was a particularly grand working area in the neo-classical style, providing the commissioners with an area of 580 sq. ft. As with the Board Room of the Admiralty, it was dominated by one, large central table around which the commissioners sat for meetings of the entire board and committee meetings chaired by the Comptroller. The model room, of which doubtless there had also been one in the former Navy Office and to which the public was now admitted, contained a beautiful collection of scale replica ships of boats which the Navy Board had had built. The purpose of the models is a mystery, with some of the models having been made before the actual ship that they represented was completed. One possibility is that the models were demonstrations of the completed boat. Alternatively, they may have been decorative pieces. A recent book by Kriegstein suggested that the models were gifts from merchant building yards attempting to gain contracts for construction work (Kriegstein, 2010). However, one exhibit that was undeniably decorative was *Sovereign of the Seas*, flagship of the Stuart Navy, which was delivered to Somerset House in 1832 having been ordered from Chatham dockyard with William Bourneville, a shipwright, the actual modeller.

Not all the rooms in Somerset House were built on a grand scale, with the offices set aside for the junior clerks being somewhat plain and lacking in space. The Victualling Board, in particular, was unhappy with some of the areas they had been allocated, writing to the Admiralty in 1805 that the lobby used by their messengers 'is but fifteen feet long by thirteen foot wide [and] is also the only place that can be used as a Public Waiting Room for Merchants, Contractors and other persons attending at this office and it is, besides, unavoidably made use of as a repository for the Secretary's department' (TNA ADM 110/52, December 1805).

Following the general move to Somerset House, one further body with naval responsibilities was created and given offices within the complex. This was the Transport Board, established in 1794 and responsible for the hire of ships for the transport of troops and stores. Although a similar board had existed between 1690 and 1724, the dissolving of that board had resulted in transports having to be independently hired by a number of government departments, with the Navy Office hiring transports for the accommodation of troops, the Treasury for transports that carried provisions and the Ordnance Board for transports that contained ammunition and stores. The creation of a new Transport Board that worked closely with those departments ensured a more efficient arrangement, with better use of vessels once hired. The Transport Board also had responsibility for sick prisoners of war after 1795, and it may have been this function that led to it taking over the functions of the Sick and Hurt Board in 1806 (Rodger, 2006, p. 475). However, this proved short-lived, with the Transport Board abolished in 1817 and the work it performed divided between the Navy and Victualling boards. In the case of the former, the hiring of transports and related work was passed to the Navy Board, with its officials transferred from that Board and its officers serving on a fourth committee. Similarly, responsibility for sick and wounded seamen was transferred to the Victualling Board.

In moving to the new premises, thought was given to improved working practices, with the Navy commissioners laying down a few rules designed to eradicate some of the improper practices that appear to have been prevalent in the former Navy Office. Among these was that of women being allowed to sit for part of the day in the main hall selling fruit and clerks having their hair cut or being shaved by hairdressers coming into the building. This was no longer considered acceptable with the doorkeepers and messengers charged with the duty of preventing 'improper persons or those who have no business there not to be admitted' and to remove those 'loitering about the premises' or 'frequenting the offices to the interruption of the clerks in their business' (TNA ADM106/2622, 31 October 1786). These minor adjustments to the rules did little to address a series of inherent problems that fundamentally prevented the boards from operating as efficiently as they might. Here the problem was not so much a willingness to improve but of failing to understand how to efficiently manage the complex military–industrial structure that was now required to support the largest seagoing Navy that the world had ever seen. This required a structural reform of the system, not a few minor adjustments.

Between them, the various boards in London managed a civilian workforce of several thousand artisans, labourers and professionals, with the bulk of these employed in the hospitals, dock and victualling yards that were located at home and overseas. In addition, and often forgotten by those who have shown an interest in naval affairs, there were sizeable clerical staffs employed in London and elsewhere. It was a task of immense and unparalleled complexity. Those tasked with its management had no model that could be used for guidance; they simply had to correct organisational inefficiencies and complications as they emerged. With no managerial training other than some of the principal officers having served at officer level in the Navy, it often took decades for problems to be recognised and further decades for a solution to be attempted. While there were many examples of inefficiency, the pioneering nature of what was being undertaken must be recognised. Although disciplinary procedures, codes of conduct and clear lines of accountability are nowadays commonplace, in the eighteenth century they had yet to establish themselves as essential tools of management.

The failure to adopt a clear principle of leadership is a case in point. Throughout much of the eighteenth century, the commissioners appointed to each of these boards took decisions in common. While certain commissioners might possess direct association with a particular branch of business, the concept of individual leadership was missing. Instead of being charged with overall authority of a particular branch, all decisions relating to any branch were taken by the respective boards as a whole, making it impossible to hold any one commissioner individually responsible for errors and omissions. Making the situation worse, none of the boards had one person with a degree of authority greater than his colleagues. The Navy Comptroller is a case in point; he was given no overriding authority over other commissioners and was seen only as having equal status to other members of the Board. This strange situation was explained by Marsh in one of his diary entries, relating to the appointment of Charles Middleton to the post of Comptroller in August 1778:

> When Sir Charles was appointed Comptroller of the Navy which some misinformed people suppose for want of knowing the Navy Board's instructions that form the words Comptroller of the Navy, that he is Comptroller of the Navy Board, which is not the case, they each member having a power to Comptrol him in any business he may want to contrary to their opinion or the public interest or service, for neither himself or any other of the Board can give any order but such must be signed by three members of the Board, and if they disagree on any business it is to be executed by the order of the majority of the members of the Board. (Diary, 30 May 1789)

It was a similar situation with regard to the Victualling Board, where meetings were chaired in rotation, ensuring that nobody could acquire the authority of leadership for more than a few meetings at any one time.

Slowly, a realisation began to emerge that clearer lines of responsibility should be developed. From 1784 onwards, the Victualling Board began to see the emergence of a First Commissioner with real authority. This came about through the insistence by the Admiralty that the commissioner in charge of the department of the Accountant for Cash should chair all meetings of the Board. As for the Comptroller, who already had the authority to chair meetings of the Navy Board, an Order-in-Council of June 1796 gave official recognition to the authority that he had slowly acquired, stating that upon the Comptroller should 'be lodged a general superintending and directing power for the regular management of the business and controlling the expense of every branch of the office' (Hamilton, 1896, p. 240). Until that time and through a lack of formal codification of his authority, the only means by which he could check and direct the general business of the Board was by sheer force of character, although his instructions and suggestions could easily be ignored by other members of the Board who were considered of equal status.

It was also in 1796 that the impossibility of one Board, albeit meeting on a daily basis, could meaningfully discuss and decide on all matters coming before it was realised. Instead of introducing the concept of single-seated functionaries, an obvious reform being touted at that time by the philosopher Jeremy Bentham, a distinct compromise was implemented, with committees established in both the Navy and Victualling offices, with each committee made up of three commissioners. To these committees was delegated the task of overseeing specific branches of the two offices, with members of each committee now deemed to be collectively responsible for the tasks overseen. Once again it was impossible to recognise who might have generated a particular decision while the practice of some board members attending very few meetings continued.

These administrative changes were part of a wider reforming movement that was radically altering and improving the bureaucracy of government. The reaction to the failures of the American War helped drive this forward, with a series of commissions examining the various departments of state. Among the earliest of these was one that enquired into fees and other emoluments paid to public servants, together with an examination of abuses in government departments. Between April 1786 and June 1788 it produced a number of reports, with the fifth, sixth and eighth responsible for the introduction of those changes through a consideration of various aspects of the civil departments of the Navy. Having taken copious evidence from a former Navy Comptroller, Charles Middleton, they not only proposed the committee system with its emphasis on collective responsibility but this same Commission deemed it 'absolutely necessary' to separate the office of secretary from the Clerk of the Acts. In keeping with its main thrust, however, the Commission also ensured that numerous fees charged by secretaries and clerks within the civil departments of the Navy should be abolished.

The charging of fees was a throwback to a much earlier age when it had been seen as a useful economy. Allowing secretaries and clerks to charge those who needed official documentation meant that they could be employed on relatively small, fixed annual salaries. In total these fees could be quite considerable, with the Accountant for Cash, an employee of the Victualling Office, reporting that in the three years preceding 1798 he had an average income of £3,169 13s 0d of which only £120 was salary. At the same time his chief clerk reported that, over the same period, his average income had been of £1,722 2s 2d of which only £60 was his salary. The greatest danger in charging fees was that it became part of a private bargain in which the two parties were advancing themselves while overriding the interests of their employee.

Irrespective of whether a post holder was receiving fees as a means of enhancing a low annual salary there was a further problem that militated against efficiency: there was no effective encouragement of younger clerks who showed efficiency or ability. This relates back to the promotion system that relied entirely upon the retirement of older clerks and a consequent succession in promotion. As one clerk retired, or left the service, those below him in seniority, and it was only men who were employed, moved up a rung. Such a system naturally encouraged lethargy, especially as clerks were rarely dismissed other than for gross abuses, such as evident corruption. In the Victualling Office in 1801 two clerks were dismissed, John Coulthred and John Halloran, both for the repeated use of disrespectful language directed towards the Accountant for Stores. Even so, in such a clear case, with numerous witnesses and the concern that their 'behaviour in a very serious degree' would injure 'the morals of the young men' working alongside the two miscreants, it took considerable time and the involvement of the Admiralty to terminate their employment (TNA ADM111/160, 30 July 1801. Re-quoted MacDonald, 2010, p. 213).

Only in 1816 was there a real attempt to encourage efficiency and intellectual ability in the naval offices through a new system of regulating the clerks that created a more developed career structure by dividing the permanent (or established) clerks into three distinct classes. All new entrants were placed on the lowest echelon, third class, with promotion to the second class dependent only upon application and ability. Within each class a separate pay structure existed, providing all clerks with an annual increment of £10 per annum until the upper limit, permitted for that class, was reached. In the case of third-class clerks, this allowed, in 1830, for a continued increase of annual salary for thirty-one years while for second and first class clerks it was twenty and twenty-five years respectively. Those selected for promotion would enter the next class on the lower limit available to that class but equivalent to the highest level of the previous class (TNA PC2/197, 30 January 1816).

In time, several more changes and minor alterations to the basic system were introduced. Much of this concerned the appointment of an increased number of commissioners, some of them with new specialist expertise. Of perhaps greater significance, however, was a recommendation by a further examining commission, the Commission of Naval Revision, that the general 'superintendence and direction of business' of each committee should be placed in the hands of the most senior commissioner appointed to each committee. At the same time the Comptroller, who had been unable to make anything but infrequent appearance at meetings of the various committees, was allowed a more general superintending role.

That an order in council of 1829 should then dissolve the committees and replace them with a system that was, in some ways, not dissimilar from that in force prior to 1796, resulted from a failure to successfully operate a system of collective responsibility. Instead, and this was where the new arrangement differed from anything previously attempted, an emphasis was placed on individual responsibility, with each of the commissioners of the two remaining naval boards, the Navy and Victualling, taking responsibility for one clearly definable area of business. It was not a situation that was to be long lasting as these two boards were abolished three years later, with the work they performed being subsumed by the Admiralty. However, in doing so, the Admiralty also adopted the new style of management, with single-seated functionaries at the heart of that particular round of reforms.

Although the abolition of the inferior boards falls out of the Georgian era, it is worth noting that while Somerset House and Wallingford House were to have been retained, it was proposed that the civilian offices move to the Admiralty, so that everything could be run under one roof. To create the necessary space within the existing Admiralty complex, the First Lord and the various junior lords were to be given new residences at Somerset House, with Admiralty House and the upper floor residences of Wallingford House entirely utilised for administration. However, this part of the plan was never carried forward. The staff of the former civilian boards, or at least those who survived the re-organisation, remained at Somerset House.

4

Conflict in the Metropolis

Wallingford House lay in London's political heartland to the west. The offices of the civilian boards were closer to the financial centre to the east. These were the powerhouses of the Navy: where decisions were taken and instructions issued. Outwardly the line of authority was quite clear; the Admiralty was the superior board, empowered by Parliament to superintend and direct the whole maritime establishment, while the civilian boards acted upon those decisions. Yet, ensconced as they were in geographically separate offices and with minimal levels of contact, there was little likelihood of the system working smoothly. Add to this the independence of authority that each of the civilian boards had managed to create for themselves together with the natural desire of those appointed to these boards to protect their independence, the outcome was sometimes nothing less than chaos. A simple dispute that might start as a mere ripple of a difference could often result in a storm of contention. So firmly held did opinions become that they had the potential for toppling a government.

That the Navy Board could enter into open conflict with the Admiralty (and even come out as victors) was a result of a quirk of the administrative arrangement that existed between the superior Admiralty Board and the inferior civil boards. Those who served as commissioners of the Navy Board had permanency of office, nothing less than a sinecure for life that could only be taken from them for proven gross misconduct. In contrast the first and junior lords of the Admiralty were political appointees, holding post only so long as the government should choose to retain them in office. Normally, on the fall of a particular administration, the entire Board would be replaced by appointees drawn from the ranks of those supporting the new government. This produced a singular lack of continuity, with twenty-five First Lords holding office between 1714 and 1830. An exception was the period 1812 to 1830 when different factions of the Tory party maintained control of the government. During this period, and as an exception to all that had gone before, Robert Dundas, 2nd Viscount Melville, held office as First Lord for eighteen years, while Sir George Cockburn, his senior naval lord, held similarly lengthy office.

Something else that weighed against the Board of Admiralty was that when it came to administering the civil affairs of the Navy, its appointed members were at a serious disadvantage. None of them on first appointment had any real knowledge of the mechanics involved in running a dock or victualling yard. Furthermore, the political nature of their appointment, combined with uncertainty of tenure, meant that it was difficult for those who made up the superior board to gain the expertise they lacked. For this reason, the permanently appointed Navy and victualling commissioners resented being told what to do by a group of 'amateurs' whose term of office was uncertain. They resorted to various underhand methods to ensure that, when it came to the civil affairs of the Navy, they would win out in any dispute.

Of course, none of this affected the ships of the Navy while at sea. Here the Board of Admiralty, having once been instructed by the Cabinet (of which the First Lord was usually a member) as to the intentions of the government, was supreme. Admittedly the First Lord might be without direct naval experience, appointed because of loyalty to the party in government, but others on the board would include those with naval experience. These were the 'professional lords', of which it was common for three to be serving concurrently and advising the First Lord on strategy. In addition there were usually two 'civil lords', who lacked professional experience but were able to undertake much of the routine daily business.

All members of the Board were of equal rank. This was a further aspect to the administrative nightmare that permeated the governance of the Navy from the London offices. No single board member had an ounce of individual responsibility for a single area of the Navy. All decisions reached had to have the general agreement of the entire board, making it impossible to blame any single member of the board for a failed decision. Admittedly, the First Lord, assuming he had the willingness or personality to do so, held some authority, and was sometimes able to steer decisions in the direction he wished. However, when the appointed First Lord had no naval background this was an impossibility, rendering the First Lord dependent for advice on his junior naval lords. Adding to the absurdity, the civilian First Lord attended Cabinet meetings and might be called upon to advise on naval strategy and how best to deploy the fleet.

A particularly valuable tool for a First Lord seeking to secure his authority was his power of patronage. Through the Board, the First Lord had the power of appointment, and was able to determine and select the duties to be undertaken by the highest of naval officers to the most junior clerk within the Admiralty. This patronage extended to the civil offices, with the First Lord able to appoint members of the inferior boards, but only when a vacancy arose. In itself, this was a problem as the appointees of one First Lord had to work with subsequent First Lords irrespective of political loyalty. Using this patronage, the First Lord was able to secure parliamentary support, with naval officers in Parliament reluctant to oppose the wishes of a First Lord, knowing that a future career, either theirs or that of a family member, was dependent on a judiciously placed vote.

Some First Lords used the power of patronage wisely, while others were less discerning. Sir Charles Wager, First Lord from 1733 to 1742, was said to be swayed by a man's ability rather than sycophantic loyalty, giving Admiral Vernon command of the fleet in the West Indies 'because he was a very good sea officer' at a time when he was highly critical of the First Lord. The *London Evening Post* of 30 January/2 February 1773 reported of the Earl of Sandwich that a vacancy at the Navy Board had been offered by him on payment of £2,000, with the same statement repeated in the issue of 13–16 February. Sandwich, in denying this slight upon his character, indicted Miller, the printer of the *Evening Post*, for libel with the case tried on 8 July 1773. Despite the case being dismissed and Miller having to pay £2,000 in damages this, together with other unsupported claims made by his enemies, have been used by earlier historians as evidence that Sandwich used patronage unwisely. In 1894, naval historian John Knox Laughton stated of Sandwich when compiling an entry into the *Dictionary of National Biography*:

> Throughout his long administration he rendered the business of the Admiralty subservient to the interests of his party, and employed the vast patronage of the office as an engine for bribery and political jobbery. Other and shadier motives were also attributed to him.

In the 1930s a further noted naval historian gave this assessment of his character:

> Nothing in the history of naval administration is stranger than the fact that a First Lord who was more regular than any other in his inspection of the Yards and more acute in his criticism of their organisation, should have been so unprincipled in his selection of men to fill those positions in which the example of honesty and diligence was most necessary, that he actually strangled his own reforms at their birth. (Murray, 1938, p. 333)

More recently, however, Rodger, in his acclaimed biography of Sandwich has put the record straight following an examination of contemporary appointment books. From these, he concluded, 'when money was offered him, he refused it with contempt'. To this Rodger further added Sandwich's own refutation of such claims, a statement that dates to 1777:

I never was, nor ever will be concerned in the disposal of any Office in which I have even the most pecuniary transaction relative to filling the vacancy. (Rodger, 1994, p. 167)

Returning to London and its perpetual inter-board conflict, although difficulties might occasionally arise because of differences in political loyalty, more often it arose from differing administrative perspectives. For, although both boards were concerned with ensuring that an efficient seagoing fleet was always available in times of national emergency, they came at the problem from totally different directions. For the Board of Admiralty the basic concern was the fighting ability of a ship once at sea. As for members of the Navy and Victualling boards they, in giving their primary attention to the preparation of these ships, were more concerned with the costs and difficulties of getting them to sea. An Admiralty instruction for a slightly lengthened or redesigned warship might appear to be a relatively easy task. However, if it turned out that such a vessel exceeded the length of the available dry docks, or that its masts were of a different dimension from that standard to its class, then a massive expenditure would result. At whatever dockyard such a vessel was to be maintained, dry docks would have to be lengthened, while a collection of suitable masts would need to be assembled at not just the building yard, but at all fleet bases, home and overseas.

At other times a dispute could arise from differing personalities. The First Lord, Navy Comptroller or the First Victualling Commissioner could be domineering individuals who could not tolerate outside interference. This was a particular issue during the period 1801 to 1804, when St Vincent was First Lord while the Navy Comptroller was the equally determined Sir Andrew Snape Hamond. The two were both noted for their lack of tolerance with St Vincent, prior to his appointment, making it clear as to how he viewed the civil departments. In fact, his view of the Navy's civil administrators was venomous to the extreme. During the summer of 1797 he declared:

If all the clerks in the dockyards were dismissed, with annuities, payable on one condition only, 'that they reside fifty miles from any dockyard', the public would benefit exceedingly.

To this, he added just a few weeks later:

You may rest assured, the Civil branch of the Navy is rotten to the core. (27 August 1797. Quoted in Bonner-Smith, Vol. II, 1927, pp. 431–2)

A factor that exacerbated the difficult relationships between the superior and inferior boards was limited contact between members. This applied socially and professionally. Members of the Board of Admiralty rarely chose to meet with those of the inferior boards to discuss any problems. Differences of opinion were normally expressed in writing, with such arguments often spanning months or even years. The members of the boards were also drawn from backgrounds that were worlds apart. Whereas all five members of the Board of Admiralty were drawn from either the upper or lower chambers of Parliament, only one Navy commissioner, the Comptroller of the Navy Board, might be so connected. As for the other members of the inferior boards, they were of a clerical and practical background, appointed because of their ability or expertise in the fields of shipbuilding, food processing or medicine.

A final exacerbating factor was the physical separation of the Admiralty at Wallingford House from the civil boards clustered on the east side of London. This was a highly inconvenient arrangement and meant that a social detachment was enforced by geographical separation. A simple meeting that might help resolve a pressing issue was rarely easily arranged. The scheme to unite the two offices under one roof had fallen through in the 1830s and this was still being lamented some years later when a senior clerk of the Admiralty, J.S. Bromley, reported:

> Even now, in time of peace, the inconvenience arising from one portion of the office being so far detached from the other, must be felt by every member of the Board who has to seek information on questions of detail. In time of war a rapid execution of orders will become indispensable, and I fear that much difficulty and confusion will ensue. I am quite certain that not an objection, which can deserve consideration, can be raised against this consolidation. The cost, whatever it may be, of providing accommodation for the whole of the Admiralty department at Whitehall would be but small in comparison with the advantages to be derived from the whole being more immediately under the eye of the Board. (Commissioners on Management of H.M. Dockyards, 1847, appendix 16, pp. 485–90)

The strategy most often adopted by the Navy Board during disputes with the Admiralty was to use their built-in advantage of permanency of office. If an instruction was regarded as ill-advised, the inferior board would often delay carrying it out, hoping that the personnel of the superior board would alter and the instruction be rescinded. Sometimes this was all that was required, a newly appointed Board often shelving policies pursued by the out-going Board.

A particularly effective member of the Board of Admiralty was Lord George Anson. He was appointed as a naval lord following his return from commanding the 60-gun *Centurion* on a mission against Spanish shipping that eventually took her on a circumnavigation of the globe. This gave Anson considerable kudos and it was a major factor in his appointment. Initially he served under the Duke of

Bedford, a First Lord without naval experience who was also new to the office. Both Bedford, and his successor as First Lord, the Earl of Sandwich, relied heavily upon Anson for advice. In June 1751, upon the resignation of Sandwich, Anson was appointed First Lord. The inexperience of Board members, all of whom had first taken office in December 1744, led them to accept Anson's advice. A wide range of naval reforms were carried out, with the work continuing when Anson became First Lord.

Conflict between the Admiralty and the inferior boards was fairly minimal during the first decades of the Georgian era but there were several periods of disunity from the mid-1740s onwards. The initial cause was complaints from naval captains that ships ordered to sea were unduly delayed while in dockyard hands. In April 1746, the commissioners of the Navy were informed that the Lords of the Admiralty 'were quite weary of the perpetual complaints' and directed that an inquiry be made into the situation that applied especially to Portsmouth dockyard. At the same time, they ordered Vice-Admiral Sir James Steuart, the port admiral and highest standing naval officer at Portsmouth, to carry out his own separate inquiry on behalf of the Admiralty. This immediately incurred the anger of the resident commissioner at Portsmouth, a member of the Navy Board and their direct link with the dockyard:

> I have received from Vice Admiral Steuart [that the] Admiralty have been pleased to order him to make an enquiry into this matter. I sincerely wish, for the good of the service, no innovations, especially of this kind, were ever to be made, and that every person in public business was not to interfere with any other, but be strictly confined to what relates to his own proper branch only. For instance, let every admiral appear to be and act as an admiral. (NMM POR/F/7, 6 April 1746)

Doubtless the sentiment was shared by his fellow commissioners. Relations between the superior and inferior board plummeted even further upon a subsequent instruction that the Navy Board direct its officers at Portsmouth to take their orders from Steuart. Not surprisingly, the commissioners of the Navy Board refused to support this demand, with the Admiralty bluntly informing the inferior board that they 'would not suffer their orders to be trifled with'. Despite a further threat that their lordships would 'take such measures as will not be agreeable to them', the Navy Board calmly informed the Admiralty that Steuart was not the best person to be given such authority. He was, as they pointed out, not 'conversant with the civil economy of the Navy' and would, if they permitted him this authority, 'rather impede than forward' the service. As it happens the Admiralty was in no position to enforce Steuart's authority, with the taking of measures 'not agreeable to them', being no more than a bluff. Indeed, a change as extensive as this would need the backing of an Act of Parliament, thus providing an opening for the opposition in Parliament to denounce the current administration as a failure.

All this did not mean the matter was closed. From Anson, still a member of the Board, but having taken command of the Channel Fleet, the Board of Admiralty received reports on a raft of problems that he encountered, including delays in getting ships ready for sea, poor food and ships being inadequately equipped for sea service. On 31 October 1746, in a letter read out to his fellow board members by one of the two office secretaries, Anson noted:

It frequently happens in winter times that Channel cruisers spring or carrying away their masts, and are sometimes obliged to wait several days till new ones are made, to the great hindrance of HM Service. I therefore desire their lordships will give direction to the Navy Board to have always a set of masts ready finished at all His Majesty's yards, for ships of the 3rd rate and downwards.

From Plymouth during the early part of 1747 Anson reported:

I found on my arrival at Plymouth that none of the frigates were clean. This, as you will easily perceive was no small disappointment to me, as I had sent previous orders to their captains to clean and hold themselves constantly in readiness to sail at a moment's warning. I feel the want of them very much in disciplining my ships; and I shall be more sensible of it if I meet with an enemy's fleet having nothing with me to repeat my signals. (Pack, 1987, p. 155)

It was from his observations of the shortcomings within the dockyards that led Board members to visit the dockyards for the purpose of inspecting them, a decision taken in the Board Room on 9 June 1749 (TNA ADM3/61, 9 June 1749).

It is easy to imagine the annoyance felt by the commissioners of the civilian boards when informed that the facilities that they managed were to be inspected and that this was to be done without any accompanying members of the civilian boards. From the Admiralty's point of view, this allowed them to communicate directly with yard officers who would be more likely to freely comment in the absence of an immediate superior. While the commissioners of the two inferior boards could do little to prevent the inspection, known officially as a 'visitation', they did ensure that the resulting instructions were delayed in being circulated to the yards with no subsequent attempt to enforce their compliance. However, the Admiralty's wish to see a reduction in the numbers employed in the yards was met with particular hostility. The six naval dockyards (Portsmouth, Plymouth, Chatham, Deptford, Woolwich and Sheerness) were employing approximately 7,000 men, a number that the Admiralty noted as being greater than that employed during the War of the Spanish Succession (1701–14). Given that the government, under First Minister Henry Pelham, had recently adopted a programme of economising, Sandwich, First Lord since February 1748, had instructed the Navy Board to reduce the numbers employed. The Navy Board had responded that this was impossible due to the returning fleet being in need of considerable repair with a larger workforce absolutely essential. The Admiralty was in no position to dispute the claim, something that changed when they had completed their inspection of the yards.

The subsequent 'visitation' allowed members of the Board of Admiralty to reach their own conclusions. They were concerned at the number of elderly and infirm workers to be found within the yards and they went on to suggest that many of these could be dismissed. In addition, they informed the Navy Board that many workers appeared to be generally indolent and that they, too, should be dismissed. On this issue, and placed under a level of pressure never previously witnessed, the commissioners of the Navy attempted to hold firm, using a combination of reasoned argument and delay. However, with the Admiralty constantly returning to the matter, the inferior Board began a programme of dismissals that would eventually amount to 895 artisans and labourers. A further Admiralty suggestion was that selected members of the workforce should no longer be paid by the day but by the amount of work completed – in other words through the introduction of piece rates, known in the dockyards as 'task work'. While it might increase output, as the day rate was paid according to attendance and not the amount of work, the Navy Board viewed piece rates as likely to lead to work being rushed. For this reason, they provided the Admiralty with a blunt refusal, stating that they were 'against any innovation', especially 'the attempting to build anything whatever by Task' (TNA ADM3/62, 2 June 1752).

Given that Jacob Ackworth, Navy surveyor since 1715, had done so little to correct the many perceived failings within the yards, the Admiralty began to hold him primarily responsible for what they deemed an appalling situation. Furthermore, with Ackworth's responsibility also extending to the design of warships, this was viewed as a second area in which he demonstrated serious shortcomings. At this point the Navy required significantly enlarged and improved ships that would better match French and Spanish ships then entering service. Apart from making such vessels more seaworthy, they would also have the advantage of mounting heavier guns. Ackworth, while conceding the need for improvements, was seen as a block on the more radical changes desired, leading to an attempt to bring about his removal and ultimate replacement.

In part, the problem was Ackworth's age. Having been appointed Navy surveyor in 1716 he had long been in a position to opt for retirement. A septuagenarian by 1740, he no longer had the stamina to perform such a massively important task, with his thinking very much in an earlier age. While the former prevented him from effectively overseeing the dockyards, his thinking went back to the more limited needs of the seventeenth-century Navy rather than the expanded global role that the Navy now undertook. Or at least that was the way the Admiralty saw it. For his part, Ackworth was concerned that in building the ships demanded by the Admiralty, he might be producing speedier and better-armed vessels but they would be lighter and less resilient. As a result, expenditure would be greater as they would require more dockyard maintenance and early replacement. However, Ackworth, through age, had become increasingly stubborn and was little open to advice, finding it difficult to seek out a more radical solution that would ensure a ship built to last while also meeting the requirements of the sea service. While the Admiralty had the power to name his successor, and even went so far as to appoint a second surveyor, Joseph Allin, who was to work alongside Ackworth, they had no authority to remove an incumbent already in office. The frustration felt by members of the superior board in London was eloquently put by Henry Legge, a civil junior lord in a written missive to the Duke of Bedford:

> … it is high time ships began to have bottoms to them & more expedition as well as better œconomy prevail'd in dockyards. This cannot happen while he [Ackworth] has any influence he will have it all. We know Sir Jacob to have so much of the nature of the Pompey the Great in him that he cannot be an equal & if Mr Allen should have so much of the temper of Julius Caesar about him that he cannot brook a superior – what must ensue but civil war added to the many indecorums and distresses the dockyards at presently labour under? Things will go on worse than ever, the same laziness, the same want of œconomy, the same aversion and discouragement to ingenuity, nothing will be suffered to continue in the yards but cousins and flatterers, and nothing turned out but bad ships and able shipwrights. (Legge to Duke of Bedford, 6 March 1746, cited Baugh, 1965, p. 90)

Only in March 1749 were matters partially resolved, this the result of an authority more superior than even that of the Admiralty: Ackworth was taken by 'the Grim Reaper' while still holding office as Navy surveyor. Allin, quite naturally, was retained in office, working with Thomas Bately, a newly appointed assistant surveyor. However, Allin was not the man the Admiralty was really seeking. He also maintained a conservative approach to ship design, forcing a further delay in the arrival of ships that were fully to meet Admiralty approval. Only in 1755, upon the appointment of Thomas Slade, following an incapacitating illness that prevented Allin continuing in office, did matters begin to ease. Slade, together with Bately, now took responsibility for the overseeing of dockyards and the design of warships. This time, the Admiralty appears to have been more careful about the man selected. Promoted from Deptford dockyard, where he had been Master Shipwright, it appears that Slade had been groomed into the post, tutored perhaps by the junior naval lords as to their perception of warship needs. Indeed, they had probably manoeuvred the arrangement, ensuring that Slade was appointed to Deptford in March 1753. This gave him proximity to Wallingford House, allowing him to pay a number of regular informal visits to garner information as to the new types of ships that the Admiralty was seeking. Leastways, within only three weeks of Slade's appointment, he had produced a design for a large two-decker warship of 74 guns (although originally classed as of 70 guns), the first of a new class of warships that eventually came to dominate the line of battle and which fulfilled the Navy's desire for ships of greater length of beam that would allow them to carry a greater weight of armament.

While these difficulties were finally resolved, further changes of government would ensure that future civilian boards with long-term, serving commissioners would fall out with their political superiors. A new level of spite and intrigue was reached in the 1770s when Navy Comptroller George Cockburn became so opposed to Sir Edward Hawke, the First Lord, that he began providing damaging information on the state of the Navy to senior politicians with whom he sympathised. His object was to force Hawke out of office so that he might be replaced by someone more amenable. Put to use by one senior politician opposed to Hawke, it was claimed that work being performed at the Admiralty was 'bungled' and the country 'was to be pitied'.

However, the very divisiveness of the system ensured that even when the superior and inferior boards were working together reasonably effectively, issues would still emerge that would undermine cooperation. From August 1778, the Comptroller was Charles Middleton, a reformer who was to make root-and-branch reforms to the Navy Board, including the production of schemes of duty that ensured every officer was fully aware of what was expected of him.

Middleton was also aware of the structural failings of the system that he believed prevented the inferior boards from effectively carrying out the work they were required to perform. Accusing members of the Board of Admiralty of lacking 'professional knowledge' and having 'a want of method of execution' in directing themselves to the management of the yards:

> All I can do at the Navy Office will avail but little if the Admiralty continues what it is at present. It is, indeed, so wretchedly bad, that, if I waited for official orders and kept within the line of duty, without pressing or proposing what ought to come unasked for, we must inevitably stand still. (Rodger, 1994, p. 163)

Of the First Lord, Middleton believed his role to be too demanding, given that Sandwich was required to oversee the workings of the entire board and give direction to the inferior boards while also being a member of the Cabinet and attending sessions of the House of Lords. Specifically directing himself to this, Middleton asked of Sandwich:

> If I my lord, who am a professional man, find myself, unequal to the duties of office I am in, with an application of twelve hours six days in the week, how is it possible that your lordship can manage yours, which is equally extensive, in three or four?

For Middleton, the solution was for the Comptroller to be a member of the Board of Admiralty and serve as an immediate adviser to the First Lord. In turn, and to ensure that the Comptroller and members of the Navy Board were fully versed with matters relating to the provisioning needs of the Navy, the First Victualling Commissioner should be a member of the Navy Board. To this he added:

> The utility of such a line of communication would [be] inconceivable to those who have not experienced the delays of office in services of despatch.

John Jervis, Earl St Vincent, proved more jaundiced than most, seeing the Navy Board at the heart of all the corruption and inefficiencies that he believed permeated the entire organisation. Unlike Sandwich and Anson, who attempted with varying degrees of reasonableness to work with the Navy Board, St Vincent simply chose to cut them out of the equation. Instead of formally seeking the approval of those who managed the dock and victualling yards, Jervis, as on the occasion of that first visitation but not those subsequently undertaken, merely informed them that the hospitals, dock and victualling yards were to be inspected. In a carefully written minute of a meeting held in the Board Room on 15 March 1801, it was clear that no area of the responsibilities held by the civilian administrators was regarded as being properly performed. It referred to expenses being 'beyond what was known in any former period', 'flagrant abuses', general 'mismanagement' and the clear implication that money was not being used 'wisely' (Bonner-Smith, *The Letters of Lord St Vincent*, p. 182).

Overall, the effect on the Navy during St Vincent's short period of office was disastrous. Fairly sizeable numbers of workers, decried as inefficient or uncooperative, were dismissed while the Navy Board was prevented from employing replacements. This left the dockyards short of workers and unable to maintain and repair the ships of a fleet that was constantly expanding. With relations between the Admiralty and civilian boards on a knife-edge, they broke down entirely in January 1803 when an instruction was issued by the Admiralty that no orders were to be given to the merchant yards for building third-rate ships. Instead they were to be built in the royal dockyards. This was a further example of St Vincent's agenda, for not only did he wish to entirely reform the civilian departments but also to reduce the power and strength of the merchant yards, which he deemed riddled with corruption:

> Were there a fair competition between the merchant builder and the King's Yards; were there anything like honesty, either in the terms or performance of these contracts – there would exist no objection to having recourse to them as often as the royal ships should prove insufficient to the demand of shipping which the Admiralty might make upon them, without necessity, and for the mere motive of conciliating a great body of interest to the political measures of the day, it is impossible for any system to be invented more corrupt, and prejudicial to the state; more pernicious to the royal dockyards; more fatal to the safety and independence of the Navy. (Bonner-Smith, *The Letters of Lord St Vincent*, pp. 456–7)

The problems between the Admiralty and Navy Board could have been minimised during any period of guaranteed peace. However, a rapidly deteriorating situation with France, leading to a reopening of hostilities in May, meant that the ability of the dockyards to work with maximum efficiency, and reliance upon merchant yards, were of paramount importance. Prime Minister Henry Addington, who had appointed St Vincent, came under increasing criticism in Parliament. The opposition under Pitt was incensed by the crusade against the civilian departments that was gradually undermining the ability of the Navy to defend the nation. In Parliament Pitt threatened that should he return to office he would 'institute an enquiry into the conduct of the Admiralty' before going on to accuse St Vincent of being 'less brilliant and less able in a civil capacity than in that of a warlike one' (*The Times*, 1 March 1804). While not responsible for the final and inevitable downfall of Addington, the criticism against St Vincent was a major factor and contributed to the return of Pitt as Prime Minister in May 1804.

Those sympathetic to St Vincent were not to be returned to power, other than for a brief period between 1807 and 1808, for some thirty years. It was only then that the debate was re-opened, with reforms carried through that were to lead to a completely new system of dockyard administration that did not involve the Admiralty having to negotiate with the commissioners of near independent inferior boards. However, this does not mean to say that there were no instances of the Admiralty and civilian boards entering into periods of dispute, merely that they were more amicably resolved. Appointed First Lord in 1812, Robert, 2nd Viscount Melville, was to remain in office until 1827, returning for a second period that lasted from September 1828 until November 1830. During those sixteen years, the longest period of service of any First Lord, he was in a position to ensure that the personnel who made up the Navy and Victualling boards were entirely to his liking. By 1822, he had overseen the appointment of all the professional officers of the two boards, leaving only a few commissioners of a clerical or business background pre-dating his own appointment.

The issue of the numbers employed within the dockyards was again raised during Melville's time at the Admiralty. Sir Thomas Byam Martin, appointed Navy Comptroller by Melville in 1816, sanctioned some very considerable reductions but wished to retain a significant number of skilled artisans. To help curtail the wage bill, Martin chose to limit possible earnings by reducing the maximum number of hours worked. This allowed Martin to retain many of those who might otherwise have been dismissed, the Comptroller believing that it would be better in the event of war to have these skilled artisans at hand, rather than conduct an urgent recruiting campaign. However, this was not to Melville's liking. Following an inquiry into the state of the dockyards that was undertaken in 1822, members of the Board of Admiralty became very concerned at the degree of overmanning. Martin was called upon to correct the situation, with the Admiralty no longer believing itself to be in a position to 'sanction longer continuance of the existing system' and requested that the yards 'be placed on a footing agreeable to the public interest' (TNA ADM1/3462, 20 June 1822).

In the event, it was one of the few disagreements between the two boards in London that was to enter the public domain, with the ageing former First Lord, Earl St Vincent, among those who chose to comment. He, as always, took a very independent view, attacking the administration in a similar fashion to his 'if all the clerks were dismissed' letter of June 1797:

> Instead of discharging valuable and experienced men, of all descriptions from the dockyards, the commissioners and secretaries of all the boards ought to be reduced to the lowest number they ever stood at, and the old system resorted to: one of the projectors of the present diabolical measure should be gibbeted opposite to Deptford Yard and the other on the opposite to the Woolwich yard, on the Isle of Sad Dogs. (J. S. Tucker, *Admiral the Right Hon The Earl of St Vincent GCB &C, Memoirs*, 1844, Vol. II, p. 425)

St Vincent, while loyal to the Whigs, the party then in opposition, also had an axe to grind. It was his intention, together with those who had been in any way associated with the Admiralty at the time of the collapse of the Addington administration, to finally bring an end to a system of naval administration that gave so much authority to the inferior boards. In Parliament evidence was produced of which politicians of an earlier decade had seemingly been unaware. James Graham, a future First Lord who was now working closely with those most opposed to the civilian boards, demonstrated that the civilian boards had a total disregard for Parliament, claiming money for one purpose and then spending it elsewhere. In words spoken on 22 January 1831 he declared:

> the entire sum voted annually by Parliament has been considered a gross sum applicable to purposes not contemplated in the Estimates, and in some items, more, and in others, less has been expended, than the precise sum allotted. (BL Add Ms 41, 368, 22 January 1831)

At Woolwich, improvements to the dockyard had been requested, but actual expenditure was considerably higher, while in such diverse areas as Leith and Bombay money, not sanctioned by Parliament, had been spent on shipbuilding. The Victualling Board took a similar approach, spending large and unsanctioned sums of money on building works at the Cremill (Plymouth) and Weevil (Gosport) victualling yards.

Although abolishment of the civil boards and the placement of the work they undertook directly into the hands of the Admiralty was undertaken in the immediate post-Georgian epoch, the necessity for taking such action was one that, in its entirety, was played out under the four Georges. Indeed, the move might well have happened earlier if one member of the Board of Admiralty during the late 1820s, Sir George Cockburn, had got his way. Recognising that the civilian boards were subverting the required economies by inflating their estimates for essential items and then spending monies elsewhere, he moved an amendment in Parliament that would have resulted in the combining of the Navy and Victualling boards under a new and much stricter arrangement that would have firmly placed them under the control of the Admiralty.

Part 2

THE DOWNRIVER NAVAL INDUSTRIAL COMPLEX

Introduction

Moving away from the administrative and bureaucratic heartland of the capital and following the Thames in an easterly direction, the Navy takes on even greater significance. Downriver, stretching out towards Deptford, Greenwich and Woolwich, was a vast, naval industrial complex. When not directly supportive of the Navy, it was home to various other enterprises that depended on the Navy for survival and continued expansion. Into the naval side of this complex, the government poured vast sums of money for warship construction and repair, the warehousing of naval stores, treatment of the sick and wounded, storage of shipboard ordnance, and the processing and supply of provisions for those at sea. Integrated into the complex, serving both the needs of private enterprise and the Navy, were numerous and varied mercantile enterprises that helped secure the finances that permitted the Navy to become a dominant global force. In this respect it was a circular and self-supporting process, for without the Navy, the extensive and necessary finances would not have been available in the first place. Much of the money was generated through the expansion of overseas trade, resulting from naval conquest and subsequent protection of the sea lanes. The outcome was that mercantile trade and the Navy grew in complete symmetry. For London, it not only ensured wealth being brought into the City but also secured the continued growth of this massive downriver industrial complex that was helping meet the two conjoined elements in their surge towards global dominance.

Limehouse Reach, a stretch of the Thames that runs from Shadwell to Deptford with a tidal flow that passes Rotherhithe on the right bank and Limehouse and the Isle of Dogs on the left, was a particularly significant element of that downriver complex. Throughout the reign of the four Georges, it was a stretch of river that was home to a large-scale shipbuilding industry, made up of numerous yards with experience in the construction of warships and large merchantmen. While many were privately financed, the largest was the government-owned dockyard at Deptford. Adding to the importance of this area, Limehouse Reach also serviced a Navy victualling yard, several timber wharves and rope walks, together with the mooring and docking facilities of the Transport Board, while providing numerous additional moorings for naval ships out of service. Finally, where space permitted, hundreds of tightly packed houses also faced onto Limehouse Reach, providing homes for the artisans and labourers who were employed within this important naval-industrial nexus. In describing the significance of Limehouse Reach, an attempt has been made to portray this stretch of water through the eyes of the commissioners of the Admiralty and Navy Board as they passed along this stretch of river on their way to observe, as they actually did, the launch of the first-rate, 112-gun warship, *Queen Charlotte*.

While the naval dock and victualling yards of Deptford lay off Limehouse Reach, these facilities can be seen as part of the naval-industrial complex known as 'Kentish London', referred to as a naval multiplex. It is a term used to cover Deptford, Woolwich and Greenwich; the first two were dependent entirely upon the Royal Navy for their growth and economic survival. Indeed, prior to the reign of Henry VIII and the establishment within their midst of two separate dockyards, both Deptford and Woolwich had been characterised by their dependence on agriculture and fishing. As for Greenwich, being the site of a royal park and a grand palace had protected it from industrialisation. Thus it was a suitable location for a naval hospital and a royal observatory.

When Daniel Defoe visited Kentish London in the 1720s he provided clear evidence of these contrasting communities, writing that Greenwich was 'the most delightful spot of ground in Great Britain'. Of Woolwich, however, he felt forced to remark that it was 'wholly taken up by, and in a manner rais'd from the Yards'. To this he added the existence of a ropewalk, 'where the biggest cables are made for the men of war', and a gun yard, 'set apart for the great guns belonging to ships'. Surprisingly, he says little of Deptford, also the home of a major dockyard but with the future victualling complex yet to be developed beyond a few meagre storehouses. In all, these government-owned undertakings were employing in excess of 2,000 workers during the early part of the eighteenth century, with this number exceeding 7,000 by the time the Napoleonic Wars were drawing to a close. To this figure, of course, can be added at least as many people dependent on these facilities: shopkeepers, merchants and publicans who met the needs of those employed by the government.

The proximity of Woolwich and Deptford to the centre of London gave the naval facilities there, but especially the dockyards, an enhanced significance.

Directly overseen by the Navy Office in London, it was in these yards that new ideas and methods were developed and trialled. This was particularly so with regard to the dockyard at Deptford, with the Navy surveyor or Comptroller able to journey from his office in London to the dockyard by river barge in less than thirty minutes. Similarly, the principal officers of the yard would frequently be called to the Navy Office to give advice on processes and procedures. In 1774, in an account of the two dockyards produced by the Earl of Sandwich for presentation to the King, this aspect of the work of the yards was duly emphasised:

> This [Deptford] and Woolwich yard being so near to the Navy Office there is no resident commissioner there, they are under the immediate inspection of the Comptroller and Surveyor of the Navy, and as the Navy Board has frequent occasion to send for the Deptford officers for information upon matters respecting the several branches of business in the Dock Yards, so the Principal officers in this yard have been usually considered as the most experienced and ablest officers in the several Branches. (BL Kings 44)

In addition to shipbuilding and the docking of ships in need of extensive repairs, which was the main role allocated to Deptford and Woolwich dockyards, the former was also the primary receiving yard for materials purchased through the London markets. Store ships carrying a great variety of items, which might include canvas, ships' sails, anchors, marine clothing, tar, turpentine or hammocks, would be offloaded and removed to the Grand Storehouse. Here it was divided into smaller lots for eventual transfer to one of the numerous lighters, launches or large transport ships hired for the purpose of shipping the items to another of the home yards, an outport or foreign station.

Of course, the siting of two naval dockyards nearly 50 miles from the open sea was a problem and explains why both Deptford and Woolwich were used primarily as building and heavy-repair yards rather than serving as operational fleet bases. In fact, the latter role would have proved totally illogical, it sometimes taking as long as six weeks for a man-of-war, heavily dependent on the appropriate winds and tides, to reach one or other of these two dockyards from the Channel or North Sea.

Indeed, it was the shallowness of the river that was proving particularly problematic, especially beyond Woolwich where there was extensive shoaling. This particularly affected Deptford, with this yard long unavailable to ships of the line. As for the building of such ships, this was still possible as at the time of their launch they required a much reduced draft through not being ballasted or having the weight of their masts and other fittings. Even for the dockyard at Woolwich there were problems, as first and second rates could only reach this yard by unloading ordnance and other heavy items of equipment at Northfleet, which lay a little above Gravesend. For this reason, and because their ships were also of some size, the vessels of the East India Company were forced to unload some of their cargoes at Gravesend before traversing the shallower waters of the Thames. Adding to the difficulties faced by the Navy, Woolwich and Deptford were unable to offer the most suitable moorings for ships that might otherwise lie off the dockyard for any length of time. This was a result of the Thames at this stretch still being freshwater, leading to the bottom of ships decaying much sooner than if they were in salt water.

5

Limehouse Reach: the Underpinning Foundation

For Londoners with an interest in the Navy, and that meant most of them, the launch of a massive new warship at the naval yard closest to the centre of the capital was bound to attract a great deal of interest. Moreover, *Queen Charlotte,* named after the wife of King George III, the Queen Consort, was the largest warship to be built so close to London. Officially rated to carry 104 guns, although she was actually to carry 112, she was due to be launched at the royal dockyard in Deptford on Tuesday 18 June 1810. She is little remembered today, possibly because the only notable action in her naval career was to act as flagship for Lord Exmouth's successful expedition to rescue European slaves from the North African pirate states in 1816, but her launch enthused all London. Thousands of people streamed from the metropolis to witness the event.

The launch was an important public occasion. Anyone who was anyone had received formal invitations to view the spectacle from temporarily erected gantries placed on either side of the slipway. Once the ship had entered the Thames, this august body would happily feast themselves at a formal banquet. Nor were those who had built the ship ignored, with the workforce given a paid holiday and the Master Shipwright the gift of an inscribed silver plate. Finally, the general public were also admitted, with the gates of the yard opened for all at 10 a.m. From that hour onwards, a constant stream of excited spectators made their way into this normally secure government complex.

Eventually, and with little experience of managing such events, the thin, red line of Royal Marines that had been detailed to keep order began to give way. Too few in number, the intense pressure of the mass of spectators proved too much. *The Times* subsequently reckoned on some 20,000 having entered the yard. Fortunately, the ceremony of naming the ship was already under way, with the various blocks and wedges that had secured the vessel while under construction having been removed. This transferred the weight of the soon-to-be-launched vessel to a sliding cradle that would, through the declivity of the slipway and the force of gravity, take her into her natural element.

Upon the signal, the 'dog-shores', the stout oak bars that held the cradle in position were removed, allowing the vessel to slide forward. Entering the river stern first, so allowing her to be more easily brought to a standstill, the resulting surge of water threatened the safety of nearby boats crammed full with water-borne spectators of the event. As for the multitude within the dockyard, so recently intent upon pushing their way forward, they were brought to an immediate standstill. Held in awe by what they were witnessing, some may have thought that the vessel had become unmanageable, a massive hulk on course to ground on the Isle of Dogs. But no such danger existed. The shipwrights of the dockyard possessed a good deal of experience in launching ships, but just in case a large anchor in the bow was ready if the vessel needed steadying. Much more important for halting the vessel were the hawsers the *Queen Charlotte* trailed, combined with the launch happening shortly before high tide. With the tide running upriver, the water flow quite naturally pushed her away from the opposite shore, allowing the hawsers to bring her to rest at the desired spot. It was here that the bow anchor was finally released; *Queen Charlotte* was safely afloat.

Most of the crowd that had viewed the launch had travelled by road, the main thoroughfare to Deptford 'almost covered with coaches, gigs, dog carts and every vessel that could be put in requisition for the occasion' (*The Times*, 19 June 1810). Also present at the launch were two exclusive and separate parties that had, most decidedly, not endured the discomfort of joining the seething masses that had taken the landward route to Deptford. They were the chief administrators of the Navy, carefully keeping their distance from each other by arriving in two separate river-going barges. Not that the word barge is a particularly appropriate term for their vessels, having little in common with the sturdy and utilitarian vessels to which this term is usually applied. Their river conveyances, sometimes known as shallops, were designed for speed and comfort. Long and narrow, with a covered compartment to the rear and a number of oarsmen seated forward, they could travel the 4 miles from central London to Deptford in considerably less than thirty minutes. Luxury vessels *par excellence*, the covered seated area was finely painted and finished with carved, wooden panelling and laid out with embroidered cushions. Of these two vessels, one was the state barge belonging to the Board of Admiralty (on this occasion carrying Charles Yorke, the newly appointed First Lord and several junior lords) and the second was the Navy commissioners' barge (with Sir Thomas Thomson, the Navy Comptroller and two Navy surveyors). Each vessel was readily identifiable by a flag flown at the masthead: in the case of the Admiralty barge a gold anchor on a red background while the Navy Board's boat had a great anchor between two smaller anchors also of gold and set on a red background.

As the Admiralty building overlooked St James's Park on the one side and Whitehall on the other, it had no obvious accommodation for a water-borne vessel. Instead, the ornately decorated barge was housed in a large empty basement underneath Somerset House and boarded via a stairwell from the Navy Board offices. From here, a large arched water gate, sited beneath the terrace that overlooked the river, permitted an easy exit for the two barges into the Thames.

It was not seen as acceptable for their lordships to come to the Navy Office to board their barge. Instead, upon instruction, it was rowed to Whitehall Stairs from where they would board. Some 150 yards from Wallingford House, it stood behind a short flight of stone steps that led down to the water. Here a substantial stone jetty, overlooked by a tall, colonnaded structure, provided an impressive point of entry that also gave their lordships somewhere to shelter.

Leaving their respective points of departure sometime around midday, both the Admiralty and commissioners' barges, on the day *Queen Charlotte* was launched, would have passed along the entire length of Limehouse Reach, before taking station at the head of several other barges, some also occupied by invited guests while others carried military bandsmen. In passing along the full length of the Reach, those on board the two barges should have been impressed by the numerous industrial enterprises that fundamentally helped underpin the country as a naval power. Whether setting out from Somerset Place or Whitehall Stairs the two barges would have headed east, shooting through the arches that supported both Blackfriars and London bridges. Their progress would have been slightly slowed by the oarsmen having to row against the floodwaters of the incoming tide. Coming within sight of the Tower, the long-time connection of this ancient fortification with the Navy might have been remarked upon. Still serving as the administrative centre for the Ordnance Board, the White Tower had, up until the 1690s, served as a store for naval ordnance and gunpowder, with this transferred by river to ships fitting out at Deptford and Woolwich.

Still within the Pool of London, the river at this point was a hive of commercial activity. On the opposing shores of Bermondsey and Wapping, a crowded line of wharves and quays were in constant use unloading ships. Those quays which were licensed by the Customs for the receipt of dutiable imports – the 'legal quays' and 'sufferance wharves' – had become increasingly clogged. They were now quite unable to deal quickly and efficiently with the volume of goods being landed. Space was at a premium with considerably more vessels attempting to use this convenient stretch of water than the number of wharves available, with many vessels anchoring in midstream. Adding to the confusion were the lighters that ferried the produce to and from the moored ships. Including the larger ships, which were to be found further downriver, the number of vessels engaged in overseas trade that used the port increased from 1,335 in 1705, to 1,682 in 1751, and to 3,663 in 1794. Even more staggering was the rise in cargo tonnage from 234,639 tons in 1751 to nearer 630,000 by 1810.

That so many ships, even in this, the seventh year since the renewal of war with France, were able to trade unhindered resulted from the resolve and might of the British Navy, as directed from London. Those ships, commanded to sea by the Board that sat in Wallingford House, with their subsequent preparation for sea overseen by the commissioners of the inferior boards, governed the sea lanes and brought in the convoys. Without the Navy, the wealth of London would have been strangled at birth rather than being allowed to flourish and grow.

Indeed, the greatest risk often run by the merchants of London was not a ship being taken but the pilferage of goods stacked on the wharves below London Bridge. Piled high, and awaiting collection by the carters and wagon masters for transfer to warehouses, security was poor, with goods left in the open for weeks on end. It was a situation that led to theft, by opportunistic thieves and organised gangs, on a massive scale. It was estimated that merchants' losses stood at around £500,000 a year, including 2 per cent of all sugar imported. Writing in 1797, the London Magistrate, Patrick Colquhoun, drew a bleak picture of this nefarious side of London life. Of the organised gangs, Colquhoun explained:

> They reconnoitred by day and made their attacks in armed boats on dark nights, cutting adrift the lighters and barges, and taking out the merchandise.

To these he added the depredations of those in authority and which comprised:

> … mates of ships and revenue officers, who would wink at the robbery of a ship, in which coopers, porters and watermen take part.

And finally, to this, he added the opportunistic thieves:

> The wine coopers [who] pilfered while opening and refining casks; the mud larks [who] picked up stolen bits, which others by concert [had thrown] onto the mud; the rat catchers employed on board ships [who] carried away produce; the lightermen [who] concealed goods whilst going from the ship to the quays.
> (Patrick Colquhoun, *Treatise on the Police of the Metropolis*, 1800, p. 414)

By 1810 it was a problem well on the way to being solved, through the construction of securer docks to the east (the West and East India Docks and the Surrey Commercial Docks), together with the creation of a marine police force that consisted of 100 men equipped with muskets, swords and pistols. With their headquarters building at Wapping New Stairs, this force was much influenced by the organisational model of the Navy, while the Admiralty gave it access to former seamen, midshipmen and a few defunct vessels.

London was the busiest and most crowded waterway in the world, and during the reign of George I this had caught the attention of Daniel Defoe. Then he had reckoned 'nothing in the world to be like it'. Marking out the area of the Pool to begin 'at the turning of the River out of Limehouse Reach and [extending] to the Custom-house Keys', of this stretch of water he wrote:

> I had the curiosity to count the ships as well as I could, *en passant*, and found above two thousand sail of all sorts, not reckoning barges, lighters or pleasure boats and yachts; but of vessels that really go to sea.

Lydia Melford, one of the prolific letter writers created by Tobias Smollett in his masterful novel, *The Expedition of Humphry Clinker*, gave her first impression of visiting London in a letter that would have been written during the mid-1760s:

> The whole surface of the Thames is covered with small vessels, barges, boats and wherries, passing to and fro, and below the three bridges, such a prodigious forest of masts, for miles together, that you would think all the ships of the universe were here assembled. All that you read of wealth and grandeur in the Arabian Nights Entertainments and the Persian Tales, concerning Baghdad, Damascus, Isaphan and Samarkand is here realised.

As the Admiralty and commissioners' barges rapidly passed through the Pool, frequently slowing to avoid hoys and other small craft or skirting round rows of anchored vessels, they would have passed, while drawing level with the Tower, *Enterprise* – a former warship that was now under the command of the Impress Service. Here, to meet the Navy's insatiable demand for seamen, volunteers and pressed men were held below decks before being taken to one of the major naval ports. Before skirting this vessel, those on board would have glimpsed St Catherine's Wharf which, although still owned by the Victualling Board, had since 1793 been transferred to the Army for bulk delivery of provisions that would then be shipped out to various garrisons.

A little further on there was a change in the landscape: the wharves and warehouses giving way to shipbuilding. This was Limehouse Reach, which took the form of a giant elongated reversed 'S'. On its banks were twelve ship repair and building yards with a further three located in the adjoining reaches of Greenwich and Blackwall. The shipyards in Limehouse Reach possessed at least twenty slips for the construction of ships and eleven or more dry docks for repairing ships. In addition, Greenwich and Blackwall reaches possessed a further five building and repair yards, at least eight further building slips and additional dry docks. In total, the Thames-side merchant yards in or around 1810 were employing roughly 4,000 artisans and labourers, and were capable of building the largest ships of the age. Admittedly, when building for the Navy Board, they were restricted to vessels of 74 guns or less, as it had been decided that any larger warship should only be built in the royal dockyards. However, when charged with the construction of East Indiamen, the long distance cargo-carrying ships of the East India Company, all such restrictions were removed. While a 74-gun ship might be rated at around 1,600 tons, evidence would suggest that the larger East Indiamen, while rated at a lesser tonnage to avoid payment of a higher tax, carried almost as much weight as the largest ships built in the royal dockyards (Parkinson, 1937, p. 130).

Of course, it could be asked why so many shipbuilding and repair yards were clustered in such a short section of waterway. There was no single reason. Playing a significant role was the Howland Great Wet Dock, sited on the right bank of Limehouse Reach and part way along the mid-section of the elongated 'S'. This was a commercial wet dock and designed to retain a full depth of water at any state of the tide for the use of ships laying up or fitting out. Named after John Howland, the original owner of the land upon which it had been constructed, it later became the particular home of the Greenland whaling ships. In turn, this had led to its renaming as the Greenland Dock with a number of blubber-boiling houses erected on the south side. The existence of such an important facility at this point of the Thames quite naturally served as a magnet for those skilled in ship repair, leading to the establishment of a number of specialised repair yards. Indeed one prominent shipbuilding family from Kent, the Wells, were particularly associated with the dock, John Wells (1662–1702) overseeing its construction while other members of the family were responsible for its management. That they also established a repair yard close to the dock was, therefore, no coincidence. To complete the story of the dock, it had by 1810 come into the ownership of William Richie, a Greenwich timber merchant and founder of the Commercial Dock Company (1807). He went on to build a series of additional docks and timber ponds, with the greatly expanded complex becoming known as the Surrey Commercial Docks.

While the wet dock had placed a premium on this as an area for the establishment of repair facilities, it was the existence of the naval dockyard at Deptford (together with a second yard at Woolwich) that helped ensure, even prior to Howland Dock, lucrative contracts for the building of large ships. The Navy Board required that ships built in a private yard should be regularly inspected for work quality by a principal officer attached to one of the royal dockyards. Once launched, the vessel would be taken to the nearest naval dockyard for fitting out and completion, including the finishing of her upper works and the stepping of her lower masts. Should the vessel have been ordered to undertake immediate sea service, the vessel would be fully masted and rigged with ordnance, provisions and a full crew brought on board. Given that so much work on a ship constructed in a private yard also required the intervention of those employed in the royal dockyards, it made little sense for the Navy Office to agree contracts with the owners of yards a long way from a royal dockyard.

The Thames-side shipbuilding yards had one further advantage when it came to acquiring naval contract work. Not only were they close to the important naval dockyards of Deptford and Woolwich but also to the Navy Office, from where invitations to tender emanated. This allowed those who managed or owned these yards to more immediately submit a tender and to support it through personal representations. This closeness also ensured greater familiarity with the organisational system and those who managed it, with the latter often sweetened through judicious gift giving. Irrespective of their success in gaining work, the private yards could not afford to become totally dependent on the Navy. Only in wartime was there enough work to ensure guaranteed survival, the period of the Seven Years War (1756–63) seeing the London Thames-side yards constructing over forty warships for the Royal Navy. In marked contrast, however, peacetime would see few naval contracts being generated, with no more than twelve warships ordered for construction in these yards during the war-free years of 1785–92.

In directing so much of their building work to this small group of shipbuilders in or around Limehouse Reach, the administrators of the Navy were creating a group of companies that came near to possession of a monopoly. It was to weaken the power of this group of builders that St Vincent, in January 1803, refused to allow the Navy Board to enter contracts with the private yards, in particular those of London, for the construction of ships as large as those rated for 74 guns. While St Vincent very much upset the Navy Board, he also angered the ship builders. Not surprisingly, they began to muster their allies, among whom was Opposition leader William Pitt. In his subsequent attacks upon St Vincent and the Addington administration Pitt was largely informed by that shipbuilding interest, with new orders for the larger naval warships soon directed to Limehouse Reach and elsewhere along the Thames upon the return of the Tories to office.

Yet this huge shipbuilding interest was set for a tumble. While they were fully employed in the final years of the war with Napoleon, this was not a situation that would long continue. It has been estimated that between 1803 and 1805 the London yards constructed some 2,500 vessels, including a number of warships. That figure fell to just 250 in 1814 (Helen Doe, 'Thames Shipbuilders in the Napoleonic Wars', 2006, pp. 10–21). In part, this resulted from the success of the Royal Navy, for it had captured so many enemy ships that their subsequent sale depressed the new-build ship market. Similarly, with the war reaching a conclusion, the Navy Board was primarily concerned with taking ships out of service, rather than introducing new vessels. But also working against the London yards was their lack of financial competitiveness, partly resulting from the higher wages paid to those employed in the Thames-side yards.

However, much of this was in the future, with few having given sufficient thought to the economic downturn that would inevitably follow upon the ending of a war that had begun in 1793. In the meantime, the shipbuilding yards of Limehouse Reach continued to prosper, with the occupants of the two barges probably noting that one of the largest of the private shipbuilders, Randall and Brent, with their yard just to the north of the Greenland Dock, had one of the Navy's future warships well in hand. It would be difficult to think that those being taken to the launch of *Queen Charlotte* would not have made a determined attempt to view this particular vessel, a 74-gun third rate for which the name 'Edinburgh' had already been reserved. With her keel laid in November 1807, she was to be finally launched in January 1811. As was customary, and underlining the advantage of being close to a naval dockyard, the vessel was immediately towed to the yard at Deptford for fitting out.

Over on the left bank, the occupants of the two naval barges would have seen on the Isle of Dogs two further shipbuilding yards. However, the dominant feature here was the West India Docks, a large complex within a secure wall that contained two wet docks – one for imports and the other for exports. It was one further scheme that had developed out of frustration with the numerous delays in bringing cargoes off the river, and the open quays and scattered warehousing that made it difficult to secure goods adequately. Immediately to the south of the newly built West India Docks was the City Canal, cutting across the Isle of Dogs. Completed in 1805, it provided a short cut for ships that would otherwise have had the inconvenience of passing along the entire length of the Isle of Dogs when bound for the wharves in the upper reaches of the river.

That the dockyard at Deptford was being rapidly approached was clear from the number of warships now visible. These included old and rotting hulks (former warships that had sometimes been converted to other uses) and newly launched or repaired vessels being equipped for forthcoming expeditions. One such vessel that had been supposedly moored was *Atropos*, the first command of Horatio Hornblower as a captain. Following his work in organising Nelson's funeral, Hornblower had been presented by the First Lord (which Forester mistakenly assumed to be St Vincent) to George III. Taking subsequent leave of his newly acquired patron at Whitehall Stairs, Hornblower makes the same journey to Deptford as already described. Deep in thought, the gig which he had hired, arrived at the far end of Limehouse Reach much sooner than he had expected:

It was a surprise to Hornblower to find that the gig was now passing the *Atropos* as she lay at the edge of the stream. He should have been all eyes to see that all was well with her and that the officer of the watch had been on the alert to direct the gig as she came down the river; as it was Hornblower merely had time to acknowledge the salute of Lieutenant Jones as the gig left the ship behind. There was Deptford Dock and beside it the enormous activities of the Victualling Yard. From a sailing barge lying beside the jetty a gang of men were at work driving a herd of pigs up into the yard, destined for slaughter and salting down to feed the Navy. (Forester, *Hornblower and the Atropos*, p. 86)

But this was the summer of 1810 and Nelson's death at Trafalgar, though far from forgotten, was almost five years past. To ensure British seaborne superiority was maintained, an extensive warship building programme was still under way, with both the Navy commissioners and the Lords of the Admiralty, having now reached Deptford, able to see the massive soon-to-be-launched three-decker lying on its slipway. A contemporary souvenir engraving provides a further insight on the day, showing the soon-to-be-named *Queen Charlotte* resplendent in her launch finery, decked out in a series of outsize flags that included two ensigns, a pendent and a jack. The engraving also shows the two state barges on the downriver side of the yard, close to a wharf wall where they would be protected from the surge of water that the blunt stern would create on entering the river. Close by were several other barges, some of them filled with military bandsmen who, on cue, would strike up the national anthem followed by other suitably patriotic tunes. The launch would also be saluted by nearby warships firing their guns to welcome the new vessel to the fleet.

Should either the two state barges or Hornblower have continued beyond Deptford, more building slips would have been glimpsed along Greenwich Reach, with the Greenwich naval hospital to be seen on the right bank. Continuing downriver they would next have entered Blackwall Reach, a mirror image in shape to Limehouse Reach, where the largest of all the private yards could have been viewed. This was the Blackwall, long associated with the East India Company through it having first been created by that company during the early seventeenth century. Despite a subsequent sale, the Blackwall Yard continued to build for the East India Company, its facilities far greater than that of any other private yard on the Thames. Consequently, it was able to meet a considerable portion of the building needs of the Company while also constructing ships for the Navy. In one year alone, 1798, the yard launched three 74-gun warships while the following year saw the launch of seven East Indiamen. Nor did the pace of work slacken off in the following years, with Blackwall going on to launch a total of thirty-six ships over the next ten years, almost half of them for the Navy. However, such figures, as impressive as they are, conceal a further important asset of Blackwall to the Royal Navy as East Indiamen constructed at Blackwall and other yards on the Thames were of sufficient strength and size to permit them to carry a considerable amount of ordnance. If attacked they were capable of putting up a good fight and they could serve as a useful auxiliary to the naval escorts that joined the East Indiamen to convoy them during war. Furthermore, and of equal importance, East Indiamen were sometimes acquired by the Navy for conversion into warships, with six newly built East Indiamen requisitioned for this purpose in 1795 and another eight so designated while still under construction. Also, there was a readiness on the part of the Company to make their vessels available as transports or for accompanying naval and military expeditions. Finally, it is worth adding that those ships through trade and the carriage of troops and supplies to India, ensured the East India Company, or at least its mechants, earned enough money to contribute considerable sums to the Treasury. This money was then used to bolster the massive shipbuilding programme that ensured the continuance of a strong Navy at sea.

THE LONDON WARSHIP-BUILDING YARDS OF THE LATER GEORGIAN PERIOD

Woolcombe and Mestaer

Positioned either side of a landing point known as the King and Queen Stairs in Rotherhithe, Woolcombe's, while concentrating on ship repair and the building of smaller merchant ships, did undertake some building work under contract to the Navy Board, launching a sixth-rate frigate, *Aquilon*, in 1786 and a 6-gun transport in 1788. Two dockyard lighters were also built, one for Woolwich Dockyard in 1788 and the other for Sheerness in 1792. Between 1802 and 1806, and possibly for a good deal longer, the yard undertook no construction of ships whether for private ship owners or the Admiralty.

A former occupant, Henry Bird Jnr, had been a regular builder of ships for the Admiralty, launching twelve under contract during the period 1740 to 1762. The first of these was *Experiment*, rated to carry 24 guns. With her keel laid on to the building slip in September 1739, the Admiralty had contracted for the vessel to be launched during the early part of the following year but construction fell behind. This should have resulted in Henry Bird paying a penalty but the Admiralty accepted that the delays were outside his control, the winter having been one of the most severe in living memory. With the Thames having frozen over and temperatures plummeting in December to -15°C (5°F) not only was a launch impossible but it prevented the arrival of building timbers from Guildford and Reading. Among other ships built by Henry Bird Jnr were *Mary Galley* and *Prince Edward*, both of 706 tons, rated to carry 44 guns and entering the Thames in 1744 and 1745 respectively. With both vessels taking just over a year to build from the laying of the keel to launch, this was a particularly busy period for the yard, with the workforce subsequently undertaking construction of a further 24-gun ship, *Nightingale*, launched in October 1746. It appears this latter vessel had not begun life as a naval warship, the Admiralty deciding to purchase her while she was under construction. It is also interesting to note that Henry Bird Jnr's father, Henry Bird, had himself been a shipbuilder, employed at Deptford Dockyard as a shipwright before accepting an invitation to move to St Petersburg where a new dockyard was being built for the Russian Navy.

William Woolcombe appears to have acquired the yard during the early 1760s when it was known as Bull Head Dock. The Woolcombe family continued to occupy the yard, considerably improving the facilities, until *c.* 1810 when it came into the hands of a shipbreaking partnership. A recent archaeological survey of part of the former site of the yard carried out by the Museum of London has helped demonstrate the layout of facilities (Heard, 2003).

The neighbouring yard, belonging to Peter Mestaer, was certainly much more dependent upon shipbuilding, having two building slips in constant use together with two dry docks. As such, it had undertaken work more recently for the Admiralty and the East India Company with *Thames* (374 tons) launched in December 1803. Originally built for the South Sea Company she had subsequently been hired by the Admiralty as an armed brig. Prior to this, the yard had constructed both the 16-gun *Pylades*, launched in 1794, and the 28-gun *Mercury* of 1779. For construction of the latter, it is recorded that Mestaer received the sum of £6,805 7s od. It was while building *Pylades* that John Lester, a caulker at the yard, was drowned in an accident in Peter Mestaer's shipyard in Rotherhithe in about 1794.

John & Robert Batson, Hill & Co. and Cox & Co.

On the opposite bank of the river were the yards of John & Robert Batson, Hill & Co. and Cox & Co. Of these, only the first two had undertaken building work for the Admiralty, with Cox & Co. seeming to concentrate on repair work. Cox & Co. was located in Limehouse, just off Fore Street (now Narrow Street), and possessed one dry dock. As for the other two yards, both on the Isle of Dogs, the Batsons constructed twelve warships for the Navy between 1739 and 1787, with their yard located immediately below Limekiln Dock. Constructed in 1666, Limekiln Dock is still a feature of this area; it was constructed to support the movement of lime and thus the area became known as Limehouse. In 1739, when constructing their first ship for the Navy, the 20-gun *Flamborough*, they were supported by the Navy Board in gaining a waiver on a penalty for late delivery. The Navy commissioners accepted that 'they were young beginners in the shipbuilding way' and their work had been performed in 'a workmanlike manner' (Banbury, 1971, p. 113). Also on the Isle of Dogs, south of the West India Dock complex, was the yard of Hill and Mellish, which opened in 1802. With three dry docks, each interconnected, it had considerable capacity for the repair and building of ships. During the four-year period 1794 to 1798, the yard launched a total of seven ships for the Navy, the largest *Naiad*, a 32-gun frigate.

Joshua Young and Edward Thompson

Returning to the right bank of the river and just beyond the point of elongation to the south were the yards of Joshua Young and Edward Thompson. Neither had undertaken building work in recent years, with the former yard having three building slips. During the 1780s there appears to have been a close relationship between Joshua Young and William Woolcombe, the two combining their resources for the construction of two naval warships, the 32-gun *Aquilon* and the 6-gun *Deptford*.

Randall & Brent

Maximising the possibility of gaining commercial repair and warship construction work was the firm of Randall & Brent. This was a major commercial undertaking, as the firm possessed three separate yards alongside this stretch of the Reach and constructed warships and vessels for the East India Company. The first of these yards was only a few hundred yards from the yards of Young and Thomson while the other two were associated with the Greenland Dock, being further south and tucked in close on either side of its entrance. In these yards, in addition to commercial repair work, some fifty warships were built between 1756 and 1810. Adding to their facilities on this stretch of water was a further tranche of land just beyond the yard on the north side of Greenland Dock, and marked on maps as Randall's Rents. Almost certainly this refers to housing owned by the company and made available to the artisans and labourers employed in its three yards. Not surprisingly, as Randall family members came and went, variations on the company name were to be noted, with the trio of yards variously trading as J. Randall, Randall & Co., Randall, Brent & sons, Randall, Grey and Brent, S. & D. Brent and Daniel Brent. As Banbury notes in his study of these Thames-side yards, 'the most we can be sure of is that the firm started as Randall and finished as Brent' (Banbury, 1971, p. 133). It was as Randall, Grey and Brent that the firm launched one particularly famous vessel that was acquired by the Navy in 1790. This was *Discovery*, the lead ship in an expedition to the west coast of North America led by George Vancouver. For this voyage, *Discovery* was fitted out at the Deptford naval dockyard.

John Wells

Located to the north of the Greenland Dock, this was the shipyard originally established by John Wells, one of the sponsors of the Howland Wet Dock. Having as its address Lower Trinity Street, a road that no longer exists, the yard had been responsible for building at least thirty ships for the Admiralty, many of these of 74 guns. It seems that the yard was closed down in 1798, following the launch of a final ship of 74 guns, *Dragon*, with John Wells becoming a partner in the East India Company yard at Blackwall. Whether this was correct or not, it was still marked on maps of 1810 as 'Mr Wells Ship Yard'.

John Dudman

The final private shipbuilding yard alongside Limehouse Reach was situated to the north of the victualling yard and was that of John Dudman. This was an extensive facility which had been established by John Winter sometime around 1704. It possessed two docks and five building slips. Since 1783 it had been responsible for the construction of at least twenty-two warships, including two third rates of 74 guns. The yard had put most of its resources into the construction of East Indiamen. Among the latter, and launched in 1801, was the *Lord Melville*, named after a future First Lord. In the event, it proved a rather unfortunate choice of name, for this was the First Lord who was forced to resign to face impeachment. The ship itself also had a delayed launch, this through the downing of tools by shipwrights employed upon her construction who were desperate for an increase in wage at a time of rapidly rising prices. Earl St Vincent agreed to support the company in its refusal to offer any increase in wages by bringing shipwrights from the naval dockyard at Chatham to complete the work.

Bronsden & Co.

The Bronsden shipyard was to the north of the naval dockyard at Deptford and entered from Grove Street. Between 1740 and 1744 four ships were built at this yard for the Navy, the contracts agreed with the Navy showing that all were built in partnership with the Wells family whose yard was but a short distance away. This yard was subsequently acquired by William Barnard.

Stacey

The Stacey yard was located at Deptford Green. Some confusion exists as to whether warships were constructed in this yard, Banbury (1971, p. 153), indicating that five were built between 1719 and 1734. However, it seems likely that they were actually built in the dockyard at Deptford where Richard Stacey was Master Shipwright. The yard was later acquired by John Buxton Junior in 1739 and by Adams and Co. from 1773 to 1785.

John Buxton Junior

Established at the Deptford Green yard formerly occupied by Stacey, John Buxton Junior built ten warships from 1739 to 1757. The launch of the first of these, the 24-gun *Fox*, was delayed due to the terrible winter of 1739/40 and the freezing of the Thames.

Adams & Barnard

A partnership formed during the 1770s, Adams & Barnard received their first order from the Admiralty in February 1771 for the construction of *Ambuscade*, a 32-gun frigate. Banbury (1971, p. 111) notes that prior to this date J. Barnard had been building ships for the Royal Navy in Ipswich. The partnership continued until about 1781 and the launch of their last warship, the 64-gun *Africa*. From then, until the formation of a new partnership with Roberts, the main proprietor appears to have been William Barnard. It seems that contract work for the Royal Navy was undertaken in two separate yards, one to the north of the dockyard at Deptford (Grove Road) and the other to the south (Deptford Green). In total, Barnard, either in partnership or acting independently, engaged in the construction of more than thirty warships between 1771 and 1813, eight of these third rates of 74 guns. Among the smaller, frigate-size ships built was *Pandora*. In 1790 she was sent to the Pacific to round up the *Bounty* mutineers but while returning with some of the mutineers imprisoned in a purpose-built cage she ran aground on the Great Barrier Reef and sank. With the wreck recently discovered she has been subject to a programme of underwater archaeological exploration. In addition to building ships for the Navy, the two yards associated with Barnard undertook a steady output of East Indiamen and in 1810 had a workforce of 350 (of whom 201 were shipwrights).

Thomas West

Situated in Deptford Strand, the yard was responsible for the construction of thirteen warships from 1740 to 1764. A contract between the Navy Board and Thomas West, dated November 1755, for a warship of 70 guns stipulated that she was to be launched in no more than seventeen months and to be paid in eight instalments of £2,900.

Blackwall Shipyard

Established during the early seventeenth century and originally owned by the East India Company, Blackwall Shipyard passed out of the company's hands during the 1650s, when it was purchased by Henry Johnson, remaining with his family until 1724 when it was leased by Philip Perry, the former manager of the yard. Eventually, in 1779, the lease was converted into a sale, and the yard was purchased by Philip Perry's son, John. In 1798, as a result of a merger of interests, John Perry, together with his own two sons and his son-in-law, George Green, formed a partnership with the Wells brothers. In turn, the Perry interest was bought out by Robert Wigram in 1810, with the firm then known as Wigram and Green and subsequently Wigram, Green and Wigram. Continuing expansion of the yard meant that, by the middle of the eighteenth century, facilities included a wet dock for the refitting of ships, two dry docks (one a double dock) and several building slips. The double dock was designed to permit two vessels to be accommodated one behind the other, with the nearest to the entrance normally undergoing repair while the one to the stern would be under construction. In 1784 the yard was described 'as the most capacious private dockyard in the Kingdom if not in the World' (Banbury, 1971, p. 116). A few years later, John Perry financed a further considerable addition to the yard, in the shape of the Brunswick Dock, a wet dock with two basins, one holding thirty large Indiamen and the other thirty smaller ships.

The yard saw a reduction in size in 1803 when the East India Dock company bought the eastern part, including the Brunswick Dock, to create two substantial docks, one for imports and the other for exports, and both connected to the Thames through a basin that was entered from Blackwall Reach.

William and Benjamin Wallis

Situated in Orchard Place, adjacent to Bow Creek alongside Blackwall Reach, the yard launched six ships for the Navy Board between 1796 and 1814 but entered into bankruptcy shortly after the ending of the Napoleonic Wars.

6

The Naval Multiplex of Kentish London

The catalysts leading to the creation of the Kentish London naval multiplex were the dockyards at Deptford and Woolwich. Created by Henry VIII during the early years of his reign, their establishment led to the creation of the various support facilities that were to make this such an important area of London for the Georgian Navy. Furthermore, despite the problems confronted by the two yards, both retained their important role in the building and repair of warships, with Deptford, although seen as the more problematic of the two yards, still clearly regarded as a major asset to the service. This was confirmed by Sandwich when he stated that while Deptford was not suited to the purpose of laying-up and equipping fleets, it was an 'exceeding convenient and useful yard for all other naval purposes'. Of its value for building ships, he added:

> It is conveniently situated for receiving timber from the interior part of the kingdom by the River Thames, therefore is useful for building both large and small ships there being a sufficient flow of water for launching them although not a sufficient depth at low water to lay the large ships on float, therefore after such are launched they are moved the first opportunity that offers for sailing them down river to be laid up at other ports. But it admits of laying up frigates and other small ships which may also be repaired here and most expeditiously equipt on urgent occasions than any other places by contract riggers to be hired on the river; as was practiced in the latter part of the last war when this method was found to be far more expeditious than by their own officers and men.

However, the drawbacks of Deptford yard were not ignored:

> It is not advisable to keep many ships here that are in good condition any length of time, because of it being freshwater, in which their bottoms decay much sooner than in salt, therefore they are usually sent to Chatham where they may

on such occasions aforementioned be rigged and equipt in like manner by contract riggers from the River [Thames].

Of Woolwich, Sandwich was much briefer in his comments:

The conveniencies and inconveniences belonging to this Yard are much the same as those of Deptford, except the inconveniency of the large ships down the River after they are launched is not so great as at Deptford. (BL Kings 44)

Although the shallowness of the Thames was mentioned, there seemed little concern that the problem was becoming more serious. So serious, in fact, that by April 1800 there was a call for the two yards to be closed, it being suggested that the delays in getting warships this far up the Thames made the yards financially unviable. Forcibly holding this viewpoint was Samuel Bentham who, as Inspector General of Naval Works, a recently created post within the Admiralty, considered the distance of the two yards from the sea, together with:

The difficulties and delays in attending the navigation of [Thames] and the want of sufficient depth of water for ships of war in the vicinity of those yards; he [was of the] opinion that it would be more advisable ... to form new ones, than to continue to incur the very heavy expense that must attend the employing of these inland dockyards for the general purpose to which they are applied. (TNA ADM7/663, June 1802)

As for where the new yard should be, Bentham favoured the Isle of Grain, since there was an existing yard at Sheerness. This idea was certainly under consideration during the summer of 1802, when members of the Board of Admiralty carried out an inspection of the proposed Isle of Grain site. Among other things, they examined the proposed ground for the new dockyard and 'discoursed with several persons' (NMM ADM B/185, 21 August 1802). It was a scheme that was never pursued, a series of test borings showing it would be impossible to obtain proper foundations for the buildings and other required structures.

The failure of the Isle of Grain scheme left the Admiralty without an immediate solution to a situation that was already reaching alarming dimensions. In a further attempt to resolve matters, John Rennie was commissioned in 1806 to conduct a full survey into the state of the nation's dockyards including those of Deptford and Woolwich. Initially turning his attention to the causes of the problem, he placed the blame on industrial developments around London, together with similar activities in various towns and villages even further upriver, causing mud to enter the Thames and feed into the navigable channels and dockyard harbours. Additional deposits were also finding their way into these waters from agricultural improvements and land drainage. Specifically though, London Bridge was identified as a major cause, responsible for staunching the flow of the river as a result of being built on massive outworks (or starlings) that allowed only a narrow tidal flow. The result, according to Rennie, was that 'the general depth of water in the Thames' appeared to be in decline:

> The constantly increasing influx of soil from London, occasions a very serious injury to the navigation of the River. Many irregular encroachments have likewise been made on its shores in its passages through London ... which checks the influx of the tide. (BL Add Ms 27, 884, f. 10)

Matters were sometimes made worse, often dramatically so, by encroachments onto the banks of the river for a range of localised projects. Such was the case in June 1828 when Oliver Laing, the Master Shipwright at Woolwich, noted that the depth of water between the moorings and wharf wall of the dockyard had decreased by 3ft in a period of only three months:

> We were at a loss how to account for this sudden decrease of water until very recently we have discovered that the late Mr Long had been superintending for the last four months the making of a strong embankment from the Ferry House up river. (TNA ADM106/1802)

As with Bentham, Rennie saw no long-term solution other than constructing a replacement dockyard at a more suitable location. Instead of the Isle of Grain, he favoured Northfleet, this having the advantage of both depth and ease of access. According to Rennie:

> From the soundings in this part of the river, which was taken by Mr Whidby, it appears, that from opposite Greenhithe to the north-eastern end of Fiddler's Reach, there are 7 fathoms at low water; in the middle of the river, below Grays, 6 fathoms; a little further down the river the depth increases to 7 fathoms; and along the lower part of Northfleet Hope there are 8 fathoms. (John Rennie, *Treatise on Harbours*, 1851, p. 56)

Despite widespread support for a new yard at Northfleet, with all necessary purchase of land undertaken by 1809, nothing was done as regards construction. Instead, this project was gradually overtaken by events at Sheerness where huge sums had to be spent on repairing a yard that was literally in a state of collapse.

These undoubted concerns had an obvious impact upon the two London yards, for while neither was to be closed during these years, there was a considerable reluctance on the part of the Admiralty and Navy Board to see any large-scale expenditure on the updating of facilities. Only during the final decade of the Georgian era were matters to change, when the two yards received a new lease of life through the development of the steam engine and its application to marine craft. With paddle steamers being built and used on the Thames from about 1814 onwards, the Admiralty was not far behind when, in 1821, it ordered Deptford to construct a purpose-built steam vessel. This was the paddle steamer *Comet*, her engines installed by Boulton, Watt & Co. from their Soho Manufactory. It was the fact of Deptford's relative proximity to the London works of Boulton & Watt that resulted in the choice of this yard for the building of *Comet*, with the engine installed at Deptford following *Comet*'s launch in May 1822. Once afloat, *Comet* proved a further asset to the two London yards, as she was employed in towing naval warships into the Thames, reducing the time taken to reach Deptford and Woolwich from the open sea and so allowing more use to be made of these yards.

However, the use of such vessels did not overcome the problem of silting. This, instead, became dependent upon a further advance brought by steam, the steam-driven bucket dredger. Directed entirely to keeping harbours and moorings free of shoaling, they replaced hand dredgers that had previously been operated by Trinity House and the Admiralty. By comparison with the steam dredger, hand dredgers were a highly inefficient method of reducing levels of silting. Able to raise only a few tons of mud each day, they were overwhelmed by the size of the task they confronted. However, even the greater efficiency of the steam dredger was not to prove a complete solution, merely stabilising the problem, with a further and far more reaching approach having to be eventually adopted.

Deptford and Woolwich yards also took responsibility for minor repair work on the Navy's growing fleet of paddle steamers. It was a logical step, as the engines for these vessels, if not manufactured by Boulton, Watt & Co. were being produced by other Thames-side companies such as Henry Maudslay (Lambeth), John Penn (Deptford) and Miller and Barnes (Rotherhithe). Therefore it was important that the dockyards undertaking repair work on such ships should be sited closest to where the engines were produced. To begin with, a building slip and dry dock had been set aside at Deptford, while at Woolwich a few additional millwrights had also been employed. This was sufficient for the undertaking of occasional maintenance work but anything more complex was beyond the capability of those employed at Deptford and Woolwich. Instead, machinery had to be removed and dispatched by river to the nearby yards that had manufactured the engines.

However, all this went against the tradition of the royal dockyards, these huge industrial complexes normally expected to undertake and complete every aspect of ship-repair work. Furthermore, it left the Admiralty unduly dependent upon the private sector, unable to guarantee fulfilment of needs during a sudden wartime emergency. To rectify this, thought was given to the creation of more encompassing facilities, with the yards at Deptford and Woolwich viewed as appropriate. Already, Deptford had constructed *Comet* and had gone on to build several more steamers. But this yard was unable to accommodate all future repair needs due to limitations of space. Woolwich, on the other hand, did have the space, being able to accommodate a range of new buildings at the west end of the yard with undeveloped land adjoining this yard also available for purchase. Not surprisingly, the choice for the nation's first purpose-built steam yard fell upon Woolwich. The new facility was to undertake engine-repair work, but the construction of engines was still to be undertaken by the nearby private yards.

Planning of the new steam yard, which would see extensive factory buildings, various work sheds and a basin for the accommodation of steamers, appears to have begun in 1825. This was a time when the dockyard wall at Woolwich, together with the mast pond, was undergoing extensive renovation while a new dry dock was also under construction. For this reason it was considered an ideal time to push forward on any other outstanding projects, with a decision to start on the new steam facilities prompted by one of the yard officers. In a letter written to the Navy Board on 30 November 1825, John Stansfield, clerk of the construction works, suggested that building of the new steam yard should be undertaken conjointly, 'so that what is done now may not have to be redone' (TNA ADM1/3412). This, in fact, was a reference to events at the Chatham and Sheerness naval dockyards, where piecemeal improvements had required extensive changes being made to works in hand in order to make way for some new overriding addition.

Both the Navy Board and Admiralty appear to have accepted Stansfield's reasoning, with construction of the new steam yard beginning in 1826. From the outset considerable thought had to be given to the steam basin, which covered an area in excess of 3 acres. This was not a simple project as it involved the digging out of a million cubic feet of soil to a depth of 27ft. The soil, once removed, was used as a back fill for the reconstructed river wall and for the filling in of the old double dock that was now being removed. As for the basin, once excavated, a surface of clay was laid to form a bottom while the sides were sealed by construction of a concrete wall. Convicts supplied the unskilled labour required. Some 400 civilian prisoners were employed at Woolwich during this period, the majority housed on the hulked warship *Ganymede*.

As well as working on the steam basin, convicts were also employed on the dockyard wall and in building the dry dock which was sited at the east end of the yard. In rebuilding the river wall, the main purpose was to straighten it, to create a smooth tidal flow that, it was hoped, would help scour the increasingly silted harbour. The project also brought additional land into the yard. To facilitate work on the river wall, a series of coffer dams were erected, allowing work to progress unaffected by the tidal movement of the river.

As work on the steam basin progressed, attention could be given to the various buildings and additional features that were to be constructed around it. Among them were a variety of boiler and work sheds, stores and engine houses. These were sited in close proximity to the cranes and mooring points of the basin, so allowing easy transfer of machinery to specific work areas. Similarly, these cranes could be utilised in the refitting of engines or the fitting of machinery to newly launched vessels.

Although completed in 1831, one year after the death of George IV, inception of the steam yard was firmly rooted in the Georgian age, placing Woolwich, if only temporarily, in the forefront of marine technology. With the yard now employing a large and highly skilled engineering workforce, it could ensure that all naval steamers were efficiently maintained while also being able to attend to emergency repair work. Unfortunately, it was soon realised that the yard was too small to fully meet the needs of the Navy. At the time of its planning in 1826 the Navy possessed five steamers. By 1831, however, this number had more than doubled, with a further twenty steamers entering service over the next ten years. Inevitably, this led to the original Georgian steam yard being superseded. From the late 1830s onwards, an expanded steam facility was constructed at Woolwich. Ultimately, the various constraints of Woolwich, notably problems of access and lack of depth, were to count against any further expansion, with Deptford and Woolwich closed in 1869.

Leaving the decline of the Deptford and Woolwich yards, let us return to their beginnings in the early eighteenth century. Deptford and Woolwich had entered the Georgian period with facilities little altered from those that had been constructed or refined during the previous century. To undertake their primary role of building and heavy repair work, the two yards possessed a number of building slips and dry docks, these facilities having seen only gradual bouts of modernising as the years wore on. An early description of the two yards is provided by Blaise Ollivier, Master Shipwright of the French naval shipwright at Brest, who was on a fact-seeking mission for his employer, Jean-Frédéric Phélypeaux, Comte de Maurepas, Secretary of State for the Marine. Ollivier was, at least technically, a spy, with his identity disguised, if not his heavy accent and limited knowledge of English. However, his right to enter the yard had been sanctioned by the Navy Board. While it may not have been realised who he was, the permitting of foreigners to enter British naval dockyards was nothing unusual, since shipbuilding technology was openly shared between nations when not directly at war.

At the time of his visit to Deptford, in April 1737, Ollivier refers to the yard as having five building docks, but this is a rather confusing assessment of the yard as he appears to be combining dry docks and building slips under the same heading, together with a wet dock. However, safer ground is reached when Ollivier states that three ships were under construction, the *Boyne* (80), *Lion* (60) and *Dartmouth* (70). The first was occupying the rear end of the double dock with Ollivier explaining the precise arrangement:

> The vessel of 80 guns which is on the stocks occupies the upper end of the dock and has its stern to the water; the other end is occupied by two yachts which are being repaired. And between the stern of the ship and the yacht is a bridge which crosses the dock at right angles, and which they take down when the ship is to be launched [sic]. (Roberts, *18th Century Shipbuilding*)

The wet dock (or basin), constructed between 1517 and 1520, was a particularly important feature of Deptford yard. Originally designed to accommodate five large vessels, it allowed warships to be fitted out in an enclosed area rather than at a mid-river mooring. The value of the facility was without dispute, with a substantial enlargement of the basin being undertaken during the early part of the eighteenth century. Ollivier, in remarking upon the wet dock, recorded it as being of 320ft long and 53ft wide with its greatest depth of water being 19ft.

A few days later, on 20 April 1737, Ollivier entered the dockyard at Woolwich, listing two dry docks and four building slips as its chief facilities, with one of the docks a double and occupied by two vessels under construction:

> One of which is of 100 guns and is placed next to the gate with its stern towards the river and the other of 90 guns is placed forward of the first. Between the stern of the 900 gun ship and the bow of the 100 gun ship there is a bridge which crosses the dock at right angles.

These were the 90-gun *Duke*, then under construction and floated out of dock in April 1739. The second, *Royal Anne* of 100 guns, was possibly in the process of being taken to pieces, allowing her timbers to be reused in another vessel. As for the four building slips, and demonstrating just how busy Woolwich dockyard was in these years, three of them were occupied with Ollivier naming the vessels as *Cumberland* (80), *Suffolk* (70) and *Essex* (60). Interestingly, the latter was actually an earlier ship that had been brought into the yard for taking to pieces so that her timbers could be re-used in reconstructing the vessel to an improved design.

While in matters of ship construction and the extent of facilities at Deptford and Woolwich, Ollivier appears to have been fairly impressed and was to advise

Left: The Painted Hall of the Seamen's Hospital at Greenwich, where Nelson's body was laid in state.

Right: Carved out of stone by Edward Hodges Baily, the figure of Nelson in Trafalgar Square was erected in November 1843. It is 18ft high, with the likeness taken from numerous portraits and busts undertaken during Nelson's lifetime.

A contemporary engraving showing the state barge (centre) that carried the coffin of Nelson from Greenwich to Whitehall Stairs.

The dome of St Paul's Cathedral, under which Nelson's body was finally laid to rest, 9 January 1806. Nelson was the first non-royal to be granted a state funeral, a further indication of the significance of Nelson and the several naval victories that he masterminded.

The Admiralty building in Whitehall, knowned commonly in the eighteenth century as Wallingford House. This engraving shows the building as it appeared following alterations made in 1826, on the instructions of the future William IV, who at that time was Lord High Admiral, giving it additional wider entrances through the removal of two of the columns.

A modern view of the Adam screen. The additional entrances added in 1826 are no longer visible due to the screen having been restored to its original design in 1923. The Admiralty complex is now used by the Cabinet, and much of the artwork within continues to have a naval connection.

The 20ft-high telegraph shutter device that was placed on the roof of the Admiralty during the 1790s.

The next shutter device in the chain was this house in West Square.

Until 1789 the Navy Office was in Crutched Friars, in this building designed by Sir Christopher Wren, completed in 1683.

Maritime carvings and reliefs on Somerset House.

This view of the quadrangle in Somerset House shows the entrance and office area allocated to the Navy Board.

Somerset House from the south or riverside, *c.* 1820. Note the water entrance (centre) through which barges belonging to the Admiralty and the civil departments would pass.

Nowadays, the water entrance to the Somerset Place complex can only be approached by road.

A drawing made for the *Illustrated London News* towards the end of the nineteenth century showing the model of the *Victory* of 1735 in Somerset House.

The Nelson Stair, originally called the Navy Stair and supposedly designed to imitate a stair on a ship.

The arched water gate of Somerset House which once fed directly into the Thames. Nowadays, it provides walking access to the complex.

Of this Range of BUILDINGS
Constructed together with the Adjacent DOCKS, At the Expence of public spirited Individuals
Under the Sanction of a provident Legislature,
And with the liberal Co-operation of the Corporate Body of the CITY of LONDON.
For the distinct Purpose
Of complete SECURITY and ample ACCOMMODATION
(hitherto not afforded)
To the SHIPPING and PRODUCE of the WEST INDIES at this wealthy PORT.
THE FIRST STONE WAS LAID
On Saturday the Twelfth Day of July, A.D. 1800,
BY THE CONCURRING HANDS OF
THE RIGHT HONOURABLE LORD LOUGHBOROUGH,
LORD HIGH CHANCELLOR OF GREAT BRITAIN,
THE RIGHT HONOURABLE WILLIAM PITT
FIRST LORD COMMISSIONER OF HIS MAJESTY'S TREASURY AND CHANCELLOR OF HIS MAJESTY'S EXCHEQUER.
GEORGE HIBBERT, ESQ. THE CHAIRMAN, AND ROBERT MILLIGAN, ESQ. THE DEPUTY CHAIRMAN
OF THE WEST INDIA DOCK COMPANY;
The two former conspicuous in the Band Of those illustrious Statesmen,
Who in either House of Parliament, have been zealous to promote,
The two latter distinguished among those chosen to direct
AN UNDERTAKING
Which, under the favour of GOD, shall contribute
STABILITY, INCREASE, and ORNAMENT
TO
BRITISH COMMERCE.

Stone memorial commemorating the laying of the first stone for the West India Docks that lay on the Isle of Dogs.

The remains of one of the building slips in Deptford dockyard, possibly the one from which *Queen Charlotte* was launched in June 1810.

The naval dockyard at Deptford in 1810, showing *Queen Charlotte* on the slipway furthest to the right and being prepared for launching.

Blackwall Shipyard. The structure in the foreground is a mast house, used for storing masts.

The Master Shipwright's House in Deptford dockyard.

Although now detached from the main Arsenal site at Woolwich, this was once the main gateway into the complex. It dates to 1829.

The Clock House in Woolwich dockyard, originally built to provide additional office space.

The steam facilities at Woolwich, with the rigging and engine storehouse dominating this stretch of water. These buildings certainly date to the early 1840s, but the plans for their construction and the addition of a steam yard at Woolwich date to the final years of the Georgian era.

This grave matted print illustrates the launch of the 120-gun *Nelson* at Woolwich on 4 July 1814.

Peter Povey preyed on seamen and their families and was brought to the Old Bailey on two occasions. He would loiter close to this statue of George III in the forecourt of Somerset House, from where he could see the door of the Pay Office. On seeing a mark, he would follow them for a short distance before conning them out of their money.

A contemporary engraving showing a wooden-legged pensioner in the colonnaded outer passage that runs along King William Court.

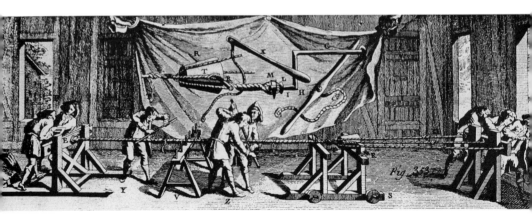

The Ropery at Woolwich, responsible for the manufacture of rope used on board naval warships, was once located at the east end of the High Street. With a workforce often in excess of 200, this illustration shows the nature of the work performed, with a large cable in the process of being formed out of three ropes for possible future use in the mooring or anchoring of ships. The artist has truncated the scene in order to demonstrate the art of rope making; the cable was much longer and required ten times the number of labourers and artisans shown.

Richard Parker, the elected leader of the seamen while in mutiny at the Nore in 1797.

Vice Admiral Cuthbert Collingwood (1st Baron Collingwood), Nelson's second-in-command at Trafalgar, lies buried in St Paul's Cathedral, close to Nelson's tomb.

Grampus, a former 48-gun Royal Navy warship that remained moored off Deptford Creek from October 1821 to Octobre 1831. Administered by the Seamen's Hospital Society, she had been loaned by the Admiralty for the purpose of caring for the medical needs of poor and destitute seamen.

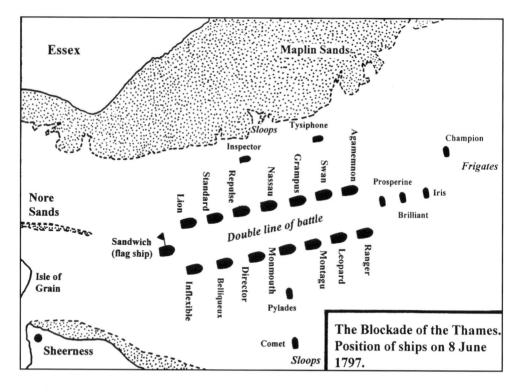

Essex

Maplin Sands

Sloops
Tysiphone

Inspector

Champion

Frigates

Agamemnon

Swan

Grampus

Nassau

Repulse

Standard

Lion

Prosperine

Iris

Brilliant

Nore
Sands

Double line of battle

Sandwich
(flag ship)

Isle of
Grain

Inflexible

Belliqueux

Director

Monmouth

Pylades

Montagu

Leopard

Ranger

Sheerness

Comet

Sloops

The Blockade of the Thames.
Position of ships on 8 June
1797.

Naval ships moored in the Thames attempted to strangle London's trade by blockading the river.

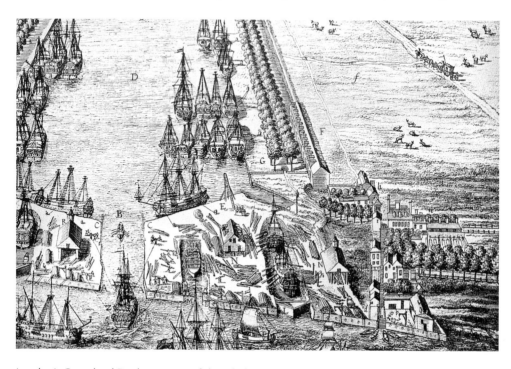

London's Greenland Dock, a centre of the whaling industry. On either side of the entrance lock
into the basin can be seen commercial yards used for warship construction and which, by the end
of the eighteenth century, were owned by Randall and Brent.

The house in Lambeth Road once occupied by William Bligh.

A modern-day view of the Royal Hospital for Seamen at Greenwich showing part of King William Court.

Lloyd's Coffee House moved to the Royal Exchange in 1774. Here, subscribing members are to be seen in the exclusive room allowed them in the new coffee room that was established on the south-east side of the building.

The Bank of England. The bank is the building on the left of the street while the building to the right is the Royal Exchange, as rebuilt and opened in 1844 and remodelled in 2001.

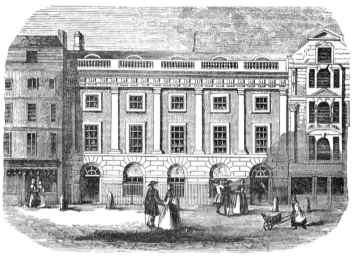

India House in Leadenhall Street. This shows the original headquarters of the East India Company, later replaced by a new building in 1726 and again in 1800 by a much larger building. The East India Company was one of the largest trading companies working out of London and liaised closely with the Royal Navy.

Naval seamen often returned from the various naval out ports with several years' back pay and (maybe) prize money. At such times they were vulnerable to the numerous tricksters and parasites that preyed upon them in the hope of acquiring some of the money they carried.

that French dockyards adopt a number of British ideas, he was critical of the condition of the two yards and the slow pace at which work was sometimes performed. In particular, he noted there to be great quantities of timber at Deptford, 'piled without order in every available space'. Much of the timber was wasted, due to it being unable to season properly and subject to wet rot. Of the storehouses, he further commented:

> There are many storehouses and sheds in the dockyard at Deptford; they are small, ill constructed and in very poor condition.

Ollivier was not in a position to assess the numbers employed within the two yards, but between them the workforce hovered around 2,000. However, this was peacetime, and the demands and pace of work were considerably less than during war. Thus, the number of workers in the two yards gradually increased over the following decades, peaking during war time and falling back during years of peace. In September 1757, some sixteen months into the Seven Years War, the total employed at the two yards was 2,342. However, by 1768, with the country in its fifth year of peace, numbers had fallen back to 1,640. Generally there was an upward trend, peaking during the Napoleonic Wars with numbers employed in the two yards having reached 3,665 by March 1814.

Of those employed it was shipwrights who formed the largest single group, accounting for approximately 40 per cent of the yard workforce. Among the tasks they undertook were assembling the frame of any vessel under construction, the laying of planks, interpreting the sheer draught, cutting templates and preparing the slipway. Despite having undertaken an apprenticeship that lasted seven years, few shipwrights were anything more than artists – guided by 'rule of thumb' over qualities of exactness. For them, if it looked right, then it was right. At Deptford, Ollivier had commented:

> I saw about 200 shipwrights in this Dockyard, yet among this whole number I scarce saw six who were good craftsmen. All of them seemed to me extremely lazy. Their tools are better than those of our shipwrights.

As for the shipwrights employed at Woolwich, he further commented that they were 'no better or less idle than those working at Deptford'. For this reason he considered the cost of labour on:

> English ships must be four times greater than in [French] yards, for not only do they pay the shipwrights here 30 shillings per day ... but they do not do half the work of [French] shipwrights.

Possibly the latter was true, but Ollivier appears to have greatly exaggerated the daily wage of a shipwright, which was 2s 1d per day!

Caulkers, who came next in order of seniority, formed a much smaller proportion of the two yards (3 per cent). They received the same basic daily wage as the shipwrights. Responsible for ensuring the water tightness of any vessels brought into dry dock, they filled the numerous seams and areas where planks were joined, with oakum. The oakum, old rope that had been untwisted and separated by oakum boys, was rolled in the palm of the hand and applied with the help of a caulking iron. Once pushed beneath the surface, the seam was filled or 'payed up' with pitch. Not that the task of a caulker started at this point, for in the case of vessels that required re-caulking, the old caulking had first to be removed by means of a 'rake' or 'hoe', an iron instrument of about 12 inches and shaped rather like a foreshortened 'S'.

Another highly skilled maritime trade was the sail maker. Working in and around the sail loft, sail makers were responsible for the manufacture of sails and other canvas items used on board ships. Deptford and Woolwich possessed sail lofts and houses for the storage of made masts, while the fir timbers yet to be converted into masts were held in mast ponds for preservation. According to Ollivier:

> There is a very large mast pond at Deptford where the unworked mast timber is preserved in water. The quantity of these spars is very great. They are fastened together in pairs with oak dogs, and for the most part stand high and dry when the tide is out.

Three other artisan trades, bricklayer, house carpenter and joiner (approximately 7–8 per cent of the workforce) were employed to maintain the buildings of the yard. House carpenters and joiners were frequently employed in the repair of timber docks, while all three tradesmen would be used in repairing and maintaining buildings within the yard. Given the considerable quantities of timber that were required in shipbuilding, a large number of sawyers were also required in the two yards.

A further distinct group employed within the dockyard were the semi-skilled labourers that included sawyers, scavelmen and teamsters (10 per cent). Between them, they undertook a series of specialist jobs that required only a minimal amount of training. As such, no apprenticeship or artisan status was attached, but each would be rewarded with a higher rate of pay and an increase in status over and above that of the ordinary labourer. Scavelmen were responsible for keeping the yard clean, opening and closing the docks, operating the pumps, digging out and cleaning the drains and removing ballast from ships about to enter dry dock, while teamsters worked as a pair and were responsible for looking after the heavy draught horses used for shifting the largest timbers around the yard. Of the three semi-skilled tasks, that of sawyer seems to be the least desirable. Working as one of a pair, they spent their entire day sawing the huge timbers and planks required within the dockyard. Throughout the day, their centre of activity would be based around one of the many saw pits spread across the yard, with one man standing within the pit and the other above. Paid at first by the day and latterly by the amount of timber sawn, the work was nearly as gruelling as that of the anchor smith. Of the pair, the top man was paid the most, as he was the one responsible for directing the two-man saw and keeping it sharpened. Ollivier described the process:

> The walls of the sawpits are lined with brick, with two or three small lodging places cut in the walls where the sawyers keep their tools. When they wish to saw up a timber they place it on rollers over one of the pits; the rollers are blocked with wedges, one of the sawyers descends into the pit, the other stands on top of the timber, and after they have sawn the full length afforded by the pit they slide the timber easily on the rollers with no need of any other device than a crow. When the timber has been sawn the planks lie so they can easily be carried away.

Remuneration varied considerably between these work groups, but other work-related factors, such as the length of the dockyard day, were identical. With respect to pay, two different rates existed: a day rate and payment by results. The former, which had been used to remunerate workers since Tudor times, was set at a less than generous level, especially when compared with those of similar trades employed outside the naval dockyards, and it remained virtually unchanged throughout the eighteenth century. As for payment by results, this was first introduced into the royal dockyards in 1758, but at that time was restricted to labourers and scavelmen. Known either as 'task work' or 'job work', according to whether it was new construction or repair work, it was not initially allowed to the skilled trades as there was a fear that it would encourage skimping. Only in 1775 was it finally allowed to virtually all classes of workers, with shipwrights at that time refusing to accept this method of payment for a further six years. In addition to pay, whether at the day or piece rate, many workers were also entitled to the perquisite of 'chips'. This was the right to take from the yard small cuts of timber, that were of no further use in the shipbuilding and repair process. These bundles consisted of timber no more than 3ft in length and had to be carried out of the gate under the arm. It was generally recognised that these bundles were financially useful, often being sold for 6d or more to town traders.

The basic day pay, which for shipwrights and caulkers stood at 2s 1d but fell to 1s 1d for labourers, was paid for the completion of a full, twelve-hour working day (6 a.m. to 6 p.m. in summer but less in winter) that included a ninety-minute lunch break. In all, six days in every week were worked, with Sunday counted as a non-working day and Saturdays finishing one hour early. Periods of overtime were also permitted, these coming in at ninety-minute and five-hour units, the former being known as 'tydes' and the latter 'days'. Overtime was most frequent in the summer, with the dockyard authorities fully utilising the longer daylight hours. During emergencies, however, even winter evenings would be worked, with artisans and labourers employed by candlelight. As for holidays, these were, more or less, non-existent. Since 1715 only four had been allowed, these being the King's Birthday, Coronation Day, 5th November and Oak Apple Day (29 May). On such days, the workforce was employed until noon but received a full day's pay.

It is interesting to contrast the picture of the two yards as presented by Ollivier with a much later description that dates to the end of the Georgian period. It appears in a supplement to the *Encyclopaedia Britannica* issued in 1824. Many of the dilapidated buildings and stores that Ollivier had identified had long been removed, with particular attention having been given to the important storage facilities at Deptford, where a new main store had been constructed soon after Ollivier's visit. Located on the south-east side of the yard, where a number of wooden storehouses had previously existed, it was a quadrangular brick building set around a central square. Of three storeys in height, the length of each side was nearly the same, approximating 210ft, while in width the sides varied from 24ft to 46ft. To this the writer of the *Encyclopaedia Britannica* notes:

> Parallel to the west front of the quadrangle [of the main store] is the rigging house and sail loft, 240ft and nearly 50ft wide, in which all the rigging is fitted for ships and stowed away, the sails cut out, made and placed in proper births for their reception as well as smaller stores of a smaller kind.

Further on it was added:

> On the eastern extremity of the yard is a long range of building called the pavilion, in which the beds, hammock and slop clothing as are kept and in which also are the Housecarpenters, the joiners and wheelwrights' shops. This building is about 580ft long by 26ft wide.

Within recent years Woolwich had seen construction of new masting facilities that included a mast pond, mast houses and a mast slip while a new smithery was under construction. According to the writer of the *Encyclopaedia Britannica* supplement:

The timber births are well arranged and the addition recently made to the western extremity of the yard will allow the stacking of several loads of timber and of classing it according to the purposes to which it may be applicable; and when the new smithery and the line of wharf wall completed, the dockyard of Woolwich will become an important and valuable naval arsenal.

Administratively separate from the dockyard but overseen by the Navy Board was the ropeyard at Woolwich. Unlike the naval roperies at Portsmouth, Plymouth (Devonport) and Chatham, the ropery at Woolwich was outside the dockyard, located at the east end of the High Street and stretching back in a north-easterly direction towards Green End. Two adjacent buildings engaged in the process of rope manufacture, one a spinning house (where rope was spun into yarn) and the other the ropewalk (where rope was formed). There were a number of smaller buildings, including the hemp and tarring houses together with several specialised storehouses. In all, numbers employed in the ropery rarely fell below 160 and would sometimes rise above 200.

The process of rope manufacture began with the arrival of raw hemp imported from northern Europe. Stored in the hemp houses that had a storage capacity of 2,000 tons, it was removed when required. The first stage in the rope manufacturing process saw it being combed, or unknotted, in a hatchelling house, the tangled hemp pulled across a board that was set with sharp pointed iron nails, known as a hatchel; this task was performed by hatchellors. The next stage was to transfer the combed hemp to the spinning house where spinners would twist portions of the hemp fibre over a hook on a manually turned spinning frame. As the frame turned, the spinner would slowly walk backwards, allowing yarn to be formed under the guidance of his left hand. At the same time, from a bundle of hemp thrown over his shoulder, and using his right hand, further hemp would be added to allow the yarn to lengthen out. The next stage was tarring the yarn. This was carried out in the tarring house, with the yarn pulled through a large kettle containing heated tar.

The tarred yarn, having been allowed to dry and wound on to bobbins, was transferred to the ropewalk, a building 1080ft in length, for the final two stages of the rope manufacturing process, combining the individual yarns into strands and then the strands into rope. The first part of the process was done by mounting the bobbins at one end of the floor and attaching the yarn ends to a rotating hook mounted on a wheel frame. The wheel frame, manually powered and mounted on wheels, travelled the length of the laying floor, drawing out yarn from the bobbins and twisting the strands together. The final stage, that of 'laying' or closing the great ropes, necessitated the strands being laid out along the length of the ropewalk floor, one end of the strands connected to hooks that could be rotated on a fixed point, while the remaining ends were attached to a wheel frame, in the case of small rope, or a larger jack wheel. To separate the strands, and keep them at a constant height, trestles were placed at intervals between the jack wheel and back frame, which were removed in turn as the jack wheel moved forward. The hooks at the fixed point and on the jack wheel were then turned by manual labour, thus twisting the frames to form rope, with the jack wheel drawn along the laying floor. As well as being inconveniently sited away from the dockyard at Woolwich, the ropery was located within a very confined space. It did not allow for any expansion while, during the early nineteenth century, this lack of space prevented some of the machinery being modernised, since the application of steam required a boiler and engine house. It was a problem, though, that had been long recognised with a plan for an entirely new ropery on land adjoining the north-west side of the dockyard having been drawn up in 1787.

The other components of the Kentish naval multiplex were the Deptford victualling yard (known as the Red House estate), the Arsenal at Woolwich and the naval hospital at Greenwich. The first of these, the victualling yard, was to the immediate north-west of the naval dockyard at Deptford and south of the Dudman shipbuilding yard. Although the early eighteenth century had seen some use of the site for naval victualling, full possession was not achieved until 1743, in order to relieve the considerable pressure under which the Victualling Board was then placed. The existing London yard, Tower Hill, which was also home to the offices of the Board, was not only operating to full capacity from the 1730s onwards but had no available room for increased manufacturing and storage facilities. Instead, other sites had to be acquired at locations more distant from Tower Hill, so creating an unworkable dispersal of facilities and workforce.

An additional problem for the Tower Hill site was that much of what was there was also ageing, with many of the structures dating to the early seventeenth century and in need of frequent repair and renovation. Year after year, references were made in the account books to the employment of carpenters, joiners, plasterers and plumbers to carry out such work, with costs in some years amounting to several thousand pounds. In 1718, for instance, the Victualling Board commissioners requested through the Navy Board a sufficient sum from Parliament to begin just one such repair programme, it being stated that many of the buildings on Tower Hill were so old and decayed as 'to be rendered almost useless' (Grainger and Phillpotts, 2010, p. 37). Four years later, more money had to be expended on the animal slaughtering house, which was only prevented from collapse by a number of judiciously placed bracing timbers. Yet again, in 1727, more money was being sought, a contingency fund of £500 necessary for repairs to almost every building. This continued into the 1730s and 1740s, with repairs continuing to be undertaken on the various stores, bakeries, dwelling houses and offices that were part of the Tower Hill victualling yard.

At Tower Hill and Deptford, for at one time they were operating alongside each other, there were clear administrative divisions, each working area directly managed by a senior resident clerk working alongside an appropriate trade master. The slaughter and cutting house, where animals were killed and the carcasses cut into pieces of 4lb prior to salting, were overseen by a clerk of the cutting house working in conjunction with the master butcher, an inferior officer of the yard. The most intense part of the year was autumn and winter, when animals were slaughtered, cut and salted, the lower temperatures aiding the preservation process. At other times of the year, much of the work was confined to the issuing and overseeing of stores. Initial purchasing of livestock was most frequently undertaken at the nearby Smithfield meat market where, it has been estimated, some 70,000 or more cattle were regularly offered for sale each year, having been brought on the hoof from as far afield as Scotland and Wales (Baugh, 1965, p. 407). The Navy, although a major purchaser, requiring several thousand oxen in any one year, was always in a position to secure its needs either at Smithfield or in one of the smaller markets that also existed in the metropolis. Animals were then brought to either the Tower Hill or Deptford victualling yards and stabled in extensive pounds before entering the slaughterhouse, with slaughtering taking place at night. Employed seasonally were the messers and salters, artisans responsible for slaughtering and the preserving of carcasses while labourers assisted in much of the heavier work. Finally, a named commissioner of the Victualling Board had overall charge of the butchery area; he was responsible for ensuring that deliveries met the contract terms and that the workmen were efficiently performing the tasks expected of them.

The bake house and beer brewery were similarly supervised, with a chief clerk who supervised the work of either a master baker or master brewer. Again, the basic raw materials were purchased in London, with the clerks responsible for receiving deliveries and accounting for their storage. As with the clerk of the Cutting House, both were subject to inspection by a named commissioner. While a bake house and brewery were to be built at Deptford, baking and brewing were tasks that were undertaken away from Tower Hill. In part, this was due to the chronic lack of space. However, a bakery did exist within the Tower Hill complex, but the constant danger of fire in the bakery inclined the commissioners to contract work out to a number of nearby bakeries. Using brick ovens, the principal product was biscuits, which were preferred to bread due to it coming in handy pieces and remaining edible for many months. As for brewing, which was a further cool-season activity; this was concentrated upon Hartshorne Brewery, partly owned by the Navy and located to the east of Tower Hill.

Apart from bread, which was packed in bags, all of the processed provisions were stored in casks. This generated a quite separate work area within the two London yards, both having cooperages for the manufacture of these containers. Simply a wooden barrel bound by hoops, they were, irrespective of size, all of the same shape: wider at the waist and narrower at the ends. The largest, known as a 'tun', could carry 250 gallons and was primarily reserved for drinking water while those of 105 gallons were generally used for the storage of wine. Other smaller sized barrels were used for butter (56lb), beer (9 gallons) and dry foods including biscuit, biscuit-meal, fine flour, pease, oatmeal, rice, currants and raisins (70–120 gallons). While the various work areas employed their own coopers, Tower Hill and Deptford had areas set aside for this work and each employed a master cooper.

The need for a unified and enlarged London victualling yard had led, by May 1742, to the opening of negotiations for the complete acquisition of the Red House estate. In that month, the victualling commissioners requested of the Admiralty that they purchase the land to create a completely unified yard that could be used for the storage and manufacture of a complete range of essential provisions. Despite Admiralty approval, outright purchase was refused by the Privy Council with the owner of the Red House estate, John Evelyn, the grandson of the diarist, agreeing to lease it for an annual sum of £500. Building work was soon under way, with a brick storehouse among the first buildings constructed quickly followed by a bakery. Not initially seen as an urgent requirement, the bakery was constructed at this point to replace one in Rotherhithe that was destroyed by fire in 1747, so confirming the victualling commissioners' concerns that bakeries should not be constructed within the confined space of the Tower Hill yard. At Deptford there was considerably greater space, allowing the bakery to be isolated from other buildings, so ensuring that in the event of fire it would not spread.

With both yards working in unison for a number of years, the total employed had, by January 1761, reached a little over 600. Of these, the largest single group, 168 in number, were employed in the various cooperages, while bakeries at Red House and a new facility at Rotherhithe were employing 130. The Tower Hill site was finally abandoned in 1787, but the new yard at Deptford continued to be developed, gaining a brewery, cutting and slaughterhouses, various residences and a further mill.

Returning to Woolwich, the Arsenal, which lay between Plumstead Road and the Thames, was also important to the Navy. Administered by the Board of Ordnance, it was here that vast amounts of naval ordnance and equipment were stored. Gun carriages and a small number of bronze cannon were also manufactured, but most naval guns, being iron, were purchased directly from private manufacturers and then tested at Woolwich. Advertised tenders, issuing of contracts and final payments were the responsibility of the Clerk of the Ordnance, an officer quartered at the Tower who was also responsible for drawing up estimates for the supply of stores to warships and the retention of all receipts for payments made in connection with naval ordnance. For the Admiralty there were several advantages in this arrangement, not least the economy brought about by bulk purchasing. Furthermore, it seems likely that a system that might otherwise have encouraged separate tendering for Army and Navy ordnance might have resulted in a degree of competition with one of these organisations probably forced to pay a higher price than the other in order to fulfil their requisite needs. Helping ensure such an outcome was the fact that most guns were identical, whether used on board ship and mounted on a sea carriage or taken to a fort and mounted on a land carriage.

However, leaving aside this simple reduction in costs, there were a number of clear disadvantages resulting from the arrangement. In particular, the Navy was entirely reliant for its supply of guns upon an organisation more or less totally dominated by the Army. All Ordnance Board members, from the Master General down, were selected only from among serving Army officers and rarely had any seagoing experience. As regards the basic gun, this was not a problem during the Georgian era, but difficulties arose as to the carriage upon which it was supported, the most appropriate being the slide mount as used by carronades. This had the advantage of providing controlled recoil rather than the unpredictable movement of the gun when mounted on the sea carriage with trucks (or small wheels). Naval historian Brian Lavery, in indicating his belief that the failure to introduce a better carriage was a possible reflection of this division between Admiralty and Ordnance Board, goes on to outline the problems associated with the standard carriage:

> Because it was mounted on wheels, it could be highly dangerous if it broke loose. There was no effective way of bringing it to a halt, and it tended to stop with a sharp jerk when the breech ropes were fully extended. The direction of its recoil was unpredictable, especially on a rolling and heaving deck, and this could be dangerous to the unwary seamen. It was not very efficient mechanically, for it was restrained too near its rear, and this probably caused it to jerk violently near the end of its recoil. (Brian Lavery, *The Ship of the Line: Design, Construction, and Fittings*, 1984, p. 153)

The ordnance facilities at Woolwich, originally established in the early sixteenth century to support the nearby naval dockyards in the arming of warships, had grown from a half-acre site that housed a few storehouses and a number of cranes into a major industrial complex. By the time the Napoleonic Wars were coming to an end, the Arsenal was employing a 5,000-strong workforce. The greatest boost to its usefulness had come about in 1671 with the purchase of a 31-acre site that was part of Tower House. Upon this land was soon to be constructed a carriage yard (*c.* 1697), the Royal Brass Foundry (1717) and a range of stores. It was within the sheds built around the carriage yard that gun carriages, including those for naval warships, were repaired and modified while the foundry manufactured brass cannons. Other buildings followed, including turning, washing and engraving houses, a smiths' shop and further carriage storehouses (with one of these set aside for sea service carriages). A further important project was an artillery barracks, much of it built during the 1730s, providing accommodation for officers and men. This too had a naval connection, as gunners of the Royal Artillery occasionally served at sea when they manned floating gun platforms, known as 'bomb ships', that were designed to carry mortars for the bombardment of shore fortifications.

By 1777, the area of the Arsenal, through the acquisition of further land, covered 104 acres, with Georgian-age building projects including a Grand Storehouse (completed in 1814), a steam-powered sawmill and an improved gatehouse. Much of this later work, in common with the building work undertaken at the naval dockyards of Deptford and Woolwich, was undertaken by convict labour. Housed in hulked warships that were well past their prime, the convicts were brought ashore each morning, manacled by ball and chain, for the commencement of their daily tasks.

A further component of the Kentish London naval multiplex was Greenwich. Most obvious in its naval connection was the Royal Hospital for Seamen, but of some significance also was the Royal Observatory. Already it has been shown that the Board of Longitude sat at Wallingford House but it was at Greenwich that some of the practical work connected with the discovery of longitude was undertaken. Founded in 1675, the purpose of the observatory was to accurately measure the position of the sun, moon and stars to help 'find the so-much desired longitude of places for the perfecting of navigation'. More complex than the use of accurate chronometers, it was the only available option prior to the invention of an accurate seagoing time piece.

For the purpose of determining a ship's longitude from the moon and stars – the 'lunar distance' method – a record of predicted positions of various celestial bodies was required, with the Royal Observatory producing data that could be tested by various naval expeditions. In fact, the Royal Navy and Observatory worked hand-in-glove to help solve a problem fundamental to global sea navigation. Even following the production of accurate chronometers, such as the one produced by John Harrison, the Navy continued to use, conjointly with marine chronometers, the lunar method into the early years of the nineteenth century. As to the Royal Navy's use of chronometers, this was also associated with Greenwich, as it was the Royal Observatory that oversaw their purchase, testing and final issuing to warships.

The Royal Hospital for Seamen at Greenwich, which could be clearly viewed from the Royal Observatory, was founded in 1694. Its purpose, as laid down by royal charter, was to provide 'relief and support [for] seamen serving on board the ships and vessels' of the Royal Navy and who, 'by reason of age, wounds or other disabilities [were] incapable of further service'. In other words, it was not to concentrate on the medical needs of seamen but to contribute to their well-being on leaving the service. Tom Saunders, the 'Poor Jack' in Marryat's novel of that title, becomes acquainted with Peter Anderson, a former gunner's mate and Greenwich pensioner, and is told that:

> the sailor who has fought for his country has much to be thankful for when he takes in moorings at Greenwich Hospital. He is well fed, well clothed, tended in sickness and buried with respect. (Frederick Marryat, *Poor Jack*, 1897 edition, p. 132)

Built to an original plan laid down by Sir Christopher Wren, by the end of the Georgian period the hospital consisted of five separate quadrangular ranges set around an inner square. Four of these were the courts that accommodated naval pensioners while the fifth was an infirmary built between 1764 and 1768. Within the buildings of each court were housed various wards, these usually named after famous ships and themselves sub-divided into 'cabins' for single occupants or small groups. Built in sequence, with the final court completed in 1751, they were each named after a former monarch, namely Charles, Anne, William and Mary. As well as Wren, a number of leading architects were involved in constructing the hospital, including Nicholas Hawksmoor and Sir John Vanbrugh. Interestingly, the architect employed in completing Queen Mary Court was Sir Thomas Ripley, the man who designed Wallingford House. A common criticism of this latter building was its overall plainness, a point also levelled against Queen Mary Court. Although, in its defence, it does blend in with the adjoining King William Court that Wren had designed.

To fund the building work and to support those pensioners who came to be reliant upon the hospital, a variety of sources were tapped into, including royal and private bequests, the right to the receipt of money from certain taxes, unclaimed naval prize money and a lottery scheme. Seamen were also required to contribute 6*d* per month to the hospital; this was seen as a welfare fund that they might themselves have to call upon at some time in the future. It was an amount additional to a payment that seamen were already required to contribute to the Chatham Chest, an earlier welfare scheme that provided for disabled seamen and widows of seamen who had died in service without a pension. Following an Act of Parliament in 1803, when it was disbursing to more than 5,000 pensions, the Chest was merged with Greenwich Hospital, a process that was completed in 1814 and by which time the fund was known as the Greenwich Chest.

The hospital, itself, was accommodating as many as 1,400 pensioners by 1752, with this number set to more than double over the next thirty years as a result of naval expansion and battles fought. Soon a point was reached when the hospital had simply run out of accommodation and was unable to accept those deserving of care until others had moved on. Fortunately though, a solution was at hand. In 1763 an Act was passed that permitted the hospital to offer 'out-pensions' to those who, on receipt of a payment of £7 per year, could otherwise survive. Again, the demand was steadily upward; a trend further advanced by the wars against revolutionary France and Napoleon, with the number of pensioners reaching 30,000 by 1820.

The original charter of 1694 had also allowed money to be set aside for the 'education of the children of seamen happening to be slain or disabled'. With concentration initially on the construction of the buildings, it was not until 1715 that attention was given to this task, with sons of pensioners supported in their attendance at Thomas Weston's academy, a fee-paying school in Greenwich that directed learning towards the science of navigation. By 1780, a separate school had been constructed on land owned by the hospital (with accommodation in a ward set aside for the purpose), and the number of supported scholars had reached 150. A not dissimilar school, the Royal Naval Asylum, was eventually to merge with the Hospital School. Established in Paddington in 1798, and generously supported by Parliament, royalty and London merchants, the Asylum first expanded into Greenwich when granted use of the Queen's House. This was a grace-and-favour residence in the possession of George III – it is now part of the National Maritime Museum – first occupied by fifty-six children in 1806. Additional wings constructed a few years later allowed for a possible 1,000 scholars, the two wings containing dormitories, teaching and dining rooms. The amalgamation of the two schools came about in January 1821. It was known from then on as the Greenwich Hospital Schools and was placed under the governance of the directors of the hospital.

Greenwich, through the hospital and its schools, was dominated by the Navy. Outpatients by the hundred, whether in receipt of payments awarded by the hospital or by the Chatham Chest, were drawn each day to the payments office to collect their quarterly awards. Mixing with these former seamen were the in-patients of the hospital, easily recognisable as they had to wear a regulation blue frock coat and tricorn hat (both formerly brown), and breeches. Add to this the increasing number of charity scholars, who were required to wear 'sailor dress'. All in all, it was hard to ignore the naval connection.

One further naval oriented group also came to Greenwich: sightseers, men and women who came to the hospital to enjoy the architecture of the hospital and more especially the Painted Hall. Located on the south side of King William Court and the original Hospital refectory, it had been given a series of magnificent paintings, executed by Sir James Thornhill (1675–1734), that depicted the Protestant succession of monarchs from William and Mary to George I. To take advantage of this, charges began to be made, which were initially used to support the Hospital School. Towards the end of the eighteenth century a more ambitious scheme was proposed to create within the Painted Hall a gallery of marine paintings. Coming to fruition in the mid-1820s, it was considerably aided by thirty-eight portraits gifted by George IV.

Governors at the hospital, all of whom were appointed by the First Lord, included George Brydges, 1st Baron Rodney (1765–71), an admiral who was later to gain considerable fame during the American War of Independence; Samuel, 1st Viscount Hood (1796–1816), who served under Rodney at the Battle of the Saintes and Sir Hugh Palliser (1780–96) a former Navy Comptroller and professional lord at the Admiralty. Through the existence of the hospital, and the high social status of its various governors, Greenwich can justly claim to mark the very beginning of the Georgian age for it was here, in September 1714, that George I took his first steps on English soil, arriving at Greenwich where he and a full retinue of German friends, advisers and servants were briefly entertained in the Queen's House, then the residence of the governor.

Nelson's body lay in state at the hospital for three days in 1806. Admiral John Byng was confined in the first-floor chambers of the Queen Anne Court from August to December 1756 before he was taken to Portsmouth Harbour where a court martial was to sentence him to be executed by firing squad. Earlier, in May, he had commanded a fleet that had failed to relieve the beleaguered British garrison at Port Mahon. It was this event that led the French writer Voltaire to conclude that in England 'it is thought well to kill an admiral from time to time to encourage the others'. Not surprisingly, this was a less than happy period in Byng's life, the garret room in which he was held being initially without furniture while an armed guard remained outside the room. Adding to his discomfiture was the placing of an iron grille over the windows and cemented metal bars across the chimney top, 'in case the portly Admiral should try to climb up to seek freedom on the roof tops' (Pope, 1987, p. 188).

A further name associated with the hospital, if only briefly, was Sir James Cook, the explorer and navigator. Two of the ships in his earlier expeditions, *Endeavour* and *Resolution*, were fitted out at Deptford naval dockyard. In 1775 Cook was given honorary retirement through being appointed Fourth Captain at the hospital and given residence. Yet, at the age of 47, Cook was unsure that he wanted to retire, writing to a friend that 'a few months ago the whole southern hemisphere was hardly big enough for me, and now I am going to be confined within the limits of Greenwich Hospital, which are too small for an active mind like mine' (MacLean, 1972, p. 149). It was for this reason that his acceptance came with a condition that if there was the possibility of more active service he would quit the position. A supper at Admiralty House with the First Lord, the Earl of Sandwich together with Hugh Palliser and Admiralty Secretary Philip Stephens, resulted in Cook enthusiastically agreeing to a third voyage at the end of which he would be permitted to return to Greenwich. This, however, was not to be, for this third voyage, an attempt to discover a north-west passage, was the one from which he never returned.

Part 3

THE SOCIAL DIMENSION

Introduction

The Navy was firmly entrenched in the social and political milieu of Georgian London. While most might proudly proclaim a great victory or mourn defeat, beyond this there was little that resembled a consensual viewpoint. In particular, there was a gulf in attitude towards service on board a warship. While officers could be recruited with relative ease, the same could not be said of the men who served on the lower decks. It is not hard to see why. Those eligible for the quarterdeck, those who commanded, were offered by the Navy good prospects and the possibility of enduring fame; for those trapped on the lower deck, life was harsh and the rewards few. Indeed, this latter group would invariably be discarded at the end of any period of service, with only the most fortunate of the most needy obtaining a berth at Greenwich Hospital. While the sons of the well connected (usually the younger siblings who would not inherit the family estate or interests) would look favourably on a career in the Navy, artisans or labourers would resort to a variety of ploys, including physical violence, to avoid incarceration on board one of His Majesty's warships. Only during peacetime, when few ships were at sea, did the majority of warship crews consist of volunteers – men who truly wished to be part of the sea service. In times of war, when the demand for men might rise from 16,000 to something in excess of 100,000, the demand for men far outweighed the number of volunteers, leading the government to sanction draconian methods of recruitment.

Exacerbating the divide, and ensuring that those of one class had clear ownership of the Navy while others were merely viewed as an expendable commodity, even acts of bravery were rarely acknowledged when performed by members of the lower deck. Instead, only the meritorious acts of the quarterdeck were seen as deserving recognition through the raising of numerous public memorials that praised a dutiful officer. A simple tour of St Paul's Cathedral or Westminster Abbey makes this point, with numerous admirals and captains memorialised in a variety of ways. At the latter, for instance, are monuments to Admiral Thomas Cochrane, Admiral Sir George Pocock (famed for his participation in the capture of Havana in 1762), Admiral Edward Vernon (the originator of the official Royal Navy 'grog' ration of rum) and Admiral Sir Charles Wager (whose chief claim to fame was his defeat and capture of a Spanish treasure squadron in 1708). Other memorials are to captains who lost their lives in battle, but these are without reference to the many men of the lower deck who also suffered and died in these actions. For instance, placed in St John the Evangelist's chapel by a grateful East India Company, the memorial to Captain Edward Cooke, commander of the frigate *Sybille*, commemorates his death when taking *La Forte*, a French frigate of superior strength, but makes no mention of the two men from the lower deck who also lost their lives in the action, nor of those severely injured. As for St Paul's Cathedral, home to the tomb of Nelson, there are memorials to captains including John Cooke of *Bellerophon* and George Duff of *Mars*, both of whom died commanding their ships at Trafalgar, and Richard Burgess of *Ardent* who died at Camperdown (October 1797). Yet, in these same battles and on board those same ships, nearly 100 members of the lower deck also sacrificed their lives, but not one of them is accorded similar recognition in London or anywhere else in the country.

Of course, it could be claimed that Nelson's funeral, through the presence of several of *Victory*'s lower-deck crew members, had a more democratic approach. In reality, this was not so. Isaac Land (2009), in his study of the British sailor during this period, indicates that they were there for the singular purpose of forming a backdrop, a symbol to appease 'the mob'. In doing so, not only had the chosen few been carefully selected but also sanitised with regard to what was to be worn, with Land quoting the words of one participant who wrote, 'we are to wear white trowsers and a black scarf around our arms and hats beside [a] gold medal for the battle of Trafalgar, value £7 1s around our necks'.

The connection of the people of London with the Navy did not end with those who served as officers or seamen on board ships of war. It stretched a good deal further, with huge numbers reliant upon the Navy. Already attention has been directed to the many thousands who were employed in the shipyards that stretched along the banks of the Thames and into Kentish London. Only some of these yards were entirely dedicated to supporting the needs of the Navy, most of the yards were heavily dependent for survival on naval contracts to supplement ship repair and building works carried out for the private sector. But of course, it went further than that. The private sector was itself dependent on the Navy for the protection of those ships that it ordered to be built; if the Navy had been unable to fulfill that duty, the ships would not have been ordered in the first place.

Fixed into this spiralling interconnected web were those who were reliant upon family breadwinners who took their income from the Navy or naval-connected employment. Here, too, there was a divide in attitude. While resentment at all levels might be directed towards the Navy for it having taken from the family hearth a breadwinner, the intensity of this hurt and any consequent anger towards the Navy was much deeper among those when the loss resulted from enforced naval service. A hot press, for instance, was a general taking of all those who were able-bodied and of seamanlike appearance. Rapidly transferred to a receiving ship that lay off Tower Stairs, such individuals would be quickly transferred to a much larger ship stationed further downriver where lay the Naval anchorage known as the Nore (close to Sheerness) for subsequent dispersal among the fleet. Families relying upon those ensnared might find their financial integrity seriously jeopardised. For the officer class, no such threat existed. Having volunteered their services and given fair warning of a likely posting, there was every chance that the family finances would be put into good order. All that had to be confronted by any dependent relatives was that of a lengthy period of separation. Even this, however, was softened for those on the quarter deck, for they at least got shore leave and might arrange a few shared weeks with a loved one when their vessel was once again in home waters.

Within London, a huge range of businesses, large and small, depended on the Navy directly and indirectly. Among the former were the owners of shipbuilding yards and the suppliers to the Navy. For the latter, the merchants based in London who were beginning to trade throughout the world required the Navy to secure trade routes. The Navy not only secured the trade routes, for it also played a highly significant role in the expansion of the British Empire, with traders quick to take advantage of the resulting new opportunities. Important city institutions such as Lloyd's, the Honourable East India Company and the Bank of England all grew through the actions of the Navy. At the other extreme, more local merchants serviced the shore-based needs of those more securely connected with the Navy. The range was considerable and encompassed tap housekeepers through to the highly respected Gieves of the Strand, which supplied senior officers with uniforms. It might be assumed that all of these, in profiting in some way from the existence of the Navy, would have nothing but respect for the service. But here existed a further divide. As many of these merchants and businesses were also dependent on the safe passage of merchant ships, they took exception to the wartime practice of pressing seamen from merchant ships while either at sea or as they entered the Thames. Another consequence was often a delayed sailing as crew numbers were replenished, combined with an increasing reluctance on the part of some to join a merchant ship for fear of that vessel being boarded by a naval press gang.

7

Those of the Lower Deck

Upon the outbreak of war or at the beginning of any period of naval mobilisation, the Admiralty would find great difficulty in manning the lower decks of the many additional ships that would now have to put to sea. While the number of seamen borne for wages during peace was usually less than 20,000, in times of war this rapidly increased by fivefold or more. In 1755, for instance, a year free of conflict, the Navy could lay claim to 17,300 seamen with this number surging to 85,000 just five years later when the Seven Years War was at its height. Similarly, the number borne in 1792 was a little over 16,000 but by 1802 had reached almost 130,000.

While many who served in the Navy did so voluntarily, particularly during peacetime, this was certainly not so when it came to periods of wartime expansion. Those enlisted on the lower decks were often unwilling participants in protecting the nation from invasion and facilitating the expansion of London's mercantile economy. For various reasons, a goodly proportion of any warship crew had not chosen to serve, with their loyalty to the Navy so much in question that few captains permitted shore leave, believing that this would result in mass desertion.

While the number of volunteers could probably have been substantially increased by improving the actual terms of service, not least the miserly wage and indeterminate lengthy periods of service, the fundamental cause was that there were not enough seamen to fulfil the needs of the Navy and Merchant services. The Navy did not have a reserve of trained seamen that could be called upon in times of need, so it was entirely dependent upon the merchant service, or those otherwise unconnected with the Navy, to make up the additional numbers. And here was the problem. The seamen available to the merchant service might be sufficient to meet its needs while allowing a limited degree of naval expansion, but there was nothing like sufficient numbers to meet wartime mobilisation. To resolve the problem, the government sanctioned forcible recruitment through the use of press gangs, with a series of Quota Acts introduced from 1795, requiring each county to recruit a fixed number into the Navy. Supplementing this, local magistrates sometimes chose to give a convicted felon the opportunity of joining the Navy rather than serving a prison term. Of course, none of these measures actually increased the pool of trained seamen, with large numbers of those who entered the Navy during periods of war being 'landsmen', men of no previous maritime experience.

For London, the Navy's hunger for men created many conflicts among the population. While the set-piece funeral of Lord Nelson might have given the appearance of a Navy capturing the hearts of Londoners, this was temporary. While there is no suggestion that the sea service lacked a degree of popularity, this should not conceal the fact that many detested the Navy. Some of those who had attended the funeral service at St Paul's Cathedral would have been owners or subscribing members of trading companies with ships that had been boarded at sea for the purpose of having some of their best seamen taken for service in the Navy. It was a dangerous practice, as it left such ships undermanned and in severe difficulty if engulfed by a sudden squall or storm. While ship owners might appreciate the protection that a powerful Navy offered, they had no love of the methods the Navy used to augment its crews. Also seated in the cathedral were members of the Corporation of London, a body that had not always been favourable to the entry of press gangs into the city. Headed by the Lord Mayor, they had even used their legal authority to prosecute the lieutenant at the head of a press or some of its members when a gang had crossed into the City in hot pursuit of a fleeing 'seaman'. Finally, there were the Londoners who were the victims of enforced impressments. Even if they had been inclined to line the route of the funeral cortege, they would have been unable to do so, for no captain would dare release them from the ship upon which they served. They were the ones who had found themselves unceremoniously dumped onto the lower deck of a warship and forced to serve, turned over from one warship to another until hostilities finally ended.

London was the Navy's most important recruiting ground. As the principal port of the kingdom for long- and short-haul merchant vessels, London, if figures existing for 1779 are reliable and typical, provided approximately 30 per cent of all recruits into the Navy (Lloyd, 1965, pp. 265–7). While these men were not evenly distributed between ships, it indicates that few naval vessels were without a fairly sizeable contingent of Londoners. Alongside the Thames, immediately to the east of the City and stretching out towards Woolwich, were the lodgings of families of artisans and labourers with a maritime association. In 1768 Henry Fielding refers to Rotherhithe as 'chiefly inhabited by sailors', suggesting that the visitor, because of the dominance of the sea, 'would be apt to suspect himself in another country' (Fielding, 1768, p. xv). It was the men of these properties who were particularly susceptible to impressment, given that the lieutenants in charge of a press gang were normally instructed to seek out 'such persons whose occupation and calling are to work in vessels or boats upon rivers'. In turn though, it was recognised that the commerce of London and the support that it gave to the Admiralty through the building of ships and the supplying of materials, would be seriously jeopardised if enforced recruitment leant too heavily upon those living in one single area. As a result, many were issued with protection certificates that ensured they could not be pressed into the Navy. However, at times of extreme urgency, when a 'hot' press had been ordered, many of those 'protections' would prove useless. Among those holding 'protections' were men employed in the naval dock and victualling yards at Deptford and Woolwich, with exemption also including some of the artisans of the private ship building and repair yards together with those in less obvious occupations such as orange porters and Limehouse biscuit manufacturers. Orange porters and biscuit makers might not seem candidates for a naval career, but anyone between 18 and 55 and who had 'used the sea' at some point in the past was liable to impressments; both groups almost certainly had former seamen in their midst.

To recruit London seamen, the captain of a newly commissioned ship would instruct a recruiting party headed by a lieutenant to establish a rendezvous. Most commonly an inn or tap house close to the river would be chosen, with the *Black Boy and Trumpet* at St Katherine's Stairs and the *Angel* in Rotherhithe popular choices. Should a suitable number of volunteers fail to enlist, a more forcible means of recruitment would be adopted. Often this involved acting upon information gathered as to where seamen might be found and a subsequent heavy-handed descent on a nearby tavern or private residence.

The alternative to a recruiting party sent from individual ships was the Naval Impress Service, a permanent organisation within the Navy. The Naval Impress Service also sent out gangs to recruit seamen but these men were permanently employed in the duty and paid additional travel money (3*d* per mile for officers and 1*d* for men) and anything up to 10*s* for every man pressed. The Naval Impress Service also sought out deserters and, for this purpose, gangs of seamen working for the Impress Service would often position themselves on the roads leading into London following the arrival of ships at Portsmouth or Chatham. Once established at a port, the service was headed by a regulating officer, either a captain or lieutenant, with a tender located nearby for the receiving of recruits. In the case of London, and for the entire period of the French Revolutionary and Napoleonic Wars, the London Impress Service was in the hands of Captain Thomas Richbell, who was assisted by a number of lieutenants. The receiving tender for the near-City area and Kentish London was normally a hulked sixth-rate frigate that was moored off Tower Stairs. At the time of Nelson's funeral, this was *Enterprise*, a vessel built by Randall's of Rotherhithe and launched as *Resource* in August 1778 but renamed in 1803 when brought to her mooring in the Thames. She was to remain here until the end of the war when she was taken out of service and broken up. From the receiving tender, whether volunteer or pressed, recruits were dispersed, with many of them taken to the Nore anchorage where *Sandwich*, a much larger receiving ship, would take them for final dispersal to a seagoing warship.

The number of men who, during periods of mobilisation, were pressed, as compared with volunteers, has long been debated by naval historians. Unfortunately there is no clear answer. The muster books of any ship will sometimes reveal whether a man was pressed or volunteered but the bulk are more often listed as having been 'turned over' from another ship, with the original terms of enlistment requiring numerous individual searches. Furthermore, a man indicated as a volunteer might well have been pressed but subsequently allowed to volunteer, so permitting him to receive two months' wages in advance together with an additional payment known as conduct money. Both were supposed to be paid only to volunteers but the money was usually paid to any man prepared to deny that he had been pressed. As a result, only the most stubborn, or those with a strong belief that they could gain release, would choose to be mustered as a pressed man. In 1776, to give one simple example, a total of 250 men were reported to have been pressed in London but, according to a newspaper report, on being brought on board a naval tender lying off the Tower, all but a few were entered as volunteers (*Caledonian Mercury*, 6 November 1776). In the late 1750s, following a request from the House of Commons, the Navy Office did produce figures that showed almost half the men entering the Navy during this wartime period, and who had entered the Navy from the shore as opposed to already being at sea, were pressed. This does not apply to the entire wartime Navy, as far more men were carried over from earlier peacetime recruitment or had joined from merchant ships already at sea. However, it suggests the Navy was heavily dependent on the impressment of men, with a possible 40,000 or more forced to join the crews of naval warships during the Georgian period.

Since so many had to be forced to serve in the Navy, it is clear that many of those living and working in London, including those with a maritime background, took a conscious decision to avoid service. The reasons are not hard to discern. Compared with service in the merchant marine, a seaman in the Royal Navy could expect to receive a much lower wage, with this only paid when the ship arrived back in England. Given that a ship might be at sea for several years, seamen in the Navy spent most of their lives on a promise; especially as it was customary for the Navy to keep back the last six months' pay to discourage desertion. Furthermore, discipline on board a warship was often harsher than on a merchantman, with naval captains having absolute authority over every aspect of the lives of those on the lower deck. This also gave any captain the opportunity to enforce his own particular whims, be they a strong conviction of the need for religion or an opposition to alcohol. There were various punishments available to enforce discipline, although the lash was the most frequently recorded. Here, the regulations stated that the number given should not exceed a dozen, but many a captain recorded in their log books four or five times this number, with not a single complaint uttered by the Admiralty. Added to all this was the risk of death or injury in battle. With all these factors acting against it, the Navy was poorly placed when it came to competing for a workforce that was, during times of mobilisation, in particularly short supply. Not surprisingly therefore, with the government unwilling to see a rise in seamen's wages and the Admiralty unwilling to relent on discipline, it was necessary for the Navy to enter into the market place with a recruitment tool that overrode the many advantages possessed by the merchant service – impressment.

While the pressing of men brought up the numbers, it was nevertheless a highly divisive ploy, resulting in outbreaks of extreme violence and considerable political and legal opposition. Beyond this, there was also the question as to whether it made financial sense. Apart from anything else, vast sums of money were required to keep the Impress Service going, a sum that might have been used in either raising the financial rewards of naval service or in the creation and training of a retained reserve force able to come forward during periods of emergency mobilisation. While nobody could agree on the exact amount that it cost to acquire seamen through impressment, there was certainly a general agreement that it was expensive. One estimate put forward by the Navy Office during the American War of Independence stated that every impressed man cost the country £100 (Southey, Vol. 4, 1833, p. 362). For others, this was much too low a figure. In a carefully worded letter to *The Morning Post* a certain TH provided a much higher figure, factoring in additional costs that had not been previously considered. In particular TH included 'the necessity to employ marines on board ship' which he, somewhat controversially, claimed arose from impressment:

> Because they are to keep the seamen in obedience it is forbidden to employ them aloft, and they consequently learn no other part of a sailor's duty but mere pulling and hauling. The marines therefore employed on board ship are so many men hired by the country, and by being made soldiers are prevented from becoming sailors. (*The Morning Post*, 12 December 1815)

However, it should be noted that Marines had other duties, being employed in assisting boarding parties, and protecting watering and foraging parties as well as helping man the guns. Although it has to be accepted that they protected the ships' officers from the crew and, for this reason, they were quartered between the officers and the lower deck.

TH included not only the cost of the Marines and their barracks, but also the men of the press gangs, the guardships, tenders and that 'many of the men procured by impressment are deserters, or are pressed two or three times', so considering it not extravagant to assert that 'for every man impressed for the country' the expense was £500 per man. This he considered 'makes every man it procures cost as much annually as it would hire two'.

While some of TH's conclusions are open to dispute, the writer was on much safer grounds when he also claimed that impressment created 'a hatred for the naval service' which arises from 'the employment of force to compel men to enter it'. Nowhere was this more obvious than in London, where it has been estimated that between 1740 and 1815 there was a total of 130 reported street conflicts that directly resulted from the appearance of press gangs (Rogers, 2007, p. 9). Usually, according to Nicholas Rogers, these centred on Whitechapel, Ratcliffe, Wapping, Shadwell, Limehouse, Poplar, Southwark and Bermondsey. However, the press gangs would also follow fleeing seamen across the City, with a number of violent outbreaks taking place along the Strand, Covent Garden, Drury Lane and the Haymarket areas. Edward Oglethorpe, writing in 1728, provides a contemporary description of the workings of the press gang in and around London at that time:

> You will see droves of the lawless fellows, armed with great sticks, force such as they think proper into the service, and knock down any who will not submit to appear before their magistrate [the officer commanding the gang] who is sometimes a lieutenant, but often an officer of the lowest rank, in an alehouse at Wapping or St Catherine's, a boatswain's, mate, or some such like judge of liberty and property. (James Edward Oglethorpe, 'The Sailors Advocate' in J.S. Bromley, *Manning Pamphlets*, 1974, p. 75)

Looking more closely at these conflicts, it is possible to provide further detail of how the press gangs went about their work in London and the violence used by the gangers and those they sought to press. Such episodes litter the pages of the London papers, with this description of an outbreak of violence in the area of Marylebone not untypical:

> Yesterday a young man, who was in the service of a gentleman in Upper Spring Street, New Road, was pressed by a press gang and taken from his master's house a considerable distance down the street. Being alarmed at the sudden change of his situation, he cried out murder, which caused an immense mob to collect. They soon opened the coach and set the servant at liberty; then they attacked the gang who endeavoured to fly in every direction. Two of them being closely pursued they took refuge in the shop of Marshal and Laurence's butchers in Durweston Street. The mob several times threatened to destroy the house; but a party of Life Guards came and escorted the refugees to the Guard House in Marylebone. (*The Morning Post*, 20 September 1808)

Such riots could result in death or injury, especially when the press gangs were confronted by determined groups of seamen who had no intention of conceding their freedom to the Navy. In March 1755 three members of a press gang dispatched by the captain of *Chichester* were attacked and nearly killed, when they were confronted at Greenland Dock by hundreds of whalers. Just over twenty years later, in November 1776, with over a hundred gangers attempting to impress seamen in Shoreditch, fights broke out in the inns and streets, with an affray breaking out in the Rose and Crown in Back Lane resulting in the landlord losing his life. Within a few days, the number of pressed men from this and other parts of the metropolis was sufficient to permit one of the tenders lying off the Tower to proceed to Portsmouth with nearly 300 men on board.

Press gangs could be very intrusive, entering uninvited into houses and onto private property while also making assumptions about a person's connections with the sea on the very slightest evidence. In November 1804 *The Morning Post* reported on one case of a false impressment that had resulted from a malicious accusation that had no truth:

> Yesterday at two o'clock a press gang entered the Library of Mr Creighton of Tavistock Street, Covent Garden, and seized upon a Mr George Dowling, a reputable youth, aged 19 who has been some time employed there as a librarian, upon the false authority of an anonymous letter, charging him with being a deserter from the Navy.

Generally, it was claimed that a seaman was relatively easy to identify through having a weather-beaten face, hard-worn hands, a rolling gait and recourse to nautical slang. Also, seamen were noted for their manner of dress: blue jacket, silk handkerchief round the neck, white trousers and silver buckles. This resulted in 'Jack Tar' being easily recognised when on shore. However, anyone who made the mistake of wearing blue and white might equally be at risk from impressment, with gangers often jumping to the wrong conclusion. Garrow, a 40-year-old insurance broker and the son of a gentleman, was taken in June 1806 while walking along Gravel Lane in the City of London on just such evidence. According to a statement subsequently made by the lieutenant in charge of the press gang, Garrow was pressed because he had a lady on each arm and appeared to be acting in a pretentious manner that was not suggestive of being a gentleman. Added to this was Garrow having 'a fine manly, open good-natured countenance' that, together with his wearing a blue coat, confirmed him, as far as the lieutenant was concerned, as a seaman. On being stopped Garrow was addressed by the lieutenant, 'Halloa messmate, what ship?' It was a simple ploy designed to trick him into admitting to being a seaman. However, Garrow quite truthfully replied, 'I am not a sailor although I have ships of my own.' Unconvinced by this answer, the lieutenant seized Garrow and demanded, 'Come. Let us look at your hands.' A struggle ensued, with Garrow hit several times by the bludgeons carried by the gangers prior to being carried off to the tender lying in the river. A complaint was laid against the Impress Service, and a judgement at the Court of King's Bench resulted in Garrow receiving damages of £50. For those less well connected than Garrow, for it was Garrow's father who managed to secure his release, the chances of a similar outcome were low. Many men were wrongfully taken and condemned to years at sea.

The press gangs and the friends of the impressed were not above using cunning and guile to achieve their aims. In October 1805 *The Morning Post* commented upon one press gang being active in Pall Mall and noted that the members of the gang 'were not dressed as sailors but in the most fashionable manner'. Given the area of the City in which they were operating it must be assumed that this was to ensure that they blended in. In contrast, a man was released from the Tower receiving ship when two of his associates, who pretended to be peace officers and came armed with false warrants, gained his release through claiming that he was charged with committing a robbery for which he must stand trial.

While most of the parishes of the expanding metropolis were open to the press gangs, this was not always so with regard to the City. Here, from the late eighteenth century onwards, there was considerable opposition, with magistrates empowering watchmen and constables to arrest the men of the Impress Service when engaged on their duties within the City. Although the City technically had no more right to oppose the press than the parishes, the press rarely operated within the City unless supported by the Mayor and Aldermen of the City during the late eighteenth and early nineteenth centuries. Due, in part, to a wider electorate, in the City the freedom of the individual was a firmly entrenched ideal. However, although impressment was objectionable that did not turn the City against naval service in general. At the outset of the French Revolutionary Wars, the Common Council of the City had been quick to offer bounties to seamen who enlisted. However, the problem for the Admiralty was that the City became a haven for seamen avoiding the press, with many flooding into it when press gangs were active. During one heightened period of mobilisation, 1795, it was stated in Parliament that 5,000 eligible seamen were estimated to be hidden in the City (*The Times*, 8 March 1795).

To try to lay hands upon those hidden within the City, press gangs used trickery to ensnare seamen within the City limits. One such ruse, which on this occasion failed to pay off, concerned four members of a gang befriending a tailor that they met on Sparrow Corner, which was just inside the City. Inviting him to join them for a drink, they crossed the road and so entered the county of Middlesex:

They then proceeded to treat him with a glass of gin, but afterwards insisted on his paying for the whole. This he refused, when they endeavoured to force him along with them. He succeeded in breaking free from them, at the loss however, of his coat, which was torn to pieces in the scuffle. (*The Morning Chronicle*, 11 September 1807)

The tailor ran back into the City, with two of the gang in pursuit, calling out 'Stop thief!' Not surprisingly this attracted the attention of one of the City's night watchmen, who apprehended all three. Brought before the Lord Mayor, sitting as a magistrate in Mansion House the following morning, the tailor was released on the grounds of his taking flight into the City. As to the two gangers, they were also released but only because the attempted impressment had taken place in the county of Middlesex. However, he added that, 'if again found pursuing a man in the City of London, even although they might have originally fallen in with him in the County, they should be severely punished' (*The Morning Chronicle*, 11 September 1807).

An attempt by the government to increase the number of volunteers came with the introduction in 1795 of a county quota that fostered bounty payments. This required each county to produce a quota of men, the number determined by the size of population and the number of seaports. This had a considerable impact on London, for it not only required the City to provide seamen but laid additional quotas upon Kent, Surrey, Essex and Middlesex; many of these men were taken from the parts of those counties that had become part of the metropolis. In order to achieve these quotas, much higher bounties had to be introduced, which were financed by local rate payers. For the City, the quota was 5,704, a number that more or less matched the estimate for seamen hidden within the City to avoid service.

The difficulty of determining from a ship's muster book whether a seaman was a volunteer or pressed can pose difficulties for those researching their own ancestors. This has proved a particular problem in my own research. I was looking into the background of a Huguenot ancestor on my mother's side with the name of John Philip Castang. He appears in March 1793 as a 'volunteer' in the muster book of the Nore receiving ship *Sandwich*, having been brought there on the impressment tender from London. Emanating from a family long connected with London, Castang's father had been a clockmaker in St Pancras with his mother running a snuff shop in Tottenham Court Road, while his brother managed a popular menagerie also in the St Pancras district. For this reason I find it difficult to understand why my ancestor should have 'volunteered' as a seaman in the Navy, especially given that he had excellent reading and writing skills, a product of his mercantile family background. Was it possible that he had been pressed but had then chosen to volunteer to receive the conduct money for which he would then be eligible? That he was immediately rated able is suggestive of his having earlier seagoing experience, possibly on a merchant ship, making it less likely that he would now volunteer for the lower deck of a warship.

A few years later William Robinson, who we know to have definitely volunteered, took the same journey out of London as that undertaken by Castang. We know this because Robinson was one of those rare seamen of the lower deck who provided an account of his life, written under the pseudonym 'Jack Nastyface'. On being sent on board the receiving ship *Enterprise* off Tower Stairs, which he joined in May 1805, Robinson admits to repenting 'the rash step' of having volunteered, all too aware that he had now lost the liberty to speak or to act and must from then on 'confine his thoughts to the hold of his mind'. His first night on board *Enterprise* was a salient glimpse of what his future now had in store:

> After having been examined by the doctor, and reported *seaworthy*, I was ordered down to the hold, where I remained all night with my companions in wretchedness, and the rats running over us in numbers.

That following morning some 200 new recruits were ordered into a naval tender that was to convey them to the Nore. Ordered down into the hold, the gratings were firmly fixed in position and marines, with muskets loaded and bayonets fixed, placed around the hatchways. Robinson continues:

> In this place we spent the day and following night huddled together, for there was not room to sit or stand separate; indeed, we were in a pitiable plight, for numbers of them were sea sick, some retching, others were smoking, whilst many were overcome by the stench, that they fainted for want of air.

Eventually, on being temporarily placed on board a receiving ship at the Nore, possibly *Sandwich*, Robinson was transferred to *Revenge*, a ship that went on to fight at Trafalgar. In providing an account of life on board a warship for a volunteer from London, Robinson, following the return of his ship from Trafalgar, was given a six-day liberty pass. This was a quite exceptional perk and only given to the most trusted. From Portsmouth he set out for London and, demonstrating just how difficult it would be for a deserter to make this same journey, Robinson was stopped on three occasions, once by a press gang and twice by military patrols. For the apprehension of a deserter, those engaged in this work, whom Robinson describes as 'men stealers' would receive £5. On returning to his ship, Robinson notes that 'a vast number of our men had run', although he fails to say how many were recaptured.

Low rates of volunteering, fighting off the press gangs and high rates of desertion were all signs that many Londoners had a low regard or even a hatred for the Navy. In addition, participation in a number of events officially classified as mutinous was a further aspect of this dislike, with the Nore mutiny of 1797 highlighting this hostility. That it involved and was supported by large numbers from the metropolis is evidenced by the initial spark having emanated from among those on board *Sandwich*, the receiving ship to which newly recruited Londoners were most usually taken. This mutiny was not an isolated incident, there having been a similar refusal to obey orders among ships of the Channel Fleet anchored at Spithead, a stretch of water between Portsmouth and the Isle of Wight. Here, crews refused to perform duty until a number of grievances that included rates of pay, harsh discipline, poor food and lack of shore leave had been addressed. Several months in the making, the mutiny broke out in April 1797 when crews refused to sail. The mutiny eventually spread to over eighty ships and nearly 30,000 seamen. Conducted in a peaceful and organised manner, many of their demands were agreed, with participants granted a royal pardon.

Given that the seamen at the Nore initially refused to take orders to show unity with those at Spithead, it seems strange that they did not return to duty in common with those at Spithead. By refusing to return to duty, the seamen at Nore placed themselves at severe risk of retribution. Their closeness to London may have been a factor; four delegates sent from the Nore to make links with the fleet at Spithead passed through the metropolis on their way to Portsmouth and on their return it is known that one of these delegates, Charles McCarthy, Irish by birth but with a good knowledge of London, met with several political contacts at a tavern in Leman Street and an attorney at law in Goodman Street. The latter was a rather mysterious character, known only as Fitzgerald, who, on meeting with McCarthy and the other three delegates, kept them waiting 'for some notes which Mr Fitzgerald was writing for them to take to Portsmouth'. Later, Fitzgerald was known to have met with other Irish seamen delegates from the Nore. It was rumoured in the Whitechapel area of London, where these meetings took place, that 'Fitzgerald always made a point of going into Town previous to giving them an answer' (TNA ADM1/3685, 17 June 1797).

The four delegates from the Nore were simply charged with making contacts with the seamen at Spithead and to offer them the support of those on board the ships anchored in the Nore. However, on arrival at Portsmouth, they discovered that agreement had been reached and the seamen were no longer in 'mutiny'. Admiral Richard Howe, the commander-in-chief of the Channel Fleet, allowed the four delegates to return to the Nore under the firm belief that in allowing them to take the news of the agreement back to the Nore, the sailors there would also return to duty. Of the delegates, two took the opportunity to desert, but

McCarthy together with Matthew Hollister did return. Passing once again through London they remained overnight, giving them sufficient opportunity, prior to the departure of the Sheerness coach, to discuss with others the developments that had taken place at Portsmouth. Any such meeting, together with the earlier one in Whitechapel, might explain why the mutiny at the Nore was not brought to an end. Instead, and against all expectations, those seamen not only continued to stand out but took a decision to extend their demands to include regular shore leave when a ship was in harbour, a moderation of disciplinary punishment and advanced payments to pressed men in common with those volunteering.

This was a quite extraordinary turn of events for not only had Admiral Howe expected the Nore mutiny to collapse but common sense suggested likewise. After all, the Spithead mutiny had involved a massive number of ships and crews while the Nore mutiny was primarily based around just three capital ships. It must be assumed that McCarthy had brought a cogent reason as to why those at the Nore should continue standing out. Furthermore, there were others, some of them elected as delegates, who were keen to adopt a more militant strategy providing they had good reason for doing so. In fact, it appears that those who were the most active in the mutiny were also those who appeared to have the closest links with various political groupings. At his court martial it was evidenced that James Smart, a pressed landsman and elected seaman delegate serving on board the naval store ship *Grampus*, had been a member of a radical political group, the London Corresponding Society, and had vented his views during political meetings in London. James Lewin, the secretary to the committee that met on board *Sandwich*, appears to have been working towards some sort of union with revolutionary France, requesting of another seaman that a hat be supplied for a seaman who was 'about to go on an embassy to France'. Later, Lewin was heard to say, when told that the ship was short of food supplies, that 'we shall go cruize on the coast of France, and there shall get provisions enough'. Thomas Jephson, another leading name, was in London immediately before the mutiny and returned with quantities of literature that called upon Irish seamen to work for the cause of their homeland. However, as this preceded the mutiny, the most damning evidence produced against him at his court martial was that of his refusal, as a bandsman, to play the national anthem. Jephson reputedly called it an 'old stale tune' and then added, 'I care nothing for Kings or Queens – bad luck to the whole of them'.

At the end of May the situation at the Nore dramatically changed when they were reinforced by the arrival of eleven ships of the North Sea Squadron. This allowed them to bring a certain degree of pressure on the government, as with an increased number of ships at their disposal they started to blockade London, with all ships entering the Thames forced to anchor that they might be searched. Those carrying perishable items were allowed to proceed while those carrying non-perishables were ordered to remain. This proved extremely successful: about 100 merchant ships were detained within the first few days of the blockade. In many ways, though, the plan was too successful. The seamen were unable to find sufficient quantities of food to feed such a large number of merchant crewmen, and so abandoned the blockade only three days after it had begun.

In London panic set in. Not only was there concern that imports into the metropolis would completely cease but an additional fear was that these heavily armed ships in mutiny would proceed upriver and bring parts of London within range of their guns. While several of the forts lying alongside the Thames were reinforced with additional cannons, the Common Council in the City of London began to encourage volunteers to join an association for 'preserving the peace', which was designed to counter any uprising in support of the seamen.

While those who led the mutiny were fairly radicalised, this did not apply to the vast majority of the lower deck. Often, it is difficult to assess their views, but an interesting glimpse into their thoughts becomes possible from letters intercepted by the Home Office. These letters provide a unique insight into the views of some of the literate personnel present at events unfolding in the Thames. While some may have been leaders, most were not. Instead, they were the passive majority, whose views ranged from total support to complete opposition. The seamen knew that letters going through official channels were being intercepted and attempted to use alternative methods for getting news to their families. As the intercepted letters demonstrate, these alternative methods did not always prove successful. Wills, a seaman on board *Leopard*, in a letter to his wife, stated that he had not sent his letter 'via the boatswain to be franked' but it was still intercepted. Similarly, Day, on board *Sandwich*, hoped his letter would arrive, when he declared he was sending it 'by long boat by stealth'.

Of these letter writers, some were primarily concerned at delayed payment of wages and others with the desire that unpopular officers who had been ejected from particular ships should not be allowed to return. Typical of this latter group was Thomas Scott, on board *Sandwich*, possibly a new pressed man, who wrote to his sweetheart at an address in Woolwich:

> We would rather die to a man than be under the cruel tyranny of Lieutenant Archibald who [has] exercised too much of his barbarity already.

Presumably this was a sentiment also shared by John Linton, a Londoner who served on *Montagu*. In a letter to an acquaintance living off Bear Lane, he wrote:

We ducked two midshipmen and the foreyard arm and tarred and feathered the doctor and turned him on shore [together] with 3 lieutenants, 1 Master's Mate, 3 midshipmen, 1 Captain of the Marines and 1 lieutenant of Marines.

In an unsigned letter another seaman on board *Sandwich* in writing to a friend or relative, a Mr Barbour of Old Gravel Lane in Wapping described how unity was maintained through the swearing of oaths:

All the seaman here were sworn too, that is to stand true one and all, till all their grievances are settled according to our proposals to the Lords of the Admiralty.

While many concentrated on the grievances expressed in the demands already made in their petition to the Admiralty, others clearly had a very different agenda and one that was much more radicalised. A number of seamen hoped that the action taken at the Nore would force the government to bring the current war to an end. It was not that they were particularly sympathetic to the French but they simply saw no reason for the continuance of the war that was then bringing great hardship to the nation while prolonging their enforced service in the Navy. Joseph B. Devonish, a seaman on board *Belliqueux* writing home to his wife living in Bath Street, Clerkenwell, clearly held such an opinion:

I wish that every method may be try'd to bring about this long wish'd for Peace, that I may once more hug you to my longing breast, and if it was possible never to part any more, I would most certainly come to you if I had a guinea to pay the expense of waterage and coach hire.

However, T. G. King, on board *Nassau*, made a much more political statement in his desire to bring an end to the war, directing his venom towards the Prime Minister: 'see what a situation Mr Pitt brought England in.'

While reflecting the opinions of a random group of literate seamen, these letters probably encapsulate the views of a much larger slice of the mutineers. None of these letters, however, appear to show any direct sympathy with the radical, revolutionary or democratic societies based in London and with which McCarthy and others may have had contact. To a certain extent, this is not surprising. Any self-respecting democrat or revolutionary would take considerable care in not reproducing feelings in a letter that (whatever precautions taken) might fall into government hands. Instead, letters containing such views would be passed on to a trusted colleague for direct conveyance to the intended reader.

Unable to continue the blockade and increasingly aware that the government was not about to concede to any of their demands, many of the mutineers began to re-evaluate their situation. Of particular significance was the role of the London newspapers. These were widely circulated throughout the country with statements made by the London press also carried by provincial newspapers. In turn, London papers were dependent upon the provincial press for important news stories that took place outside the metropolis, with printers of many of the London newspapers carrying directly copied items from a range of provincial newspapers to which they subscribed. In reporting the actions at Spithead, the London press often acted in a neutral way, not only reporting on events taking place but printing letters written by the seamen in defence of their actions. *The Times*, on 24 April, carried two accounts written by the seamen, the first of these a detailed breakdown of the reasons behind their demands and the second a response to an earlier vilification of their actions that had appeared in another London newspaper, *The Sun*. Whereas the seamen at Spithead gained public support through favourable newspaper coverage, this was denied to those at the Nore through a piece of government legislation that made it a felony to communicate with or be on board a warship named as being in a state of mutiny. This made it virtually impossible for seamen of the Nore to publicise their version of events. From now on, the only accounts available to the press would be based on hearsay or ministry-produced, carefully massaged accounts. Furthermore, the seamen on board those ships at the Nore were also reading the newspaper accounts that told of government intransigence and military preparation that was clearly aimed at bringing a violent end to the mutiny.

Isolated from their supporters in London and with the government cutting off food supplies, an increasing number of seamen began to recognise that surrender was the only available avenue. On some ships fighting broke out as those who favoured struggling on clashed with those who were less certain. First one ship and then another came back to the Navy, with all eventually surrendering. But, unlike Spithead, no concessions were made and no royal pardons issued. Instead, an incensed Admiralty determined on retribution, with 400 seamen detained for punishment. While the majority were eventually pardoned some fifty-two were condemned to death (of whom twenty-nine were hanged) with a further twenty-nine imprisoned and nine flogged.

The government, in preventing the newspapers publishing anything favourable to the striking seamen, was clearly effective. While public support for the seamen at Spithead had been considerable and was aided by a sympathetic or neutral press, matters were quite different for the strikers at the Nore. This not only undermined the resolution of those at the Nore to remain firm, but it couched the views of friends and relatives on shore. While the seamen were writing letters attempting to explain their actions, they received letters that pleaded with them to think again. Some of those writers were clearly influenced by newspapers that were no longer permitted to print material emanating from the seamen. Among those affected by what they had read in the press were the parents of William Green, a seaman from Greenland Dock serving on board *Montagu*:

> We are sorry to hear from the newspapers that you are all in disobedience. We hope that with the blessing of God you will all return to your duty and not to be led away for to come to an untimely end. Pray be careful what you say and keep your mind to yourself.

Peter Cudlip of Union Street in Deptford received similar advice from his brother:

> Let me beg of you to be true and loyal to your King and Country [this is] a time when every brave and true Briton ought to come forward as one man to resist it and frustrate every attempt of the enemy of this happy island.

One letter, however, does imply an interest in the wider political context of the age and offers no suggestion that the recipient should break with his fellow seamen. Richard Reddy, who has a London address, writing to Michael Delaney of *Britannia*, informs him of an emerging crisis in Ireland. However, sympathetic or otherwise, the writer was no activist, indicating his own desire to go to sea, intending to join the Navy or the East India Company. Of matters in Ireland he informed Delaney:

> Ireland is in proper confusion; and indeed I lately heard from a person come from thence that two delegates had arrived there from France and that the boys of the Shamrock had sworn blood that they will join them.

The forced impressment of seamen did not just affect those taken for service in the Navy but also those left behind. There might be no witness to the pressment, and thus no explanation of a sudden disappearance for a bewildered family. The dependants of a newly pressed man might now find themselves quite penniless. It was a not unusual situation, with Oglethorpe, in his pamphlet of 1728, making the point that those with dependants were more, rather than less likely, to be the ones subject to impressment:

> A poor fellow, who perhaps hath six or seven children and makes hard shifts to bring them up by labouring in lighters, fishing boats, or plying as a waterman, and is not willing to leave his family to go a long voyage, is the first who is laid hold of; while the single man, who is the fittest for sea, can leave his place of abode and hide himself till the press warrants are called in, or else go into foreign service; and oftentimes the father of a hopeful family is hurried into a

king's ship or press smack, and his children immediately left without subsistence to seek charity, thus many become shoe cleaners and vagabonds, instead of being bred up as sailors. (Bromley, *Manning Pamphlets*, p. 75)

A particular injustice resulting from the impressment of a husband was that of Mary Murphy, an attractive 26-year-old redhead with a distinct Irish brogue. While living in London, her husband was forcibly taken into the Navy during a hot press conducted in early 1771. With no income and two children to support, she was forced to beg on the streets but eventually, although most agreed as to her honesty, resorted to theft. Caught in the act of stealing four remnants of muslin valued at 30s from a linen store on Ludgate Hill, she was tried at the Old Bailey and found guilty. Sentenced to be executed, she was hanged at Tyburn on 16 October that same year.

Whether pressed or volunteered, much depended on the actions of the man now forced into the Navy as to how his dependants fared. Some used pressment as an opportunity to disappear, refusing to make any further contact. Unless a man was pressed to a ship that was immediately sailing, there was always the possibility of writing a letter that might quickly reach home. Even an illiterate man might get a fellow seaman, at a possible cost, to write the letter for him. This would at least alert those on shore as to what had transpired. Knowing the name of the ship, it was possible for those on shore to learn the subsequent whereabouts of the vessel, since the information appeared in the London newspapers. This was the least a man could do for those who depended on him. Far more significant however, was ensuring that those on shore were financially secure. This could be done through arranging for a portion of their wage to be paid to their dependants. During the early part of the eighteenth century this would need to be an ad hoc arrangement, a sympathetic officer sometimes transferring money through his own bank account. Only from 1758 onwards was this regularised, with the Navy Pay Office organising payments on request. This was further improved in 1795, when a named dependent was allowed to collect a remittance every twenty-eight days, even if the ship had not been paid. In addition, pensions were occasionally available to the dependants of men killed in service.

Unfortunately for those on shore, the number of seamen offering to make payments to wives and mothers was relatively small, with one estimate based on pay books from sample ships indicating that only one in twenty made any remittance (Rogers, *The Press Gang*, p. 78). There is evidence of seamen using the opportunity of naval service to break with a wife, or at least the woman with whom they had been living. While some liaisons would have been officially sanctioned through a church ceremony, many of those 'married' to seamen lacked such regularisation, so placing the woman (and any children) in an even more precarious situation. Compounding matters, seamen would sometimes enter into a new relationship, sometimes resulting in bigamous marriages. This might only become apparent after the man's death, when both wives attempted to claim his unpaid wages or other payments due as a result of naval service.

Not that it was only the man who might begin a new relationship. Women, forced to survive without their former 'husband', might begin a new relationship. Out of contact with his wife for five years, a seaman who had the fortune of being part of the crew of the frigate *Active* when she participated in the capture of *Hermione*, returned to London to find that she had recently taken a new husband. Considered a newsworthy event, given that the returning seaman had pockets brim full of money, the story reached the pages of several newspapers, including the *Oxford Journal*:

> The tar pleaded his prior right, and insisted on having his wife back again, which the new husband readily agreed to. The sailor, putting his hand in his pocket said, 'here friend, accept of a couple of guineas of the service you have done my wife;' and afterwards set out with her ... in a landau and four for Portsmouth. (*Oxford Journal*, 9 April 1763)

Wives and mothers suffered as much as their husbands and sons when the press gangs were successful in hunting down seamen and transferring them to the Thames receiving ship. Bereft of a secure income and often responsible for several children, they were a further component of the London social milieu that had little liking for the Navy. While men could often direct their anger to the source of their problem, the Navy, this was not possible for dependants. If they were not in receipt of regular payments and were unable to find suitable work or gain the sympathy of a charity, there was often little left apart from theft and prostitution.

8

The Officers of the Quarterdeck

The quarterdeck was the part of a warship occupied by the men who commanded. A raised area to the rear of the main mast, it was an exclusive area of the ship. Warrant officers, other than the master who was responsible for navigation, were infrequent visitors to the quarterdeck, although they might be called here to receive instructions. The quarterdeck was the province of the captain, an area where he might claim a degree of privacy. The captain's quarters, and those of the officers, were beneath the quarterdeck, with space allowed commensurate with rank. The captain had possession of the great or main cabin that was always located at the stern of the ship. While the actual area allowed for accommodating the captain might vary according to the size of the ship, most vessels also provided him with an additional sleeping cabin. As for the lieutenants and the ship's master, the cabins set aside for them were much smaller, and were immediately forward of the great cabin.

Although the officers of the quarterdeck might be associated with London, their association was more often a result of Navy service than a prelude to it. In particular, an officer seeking promotion or a new command needed to live near the centre of London to facilitate the regular personal contacts at the Admiralty necessary to secure advancement. In peacetime, with few ships required, only officers with influence and persistence could secure such positions. To be any distance from London was a clear disadvantage. For the particularly well-connected Augustus Hervey, the future 3rd Earl of Bristol, a brief stay in London during the summer of 1746 following service as a lieutenant in the West Indies was essential if he was to gain a much sought-after captaincy.

One problem that immediately confronted Hervey in his campaign for promotion was the need for suitable residence, and one befitting his status. The family estate was no use as the large house at Ickworth in Suffolk was too distant. Furthermore, as Hervey noted in his *Journal*, no other member of the family at this time, 'kept a house [in London] for me to dine at'. It was Hervey's tailor, Mr Volls, who came to his rescue, offering him lodgings at the Golden Ball in

Pall Mall. Now resident in one of the most fashionable areas of London, Hervey began to call upon a number of senior members of the government and others with whom his family were in alliance or owed favours; he eventually secured command of the sloop *Porcupine*, then on the building slip of Taylor's yard in Deptford. It was not until 20 September 1746 that she was to be launched, with Hervey among those who witnessed the event.

A further delay ensued while the vessel was fitted out, a task that occupied a further six weeks. This was a lengthy period of inactivity for Hervey, given that he had been in London since mid-August, with the young naval officer feeling himself trapped and forced to seek ways to amuse himself. To while away the time he attended a number of dinner parties and spent at least one evening at Whites, then located in Chesterfield Street, a gambling house described by Jonathan Swift as the 'bane of half the English nobility'. Frequent visits to the theatre also helped pass the time, although the performances on stage were not necessarily Hervey's primary interest, a fact borne out by an admission that appears in his already quoted *Journal*:

> Being young and much about it was not surprising I got hold of some things; [Caterina] Galli and [Signora] Campioni, both famous in their way on the stage, admitted my attentions. The latter was beautiful, and as she would accept of nothing from me being kept by the Count Haslang, I found it most suitable as well as most agreeable to stick to her; which I did, and only when I went away gave her a diamond ring. (Augustus John Hervey, 3rd Earl of Bristol, *Augustus Hervey's Journal*, 1953, p. 44)

This suggests Hervey was a regular at the Covent Garden Theatre, as Caterina Galli, an Italian operatic mezzo-soprano and Signora Campioni, an operatic dancer, regularly performed there. It is easy to understand why the bored young naval officer spent much time with these two women, for they were beauties of the age. Signora Campioni, in particular, was noted for her charms (rather than her dramatic performances) while she was blessed with a husband who overlooked her occasional transgressions. Caterina Galli, with whom Hervey appears to have spent less time, was later to become a close friend of fellow singer Martha Ray, the longtime mistress of First Lord Sandwich. Galli accompanied Ray on the night that she was murdered following a performance of the comic opera *Love in a Village* at Covent Garden in July 1779.

For others of the quarterdeck, a connection with London was often formed at the end of a seagoing career, with some senior officers appointed to one of the many administrative offices that were centred on the metropolis. Of these, an appointment to the Board of Admiralty might carry kudos but it lacked permanency, while those appointed to one of the civil boards of the Navy or to Greenwich Hospital stood little risk of removal. In whichever case, appointees acquired an opulent London residence through their period of office.

According to Lincoln (2002), a surprisingly high number of naval officers entered Parliament, requiring them to obtain lodgings close to Westminster, with a total of seventy-nine serving officers sitting in the House of Commons between 1754 and 1790, with the highest number, twenty-three, entering the House of Commons after the general election in 1784. That they were in Parliament in the first place was a product of the patronage system, with naval officers encouraged to enter Parliament to support the governing administration. Effectively it was a purchased vote, for naval officers were dependent upon the government for any future naval appointment and would vote with the government to ensure that they were favourably considered when new seagoing appointments were available. These same seagoing officers in Parliament could also use their position to gain for a son or a friend a clerkship in the Navy Office or a midshipman's post on a newly commissioned ship.

The connection between London and a proportion of the officer class is especially well demonstrated by William Locker. His association with the metropolis was life-long, broken only by periods of service at sea. Locker's decision to enter the Navy at the age of 14 appears surprising. His immediate family had no connections with the sea, his father and paternal grandfather having trained as lawyers and consecutively holding the post of clerk to the Leathersellers' Company; this was a prestigious position as the clerk was responsible for the day-to-day running of this powerful city livery company. On his mother's side there was a strong association with the Church: his maternal grandfather was a cleric and a distant uncle had been Dean of St Paul's. No doubt William's father, John Locker, could have acquired for his son a lucrative position within the Leathersellers' Company in the way that his own father had done for him. However, Locker was taken with the sea, an ambition that his father eventually came to support. Born in February 1731, the future naval officer went on to attend the nearby Merchant Taylors' School. His interest in the Navy was apparently fostered by Charles Wyndham, a relative on his mother's side. A naval captain, Wyndham had taken command of the 70-gun Kent that had been launched at Deptford in 1746 and he allowed the 15-year-old Locker to visit while she was fitting out in the Thames. This clearly excited the youngster's imagination, with an agreement that Locker could join the two decker as a 'captain's servant'.

Locker was on course for rapid promotion, for being a captain's servant meant he was under the eye and patronage of the most powerful person within the ship and would thus receive the necessary training and opportunity to reach the rank of lieutenant. However, such high hopes came close to being dashed within a few months when Wyndham, overwhelmed by recurrent attacks of gout, was invalided out of the service. This left Locker without the secure future that had been so entirely dependent upon Wyndham's influence and might have resulted in his leaving the Navy with an unfulfilled ambition. Fortunately, Locker's enthusiasm and ability had not gone unnoticed, and the youngster was able to rise through the ranks, serving in command positions during the Seven Years War and the American War of Independence. In doing so, his health was to suffer immensely, a severe leg wound and malaria forcing his own eventual retirement from active service.

Returning to dry land in 1779, Locker settled in Kent before acquiring a house in Kensington. Here, on the outskirts of London, he began a regular correspondence with a number of those who had served under him. Among them was Horatio Nelson, one of his former lieutenants, from whom he received over the next twenty or so years a regular flow of letters. Nelson had a great deal of respect for Locker, with one letter written in 1799 particularly fulsome in its praise: 'I have been your scholar, it is you who taught me to board a Frenchman by your conduct, it is you who always told me "lay a Frenchman close and you will always beat him".'

Locker returned to naval service in 1792, when he was given command of *Sandwich*, the Nore receiving ship. Just eighteen months later he was given a much more generous position, when he was appointed Lieutenant Governor of the naval hospital at Greenwich. While this position was reserved for those at the end of a long period of service life, it was no sinecure, as the holder had responsibility under the governor of the hospital for the efficient running of the establishment, with four captains, eight lieutenants, two chaplains and a treasurer all reporting directly to him. It was Locker who first suggested that the Great Hall of King William Court at Greenwich should be transformed into a gallery for marine paintings to commemorate the eminent services of the Navy. Due to the continuing war with France, the idea, while seen as having much to commend it, was not at the time pursued. However, in 1823 it was again proposed, this time by Locker's son, with the idea then accepted and the collection of various paintings begun. George IV was among those who provided support, donating an extensive and valuable series of portraits of celebrated admirals that had been previously held at Windsor Castle and Hampton Court together with other paintings held at St James's Palace and Carlton House. Others also began to give pictures and, in the course of a few years, the walls of the Painted Hall were adorned with portraits of naval commanders and representations of their actions.

It was while at Greenwich that Locker found time for other matters dear to his heart, among them the Amicable Navy Club and the Institute for the Improvement of Naval Architecture. The Amicable Navy Club had begun life in 1739, the outcome of a meeting of a number of naval captains who, at that time, were frequenting Will's Coffee House close to the Admiralty. Then it was a political organisation, its original purpose being to oppose actions taken by the government that might 'deprive them [officers in naval service] of the liberty [that] other British subjects enjoy'. Successful in accumulating funds, it was agreed by its members that much of this money should be used for the relief of widows of Navy captains, as it was recognised that there was an increasing need to support naval officers, their widows and children, when they had fallen upon hard times. Over time, however, the Society had become more or less defunct. Locker was determined to reinvigorate it. In this he was successful, gaining the support of many leading admirals, including St Vincent, Barham, Nelson and Gambier. Later, following Locker's death, it became the Naval Charitable Society and in 1838, due to William IV being a member and a patron, it was incorporated by charter and became known as The Royal Naval Benevolent Society.

Less successful was Locker's involvement with the Institute for the Improvement of Naval Architecture. Established at a meeting held at the Crown and Anchor pub in the Strand on 14 April 1791, Locker was one of its earliest committee members. Its object was 'to encourage every useful invention and discovery [for the improvement of naval architecture] as far as shall be in their power, both by honorary and pecuniary awards'. Despite having the Duke of Clarence (the future William IV) as its honorary president and a secretary located in Westminster, the Society failed to prosper and eventually disappeared. Locker, while lieutenant governor, also started collecting material for a formal written history of the Navy, using his position to talk to many former seamen. This resulted in a series of biographical anecdotes that was eventually passed to John Charnock for use in his *Biographia Navalis*. It was while in post at the naval hospital that Locker suffered a series of severe strokes which claimed his life on 26 December 1800. His funeral, held at Greenwich, was attended by many senior naval officers before the body was taken to the family tomb at Addington in Kent. Nelson, who at that time described Locker as his 'much lamented friend', was among those who accompanied the cortege on part of its passage from Greenwich to Addington.

Edward Berry and Sir Thomas Bladen Capel, two of the captains at Trafalgar, were born in London. Prior to that battle, Berry had already formed a strong association with Nelson, fighting alongside him at Cape St Vincent and the Nile as well as commanding the 74-gun *Agamemnon* at Trafalgar. Berry was fortunate that at a young age he had gained the patronage of Lord Mulgrave, a lord of the Admiralty, through an uncle who had once tutored Mulgrave. If it had been otherwise, Berry might well have had a rather bleak future in the Navy as his father, a respected member of London's mercantile community, had died young, leaving Berry, a brother and five sisters, together with a widow, to look after themselves. Berry was a particular favourite of Nelson and accompanied him to St James's Palace in September 1797 for Nelson's investiture with the Most

Honourable Order of the Bath. At the time, Nelson was still recovering from the partial loss of his right arm during an assault on Tenerife two months earlier, the King tactlessly noting, 'You have lost your right arm.' Nelson, singularly unphased, simply retorted, 'But not my right hand', as he gestured in the direction of his colleague and he went on to add, 'as I have the honour of presenting Captain Berry'.

Capel, for his part, through possession of a clear aristocratic pedigree, had a much more assured beginning to his naval career, being the fourth son of William Anne Capel, the 4th Earl of Essex. Born in 1776 in the family's town house in Hanover Square he was, from the outset, highly favoured, and taken onto the books of HMS *Phaeton* at the age of 5. This provided him with a fictitious amount of sea time that allowed him to rise rapidly through the ranks when he finally did go to sea. At Trafalgar he commanded the frigate *Phoebe*, a vessel used for the repeating of signals between ships. However, Capel had also been with Nelson at the Battle of the Nile and had then been charged with taking the news of the battle to London, with Capel arriving at the Admiralty on 2 October 1798. On that journey to London, in addition to the dispatches from Nelson, he brought with him the sword of the senior surviving French Admiral, which he went on to present to the Lord Mayor of London.

Towards the end of their naval careers, Berry and Capel had been appointed to command royal yachts. This was an honour reserved for officers who had undertaken meritorious service, so ensuring that they received a continuance of their naval pay rather than the half pay given to a retired or semi-retired officer. Furthermore it reaffirmed their connection with London as those appointed to the royal yachts were expected to have a residence close to Deptford, the naval yard responsible for mooring and maintaining these vessels. In the years following the fall of Napoleon, there were approximately five royal yachts which were used for the conveyance of the royal family and certain favoured state officials. For Berry, his command, which he held between 1813 and 1814, was *Royal Sovereign*, built for George III, and launched at Deptford in 1804. By all accounts she was a particularly magnificent vessel, fitted with all the comforts imaginable and encrusted with lavish gilt carvings. In 1816, following an extensive refit that was also undertaken at Deptford, a lengthy description of the vessel appeared in *The Morning Post*, with much attention given to those extensive carvings. Particularly impressive was the King's room, approached by way of a passage that was finished in white with gilt panelling and carved pilasters:

On entering the King's Room, the mind is struck with surprise by its elegance. The roof is mahogany and gold panels; the sides are crimson damask panels, with gold framings; round the room are twenty beautiful carved figures, representing the four elements, the cardinal virtues and the arts and sciences, all of which are placed on mahogany and gold pedestals, surmounted by ionic caps. (*The Morning Post*, 10 August 1816)

Some nine years later, *Royal Sovereign* was under the command of a further Nelson-connected officer, Sir William Hoste. Hoste was with Nelson at the battles of Cape St Vincent and the Nile, and he went on to achieve his own command success at the Battle of Lissa in 1811. Appointed to *Royal Sovereign* in 1825, his command embraced the period in which the yacht was used by the Duke of Clarence in his role as Lord High Admiral, with the vessel carrying the duke on his inspections of the royal dockyards. As always, sailings began and ended from the Thames off Deptford, with the following description of the departure for Plymouth appearing in *The Morning Post*:

> His Royal Highness the Duke of Clarence left his residence at the Admiralty on Saturday morning, at nine o'clock accompanied by W.R.K. Douglas, Esq, one of the members of the royal Duke's Council, John Barrow, Esq., the Second Secretary. His Royal Highness and suite arrived at Deptford about ten o'clock, and, after a brief inspection of the yard, they embarked on board the Royal Sovereign yacht, commanded by Sir William Hoste, and proceeded down river accompanied by the Lightning, government steam vessel, and the Comet steamer; the latter takes Sir Byam Martin, the Comptroller of the Navy, to Plymouth, the first of the out ports which his Royal Highness intends to inspect. (*The Morning Post*, 9 July 1827)

Thomas Capel's appointment, in December 1821, was to the *Royal George*, the yacht normally reserved for the exclusive use of the King. While no larger than a sloop, she was actually registered as a third rate, equivalent to a 74-gun ship, this for the simple purpose of allowing Capel to draw the same wage to which he had been entitled as an active-service captain. It was a dream command with a hand-selected crew and only the elite of the elite allowed to board. In the summer, when the King most often undertook his 'aquatic excursions' away from London, the south coast was a frequent destination, with a Royal Marine band from Portsmouth an absolute necessity. On such occasions, *Royal George* would be joined by a cluster of yachts carrying other members of the royal family. Capel was to have been appointed to a new command, the 1,071 ton *Apollo*, a former frigate which was converted into a royal yacht and which towered over all the other yachts. However, she came at such considerable cost that she was paid-off soon after being brought into service. (*The Morning Post*, 5 May 1823)

St Paul's Cathedral is the final resting place or memorialises many naval officers of the period. Many of these were colleagues to Nelson, with several memorials within the cathedral to those who fought alongside him in his various battles.

Among these is Vice Admiral Cuthbert Collingwood (1st Baron Collingwood), who lies close by the tomb of Nelson; a good pairing as Collingwood was his second-in-command at Trafalgar and succeeded Nelson in the command of the Mediterranean fleet. He died of cancer on 7 March 1810 while on board his flagship *Ville de Paris* which was then off Port Mahon. While he was not to be accorded a state funeral, it was immediately determined that his body should be brought home for burial in St Paul's. As had happened with Nelson, Collingwood's remains were first brought to the Painted Hall of the naval hospital at Greenwich before being taken to the cathedral on Friday 11 May. The funeral cortege was accompanied by many officers and pensioners of the hospital, including its governor, Vice-Admiral Sir Samuel Hood (1st Baronet Hood), with the cathedral crowded beyond capacity by those who wished to pay their respects.

Although many Georgian naval officers lived in London, only three, William Bligh, Thomas Cochrane and Horatio Nelson, are accorded blue plaques. For Nelson, the blue plaque is in Bond Street, a temporary lodging occupied from September 1797 until March 1798, in which he resided following the loss of his right arm at Santa Cruz de Tenerife. The wound, being slow to heal, saw frequent consultation with Dr Benjamin Moseley, a military physician who Nelson had known in the Caribbean and who was then practising at the Royal Hospital Chelsea. The Bond Street residence also placed Nelson within easy reach of those points in town that a much feted naval officer was expected to attend, including the Guildhall, where he was presented with the Freedom of the City, and St Paul's Cathedral, where he attended a service of thanksgiving for naval victories. From Bond Street, Nelson could also visit William Locker at Greenwich Hospital, where he was sketched by Lemuel Abbott, a famed painter of naval officers and from which several portraits resulted, including one that was recorded in 2007 as being in the Terracotta Room of number 10 Downing Street and another on display in the Lloyd's building in Leadenhall Street.

Another address associated with Nelson is 17 Dover Street (to the north of Piccadilly), which he occupied towards the end of 1800 until his departure in March 1801 for the attack on Copenhagen. It was here that his marriage to Frances Nisbet finally ended when, over the breakfast table, she gave him the ultimatum that she was 'sick of hearing of dear Lady Hamilton and am resolved that you shall give her up or me'. Frances may not have been the most loving of wives, but Nelson had certainly placed her under a good deal of strain, inviting Emma Hamilton, and her compliant husband to dinners at Dover Street and expecting his wife to enter into polite conversation with her rival. Although Frances continued to live at Dover Street after Nelson had returned to sea, she left her husband after that fateful breakfast conversation. Nelson was unwilling to give up his mistress, who was then heavily pregnant with his future daughter.

Although Nelson purchased Merton Place in September 1801, a country estate in Merton (now part of south-west London), where he lived with Emma and Sir William Hamilton, he still retained lodgings in London. For a time this was in Piccadilly but when the lease expired he also stayed at Gordon's Hotel in Albemarle Street. This gave him the opportunity to frequently visit the Admiralty and senior government ministers, providing the latter with advice and information on the progress of the war at sea. It also meant that, having been raised to the peerage as Baron Nelson of the Nile, he could take his seat in the House of Lords. While not a regular attender, he did make a few speeches, but these did little to enhance his prestige and it might well have been better if he had chosen not to rise to his feet. One of his earliest interventions related to the Treaty of Amiens, which had brought a temporary end to the war with France and which required Britain to relinquish control of Malta, Minorca and the Cape of Good Hope. In private, Nelson had greatly mourned the handing over of these important naval strongpoints, but foolishly declared in Parliament that the last of these, the Cape, was 'little more than an outmoded tavern on the way to the East Indies' while Malta was condemned of little value. One can only assume that Nelson, in making this declaration, was trying to purchase favours from Henry Addington who had recently replaced Pitt as Prime Minister. William Huskisson, the former Under Secretary at War, neatly summed it up in a letter to Henry Dundas, a future First Lord, when he wrote that Nelson might have convinced himself 'that a seaman could find a tavern nearer home than the Cape of Good Hope, and if Malta is not to be considered because it does not serve to block Toulon, we must be obliged to conclude that no station in the Mediterranean is a good one'. Finally, he went on to ask, 'How can ministers allow such fools to speak in their defence?'

Wherever Nelson was seen in London during the years leading up to Trafalgar he was sure to attract a huge crowd, no more so than in the late summer of 1805 immediately prior to his re-joining the British Fleet off Cadiz. Benjamin Silliman, an American chemist who was at that time visiting London, describes his own satisfaction in glimpsing Nelson while in the Strand, 'in company with his chaplain and, as usual, followed by a crowd'. Silliman then went on to comment:

> Lord Nelson cannot appear in the streets without immediately collecting a retinue, which augments as he proceeds, and when he enters a shop, the door is thronged until he comes out, when the air rings with huzzas and the dark cloud of the populace again moves on and hangs about his skirts. (Benjamin Silliman, *A Journal of Travels in England, Holland and Scotland*, 1801)

William Bligh, the man forever associated with the *Bounty*, has a blue plaque in Lambeth Road. He took up residence there because he had to call upon the

Admiralty when seeking a ship to command. His appointment to *Bounty* in August 1787 also required him to be present at Deptford where she was being modified. The intention was that she should sail to Tahiti and collect breadfruit plant, a high energy, easy-to-grow food that was to be deposited at the botanical gardens in Kew. From there, following a programme of nurturing and development, it was hoped that the plant could be transplanted to the Caribbean, where they might thrive and serve as a source of food for British slaves. It was the mutiny that ensured the first batch of breadfruit never reached England. Bligh headed a second and ultimately successful expedition that returned in August 1793, having first taken samples of breadfruit direct to Jamaica. To defend his name and market his own version of the events surrounding the mutiny, Bligh took up permanent residence in the capital, purchasing the house in Lambeth Road that is now marked with a blue plaque. Here he was to remain, with absences for sea service and a short stint as Governor of New South Wales, until the death of his wife Betsy in 1812, with Bligh then moving to Farningham in Kent. However, husband and wife are buried in a family plot in the church grounds of St Mary's Lambeth, now the Garden Museum. Their tomb, which still survives, is topped by a breadfruit.

Thomas Cochrane has a much greater association with London. A blue plaque marks his place of residence at Hanover Lodge, a Grade II listed building in Regent's Park. Cochrane, though, did not occupy this house until later in life, having a number of earlier lodgings that were generally closer to the Admiralty and the Palace of Westminster. Very much the naval hero, Cochrane was famous for a series of single-ship actions that placed him at the forefront of public attention. Among the earliest of these was the taking of the Spanish 32-gun frigate *El Gamo*, a vessel armed primarily with 24-pounder carronades. In contrast, Cochrane commanded the much smaller *Speedy*, a 14-gun sloop armed with 4-pounders. Given the unbelievable odds, it was maybe an action that Cochrane should have avoided. Yet, it was he that chose to attack the Spanish vessel, first hoisting the American flag to confuse his prey – a legitimate *ruse de guerre* – before replacing it with the British ensign. Surprisingly, it was the *Speedy*'s diminutive size that really worked to Cochrane's advantage, with two Spanish broadsides completely missing the target. As the two vessels closed, the great difference in height resulted in the Spanish ship not being able to depress her guns sufficiently to bear on her adversary. On the other hand, *Speedy*'s tiny guns, now that they were within range of the frigate, proved devastating, sweeping the decks and disabling many of her crew. Finally, although fewer in number, the crew of the British sloop once aboard the Spanish frigate, overwhelmed her crew and forced them into the hold.

Given the audacity of the attack and its successful outcome, it naturally caught the imagination of those in London. Having been reported in detail in all the London papers, *The Morning Post* went on to describe the action as proof of 'the astonishing superiority of the English over the Spanish Navy'. Hundreds flocked to the public rooms in Lower Brook Street where the fashionable marine artist, Nicholas Pocock, had placed on display a painting that accurately depicted the final moments of the action. Despite his undoubted public popularity, Cochrane was no favourite of the Admiralty. He was disliked by the establishment because of his frequent unearthing and criticism of administrative shortcomings. St Vincent was a particular target of Cochrane's disapproval and recriminations, accusing him of using his position to further the career of undeserving friends and those who would return favour for favour. This, in turn, explains why St Vincent, during his time as First Lord, was so reluctant to provide this dashing commander with a suitable ship at a time when the country was in need of experienced officers.

To provide a more public platform for his attacks upon those who administered the Navy, Cochrane entered Parliament. While elected in 1806 for the Devon seat of Honiton, it was a spectacular campaign in May 1807 to represent the electors of the City of Westminster that really marked the beginning of his political career. While most constituencies, including that earlier seat of Honiton, were in the pockets of the rich and powerful, with borough managers able to influence and bribe the small numbers who had the right to vote; this was not so in the City of Westminster. Here were to be found over 10,000 registered voters, the result of all male ratepayers having the right to vote in a constituency where most were ratepayers. To win it was necessary to argue a case rather than splash the cash. This was just how Cochrane wanted to play it, for it gave him the opportunity to expose numerous naval shortcomings, with each and every one of his speeches duly reported in the London newspapers that were then circulated throughout the country. Establishing his principal committee room at Richardson's Hotel in Covent Garden, a number of other committee rooms were established in several coffee houses in the Westminster area, including the Navy Coffee House in the Strand and the British Coffee House in Cockspur Street. Cochrane soon became a familiar figure and one to whom people were prepared to listen. He spoke of ships unsuited for sea, of merchants who only received contracts because of votes they possessed in Parliament, and officers appointed through influence and not ability. That Cochrane was also a naval hero was not forgotten, with a song specially written for his campaign neatly driving this home:

> All hail to the Hero – of England the boast,
> The honour the glory the pride of our coast
> Let the bells peal his name, and the cannons' loud roar,
> Sound the plaudits of Cochrane, the friend of our shore.

Come the election, Cochrane gained 3,708 votes with Francis Burdett, a leading reformer of the age, also returned with a vote of 5,134.

That year, following the General Election in which Cochrane had won his Westminster seat, Parliament opened on 7 July. In the debate on the King's Speech, Cochrane launched a broadside against the use of parliamentary influence, especially the gaining of lieutenancies and other positions in the Navy through a well-directed parliamentary vote. Much more serious was his demand that Parliament look into the loss of two naval vessels, *Atlante* and *Felix*, which were overwhelmed by heavy seas while operating with the Channel Fleet. According to information available to Cochrane, both ships had long been in need of extensive repairs and should not have been allowed to remain at sea. Cochrane had actually boarded *Atlante* shortly before her loss, relaying the serious condition of the vessel to the squadron commander. No order to return home was given, resulting in a tragedy that Cochrane wished to demonstrate could easily have been avoided.

Such a public condemnation of the Navy was not something the Admiralty relished. Furthermore, they had the means to gag Cochrane; they simply ordered his return to sea. Given a posting that took him to the Mediterranean, Cochrane was absent from Parliament for twenty months, returning in May 1809. By then, he had another concern that he wished to pursue: the outcome of an attack some weeks earlier on a French fleet anchored in a protected stretch of water between La Rochelle and Rochefort, and known as Basque Roads. It was an operation in which Cochrane had been a major player, leading a part of the operation that had seen fire ships and vessels packed with explosives entering the anchorage and scattering the enemy fleet with several of their battleships running aground. This left them totally vulnerable to the main British fleet led by Admiral Gambier. However, no advantage was taken of the situation, with Gambier simply holding back and observing events from a distance. Napoleon, when later in captivity on St Helena, referred to Gambier as an *imbécile*, believing that if the British fleet had followed through, then every one of the French battleships would have been destroyed. Cochrane, upon his return to London and his Westminster seat, was incensed that Gambier was to be given a vote of thanks, attempting to use the occasion to highlight the admiral's failure to confront the enemy at such an advantageous point in time.

As an independent working against the powerful governmental machine, Cochrane was generally out-manoeuvred but he did manage to ensure thirty-nine members voted against the motion. Subsequently denied command of a further ship as retribution for his public criticism of Gambier, Cochrane had the opportunity to spend more time in the metropolis, taking up residence with an uncle whose house was in Portman Square before acquiring his own house in Green Street, off Park Lane. Among issues that he took up was the administration of prize money, which saw those responsible for overseeing payments allowed to cream off large sums that might otherwise have gone to the seamen who risked their lives to make the capture. During this period, Cochrane also revealed to the House the unfairness of the naval pension system, which allowed relatively small amounts to seamen who had lost one or more limbs in battle as compared to payments made to senior officers or even the staff employed at the Admiralty and Somerset House. In one example presented to the Commons, he referred to seamen, upon the loss of one leg, being entitled to a payment of £40 while the First or Second Secretary at the Admiralty 'in full health' might receive an annual pension of £1,500.

That Cochrane, prior to his return to Parliament in May 1809, had been involved in the action fought in the Basque Roads was the result of a direct request made to him by a newly appointed First Lord, Henry Phipps, Earl of Mulgrave, who held this post from 1807 through to 1810. At the time the naval war had taken a turn for the worst, with a number of French battleships having out-manoeuvred the British blockading squadrons off L'Orient and Brest, allowing them to join forces in the Basque Roads anchorage. Here they were poised to descend on British convoys in the Atlantic or attack the West Indies. Anything was possible and the threat had to be immediately neutralised. With Cochrane having returned to Plymouth in March 1810 following a series of highly successful assaults on French forces along the coast of Spain, he was considered the most obvious person to plan and lead an attack on the French ships in the Basque Roads under the protection of shore batteries. Summoned to the Admiralty in London by telegraphic message, his meeting with Mulgrave was in complete contrast to the earlier meeting with St Vincent just six years earlier:

> On presenting myself at the Admiralty, the First lord (Mulgrave) did me the honour to consult me confidentially as to the practicality of disabling or destroying the French squadron as it lay at anchor under the protection of the batteries of Isle d'Aix, where, as his lordship told me, the commander-in-chief did not consider it prudent to attack them. (Thomas Cochrane, *Memoirs of a Fighting Captain*, 2004, p. 147)

The outcome was the plan to attack the French using fire ships and explosion vessels, with Cochrane to take command. However, it was a temporary rapprochement with the establishment that was quickly dashed upon Gambier's failure to provide effective backing, with those supportive of Gambier able to get their revenge five years later. This was in 1814, when Cochrane became implicated in the famous Stock Exchange scandal. Cochrane was implicated in a plan to bring a sudden increase in the value of certain shareholdings through a false rumour that Napoleon had been assassinated and the French had surrendered. While this news spread across London, Cochrane's financier sold a number of his shares at a considerable profit. It seems clear that some of Cochrane's friends and associates were involved but Cochrane himself appears entirely innocent. Nevertheless, in the subsequent trial, with a rigged jury and a highly biased judge, the evidence against him was carefully massaged and Cochrane was sentenced to a year of imprisonment. He served this in the King's Bench Division in Southwark.

Cochrane was not the only quarterdeck officer to represent the Westminster constituency in Parliament. In 1784, the far from radical Samuel Hood, the future 1st Viscount Hood, became one of its two members when he successfully defeated Charles Fox, leader of the Fox-North coalition. Having acquired a heroic status while serving as second-in-command at the Battle of the Saintes (April 1782), Hood's supporters believed his name alone would secure victory. The King and Prime Minister, William Pitt the Younger, would baulk at nothing to see Fox defeated and, for this reason, persuaded Hood to stand. The resulting campaign proved bitter and hard fought, with Hood securing first place but Fox narrowly securing the second seat. Hood, during the campaign, traded heavily upon his recent naval successes, with his main committee room at Wood's Hotel strung out with 'ensigns of the French and Spanish nations taken by Admiral Hood during the late war'. To help drive home the point, a band played patriotic airs such as *Britons Strike Home!* Hood used large amounts of government money to persuade voters to his cause, employing seamen who acted as if they were still fighting the French rather than supporting their Admiral in a democratic election:

> Yesterday [Monday 5 April] another tumult happened in Covent Garden, between the sailors and a body of chairmen, in which many were hurt, and two of the former are reported dead of their wounds, and four so desperately bruised that they cannot recover. In Friday's tumult, a gentleman had his arm shattered to pieces; and on Saturday three fingers of a boy were cut off. (*Caledonian Mercury*, 10 April 1784)

Fox also fought a fierce campaign, which was overseen by Georgiana, Duchess of Devonshire, who was believed by some to be his mistress. She gained at least one vote for him when she deliberately bribed a shoemaker with a carefully placed kiss.

Two Londoners who might have ascended to a more senior rank in the Royal Navy were Peter and John Butt, the sons of Peter and Grace. Both of them had the Navy in their blood, with their father Clerk of the Survey at Deptford dockyard. As such, the two boys would have regularly witnessed from the windows of the dockyard house that the family occupied the comings and goings of naval vessels. No doubt, it was this that fired them to join the Navy. But life at sea was harsh, even for those of the quarterdeck, and both men died in service before the age of 30. Peter, the eldest of the two, was only 17 when he died of wounds sustained during the Battle of the Saintes (1782). His death, which was long, lingering and painful, occurred some eight weeks after the battle. John, the second son, was drowned while in command of an armed ship in the North Sea in September 1799. With both sons buried at sea, the parents were only able to memorialise their children through inscribed stones placed in the churchyard of St Nicholas', the Deptford parish church.

John Philip Castang, who was mentioned as a volunteer on board the *Sandwich* receiving ship at the Nore in 1793, gained a rather fortuitous appointment. One of the ships seeking crew was *Agamemnon*, commanded by Nelson. Castang was one of those sent over to the *Agamemnon* and, although rated as an able seaman, he was given the much more favoured post of captain's clerk. It is not impossible that Captain Locker, the commander of *Sandwich* and a close friend of Nelson, might already have been asked to identify a possible candidate for this post. Castang came from a successful small-business family and had the necessary reading and writing skills. This appointment proved to be a considerable break for the 25-year-old Philip Castang, as it immediately took him from the crowded and unwholesome lower deck to the quarterdeck and a separate cabin that adjoined the future national hero. Castang was to remain with Nelson for six years, transferring from *Agamemnon* to *Captain* in June 1796 and being raised to the more prestigious post of Captain's Secretary upon Nelson being appointed a Commodore. Finally, as reward for his service to a man who, by that time, had become a household name, Castang was warranted to the office of purser (putting him in charge of supplies carried on board) in July 1797 and appointed to a 14-gun brig sloop. Because of that six-year association with Nelson, it is possible that Castang was present in London for Nelson's funeral, as his ship, by then a 34-gun frigate, was held at Portsmouth for extensive repair work.

As with ratings of the lower deck, the families of the quarterdeck also suffered, but not necessarily to the same extent. In the main, this was because the officers' departure for sea was likely to be planned, allowing time for financial affairs to be arranged and the needs of the family carefully settled. Of course, the level of security might differ according to the status of the officer, with an aristocratic family likely to meet with fewer financial problems than a family being supported by a lowly and unconnected warrant officer. Nevertheless, all on the quarterdeck, regardless of status, were in a position to ensure immediate and regular remission of their Navy pay – if that was required – to a named person on shore.

While a regular income might ease the pain of separation it did not remove the resulting stress. Letter writing was a comfort, given that those of the quarterdeck had a level of literacy that was only occasionally replicated on the lower deck. The frequency of letter writing varied according to the nature of the individual, time available and the possibility of letters reaching their intended recipient. Edward Codrington, one of Nelson's captains at Trafalgar, was a regular letter writer, his wife Jane having remained at their home in Berkeley Square. These letters frequently confirm the pain of separation and the frustration of not being able to instantly communicate, especially when Codrington learnt that his wife had developed an irritating cough. His fear was that she might have developed tuberculosis, the major killing disease of the age, referring to a female acquaintance who had succumbed to the disease, 'though you may be as fat as she is lean, I cannot be quite at ease under such circumstances' (NMM COD 21/1a, 26 May 1809. Re-quoted from Lincoln, 2011, p. 67).

Betsy, the wife of William Bligh, underwent long bouts of unhappiness as a result of her husband's frequent absences, with his sea service taking approximately half their married years. So desperate did she become that she attempted to gain an appointment for him at Greenwich where she hoped he might serve as a captain at the naval hospital. To this end she wrote to Bligh's patron, the scientist Sir Joseph Banks, to see if he could obtain such a position for her husband. Banks, in 1795, certainly wrote to the First Lord, at that time the 2nd Earl Spencer, pointing out that Bligh's health was much in decline, partly through the lengthy open boat voyage after the mutiny on the *Bounty* and also from further sea service in the Pacific and North Sea. However, Spencer declined the request, with Bligh appointed to the 64-gun *Director*, which, under Bligh's command, saw its crew participate in the Nore Mutiny (May–June 1797) followed by her presence at the Battle of Camperdown (October 1797).

Betsy may have found some comfort from seeing her husband during periods when his ship was in one of the home ports. Given that he was temporarily removed from his ship, *Director*, by the Nore mutineers during the early summer of 1797, she had the thrill of his unexpected return home then. But lacking the affluence of an aristocratic family, she was in no position to make her way regularly to the home ports where Bligh's ship might have moored. A similar problem confronted William Wilkinson, a ship's master in the Channel Fleet with a home in Church Street, Kensington. Sally, his wife, frequently indicated in letters her desire to travel to Portsmouth where his ship regularly returned but she also recognised that the costs were prohibitive. Nevertheless, Sally did make several visits to Portsmouth, with one undertaken in 1808 carefully planned out by her husband in a letter that advised her to catch in Kensington a coach that left from Fetter Lane and which would take her to the India Arms in Portsmouth (Lincoln, 2011, p. 122).

In total contrast to Bligh and Wilkinson was Alexander Hood, 1st Viscount Bridport, who had a London house in the highly fashionable Harley Street and a family estate at Cricket St Thomas in Somerset. Brother of Samuel Hood and commander-in-chief of the Channel Fleet from 1795 until 1800, he was able to arrange for his wife to meet with him regularly when the fleet he commanded came into Portsmouth, informing her on one occasion that if she arrived before his ship had returned she was to take accommodation in the Crown Inn. Vice-Admiral Thomas Fremantle, another with a house in London, also arranged for his wife to regularly travel the Portsmouth Road from London but, on one occasion, matters went astray when they passed each other *en route*, Fremantle having taken the mail coach to London while his wife was heading towards Portsmouth. For Jane Codrington, wife of Thomas Fremantle, then a naval captain, at least one journey to meet her husband was simplified as her husband was able to arrange for her to be collected from Chatham by the dockyard commissioner's yacht.

It was the long bouts of separation, accompanied by uncertainty as to when a reunion might occur, that occasionally drove a husband or wife into the arms of another. Most celebrated, of course, is Nelson's affair with Emma Hamilton, with the two living openly together in London. Most chose to avoid such openness, aware that the attitudes of others could seriously damage promotion or standing in society. The young and energetic Augustus Hervey, apart from his affair with an operatic performer, threw himself into a staggeringly large number of illicit relationships. These appear to have been prompted by a lengthy posting to the Caribbean while his wife's 'conduct was not altogether as Vestal like as I would have wished'. Lieutenant George Hayes, upon returning home to Deptford after a year's absence in the Mediterranean had a not dissimilar experience with his wife, finding her not only to have given birth to a child but to be living with the father in Hoxton. Claiming that she had been abducted, for which there was little evidence, she attempted to return to her husband but he rejected her. Instead, he filed for divorce and was eventually awarded this and £400 damages.

Part 4

MERCHANTS, TRADESMEN AND PROFITEERS

Introduction

London's connection with the Navy was all encompassing. It went well beyond the administrators of the sea service, the docks and the victualling yards that lay alongside the Thames, and the many Londoners (by birth or subsequent residence) who had once served or would serve on board a ship of war. The London naval connection also included the City merchants and the many thousands of other Londoners involved in trade. All were inter-connected with the Navy, dependent on the service for the security of existing seaborne trade and for future expansion. Indeed, it would be no exaggeration to say that all in London gained in some way from the wealth that poured into the capital and continued to do so only because of the protecting hand of the Navy and the global reach it had achieved by the end of the Georgian epoch.

For some London merchant traders, of which there were 16,000 listed in the *Universal British Directory* of 1791, this connection was markedly more direct. The Navy had an almost unquenchable appetite for materials, be it for the construction, maintenance and fitting out of warships, or for the basic needs of those who served on board. This trade was immensely lucrative and, despite the dispersal of many of the naval yards away from London, it was very much centred on the capital. With London traders particularly well placed to negotiate contracts at the Navy and Victualling offices, it was an area of business that had produced some of the wealthiest merchants in the City.

While not all London merchants dealt directly with the Navy, many of those who traded were just as dependent on the Navy whether the nation was at peace or at war. If the former, there was the problem of piracy, with the Navy mounting expeditions to eradicate this menace. In 1828, to provide one example, a counter force had to be sent to the coast of South America where privateers under the flags of Buenos Aires, Brazil and Colombia were plundering British ships. In time of war, the Navy was paramount, serving not only as the nation's first line of defence but the force holding open sea lanes, protecting convoys and eliminating the enemy fleets that might otherwise have destroyed London's commercial interests.

While imports always had to cross the sea, much of the nation's domestic trade was also seaborne, with hundreds of coastal vessels running between London and the countless small ports that ringed the British Isles. This was a result of the poor state of roads, with coastal trading vessels providing savings in time and cost. Among the most essential commodities to arrive by sea in London were coal, corn, meal and most basic foods. Should an enemy neutralise the Navy, it could then destroy or prevent the sailing of a large proportion of these vessels, bringing not only foreign trade to a standstill but threatening the very survival of London. To counter such a possibility, it became necessary to restructure the composition of the fleet. Whereas, during the early part of the eighteenth century, the emphasis had been on a fleet primarily composed of the larger warships that could engage other similar ships in battle, the latter years of the century saw the introduction of a greater number of smaller vessels that were deployed in convoy duties and the general protection of merchant shipping.

Although substantial losses of merchant ships were recorded in the various wars of the eighteenth century, the actual numbers were never so great as to seriously threaten the survival of the country or its merchant economy. However, the potential for disaster, should the Navy have failed in the task of keeping the sea lanes open, was clearly demonstrated by the impact of Napoleon's 'Continental System', an economic blockade of Britain that operated between 1806 and 1812. As a result of the ports of the French Empire and its dependencies being closed to British shipping, overseas trade fell from £48 million to less than £35 million. This resulted in the closure of many London businesses, with the shipping industry taking the hardest hit. Making matters even worse was a series of disastrous harvests that led to staggeringly high food prices, bringing the nation to the brink of starvation. Ironically, the Royal Navy also contributed to the crisis, as it was responsible for the loss of the USA as a trading partner; the latter declaring war on Britain in retaliation for the forcible boarding of its vessels by British naval crews who were enforcing a similar blockade against the French Empire. A not dissimilar loss of trade, and probably one much more severe, would undoubtedly have resulted from a failure on the part of the Royal Navy to control the major mercantile sea lanes. This confirmed the essential link between London and its merchant traders.

9

Finance and the City

The close link between the Navy and its various contractors is nowhere better illustrated than the supply of meat. Contracts were generally divided between the supply of livestock that was slaughtered and preserved in London, and cut and salted meat. For several decades the Mellish family held contracts to supply the bulk of the Navy's fresh meat. Given that the contract might require the provision of many thousands of oxen and sheep each, resulting in a turnover in excess of £70,000, this was big business. Despite the contract being subject to open tender, Samuel and Peter Mellish provided the bulk of the Navy's fresh meat during the Seven Years War and the American War of Independence, with a further generation of the family, Peter and William, doing likewise during the period of the French Revolutionary Wars and beyond. In addition, the earlier generation of the family had also managed to extend their dealings with the Victualling Office through the hiring out of ships for the transporting of meat and other comestibles to stations abroad (Knight and Wilcox, 2010, p. 129f and MacDonald, 2006, pp. 56–66).

One advantage possessed by the Mellish family that contributed to their ability to hold on to the lucrative fresh meat contract was that they lived in the metropolis and had good connections with the City. Peter, of the second generation of the family, was liveryman of the Butcher's Company, as was his brother Peter. The latter was also Sheriff from 1798, rising to alderman status. He had a sizeable family residence in Bishopsgate within five minutes' walk of the Victualling Offices alongside the Tower. As for the trade in which the family were primarily engaged, the Mellish dynasty possessed slaughterhouses in Shadwell and on the Isle of Dogs which were used for the slaughter and salting of animals when the Victualling Board facilities were under pressure. The family also acquired interests in shipbuilding through the shipyard of Hill and Mellish on the Isle of Dogs.

As to how the Mellish family could retain the bulk of the fresh meat contracts for such a long period of time, the development of a cosy relationship with the clerks and the officers of the Victualling Board, where they frequently mixed and the clerks took advantage of hospitality from the Mellish family, must have been a factor. A hint of this exists, with William inviting the clerks of the Victualling Office to an annual beef dinner. These clerks were, as MacDonald (2010) shows, also the regular recipients of between two and eight dozen bottles of Madeira or port while Peter Mellish left £500 to 'Richard Harman of the victualling office' in his will. As for the number of times that victualling commissioners, especially those responsible for contracts and the cutting house, attended dinners and other occasions at Peter's Bishopsgate house or a further residence that the family had in Shadwell, that is not recorded.

The contract to supply salted meat to the Navy for the final three decades of the eighteenth century and into the Napoleonic Wars was held by Charles Flower, a man who extended his contracts with the Victualling Board to include the provision of butter and cheese. A resident of London, with a house at Russell Square, it is clear from a leasehold advertisement that he often worked from home, where he retained a suitably equipped office. Through holding East India Company shares and as an insurance underwriter through Lloyd's, he was well connected with the City, so much so that he was elected Lord Mayor in 1808, having served as a sheriff since 1798. It was from Ireland that most of the commodities he supplied to the Victualling Board were drawn, with agents there undertaking the purchase of livestock and overseeing the slaughter, salting and cutting prior to it being transported by sea to London or a designated victualling yard. As with the Mellish family, Flower's ability to retain supply contracts with the Victualling Board over such a long period of time was in part the result of being close to the Board offices in London (Knight and Wilcox, p. 165 and MacDonald, 2006, pp. 65–6).

It was the close relationship with the Navy Board that probably saved Flower from losing his lucrative right to supply salt meat to the yard at Deptford when, in 1794, it was discovered that he was supplying beef of very sub-standard quality. Following the opening of several casks, it was shown that these contained meat adulterated with marrow bone and neck pieces, with the quantities of salt used to preserve the meat being inadequate for the purpose. An entire consignment of 1,268 large casks was returned, with Flower required to replace them with beef of the agreed quality. Despite this clear attempt on the part of Flower to deceive the Victualling Board, he was given a further contract to supply preserved beef only a few months later.

It was probably a series of similar deceptions practised on the Victualling Board and elsewhere that gained Flower a somewhat dubious reputation, with a Rowlandson cartoon of 1809 depicting him as a sunflower growing out of a tub of rancid butter perched on two rounds of mouldy, rotten cheese (MacDonald, 2006, p. 242). This was two years after Flower had claimed to be unable to fulfil a contract with the Victualling Board at the agreed price for supplying 1,000 tons of butter and cheese, claiming that the market price had risen dramatically as a result of a dry summer and the effect of the Continental Blockade. Flower offered to pay the required penalty for cancelling the contract but then entered into a further contract in which the butter and cheese was to be supplied at a higher price. Subsequently the Victualling Board was informed that Flower had, at the time of cancelling the contract, a sufficient quantity of butter and cheese in store, only releasing these to the Victualling Board once the new contract had been signed (Knight and Wilcox, 2010, p. 105).

The Navy Board also came to rely on a restricted number of merchants for the supply of materials for the construction and repair of ships, with timber the most important. Whereas in the early 1770s the Navy Board had divided the supply of English timber, particularly oak, between twenty-eight different contractors, this number was gradually reduced over the following years, with the trade eventually dominated by John Larking. A long-time resident of London, he had at different times houses in Holles and Welbeck streets, each furnished with sufficient office space for his own use and that of a clerk. In addition, he also owned Clare House; a country estate set in its own grounds just outside the village of East Malling in Kent. A trade with enormous potential profits, the timber contract that he had acquired was worth as much as £450,000 in any one single year, so explaining why he could afford the lavishness of both a town house in a fashionable quarter of London combined with a sumptuous country residence. Furthermore, with Larking, who often worked in close relationship with a second City merchant, William Bowsher, having secured his position as the single most important contractor for timber to the Navy, he was able to increase his profits through a virtual dictation of the price that he required for each measured load of timber. St Vincent, while First Lord of the Admiralty, believed the situation to have arisen through the complicity of the Navy Board, suggesting that bribery was the root cause. However, it should also be made clear that Larking, irrespective of any profit motive, would certainly have had to increase his prices as the available stocks of English timber, while diminishing through demand, were often only to be found in more isolated areas that had not previously been harvested, so escalating both felling and transport costs. As for Larking retaining contracts through bribing the commissioners of the Navy Board, this is somewhat more debateable and credence also needs to be given to the interpersonal relationships that developed between the various individuals involved. This is not to say that Larking or Bowsher did not attempt to bring undue influence to bear, with a former Comptroller of the Navy Board, Sir Charles Middleton, declaring to a government commission of inquiry in 1806 that 'several presents were offered' to him by 'persons who were candidates for Navy contracts' but he had always declined such gratuities.

It was the ability of certain contractors to retain their right to supply the Navy over remarkably long periods of time that drew the attention of St Vincent while he was serving as First Lord. Recognising the potential for fraud, his administration oversaw the introduction in 1802 of a commission to 'examine irregularities and abuses' with its third report considering the contract for coopers' wares for the dockyard at Woolwich. At that time the contract was held by two brothers, Michael and John Hedges, with their family having held the same contract since 1714. However, unlike some of the other long-held contracts, there was clear evidence of fraud, with the two brothers found to be claiming for items never delivered and for work not undertaken. As a result of the investigation both brothers received a six-month prison sentence, with the first month of the sentence requiring that they be placed for one hour each day in stocks immediately outside Somerset House.

It was the fact of some merchants holding naval contracts for lengthy periods that led the writer of a history of the naval administration under St Vincent, published in 1827, to conclude:

> the contractors of the Navy Board are one body of men; one favoured corps, unpolluted by the casual admission of any uninitiated competitor. Their contracts are the estates of families. They descend like college leases, from generation to generation; and are more regularly and more beneficially renewed! (Anon, 1827 see Smith, 1927, p. 462)

Of the many hundreds of London merchants who acquired contracts issued by the various civil boards, the majority did so under open competition. Initially, the relevant board invited tenders through the placing of an advertisement in a number of newspapers that included the date by which any submitted tender must be received at the appropriate office. On receipt, each tender, having been placed in a sealed envelope, was placed into a locked box. This was only opened when the deadline had expired with the merchant offering the lowest prices accepted, but only if he was able to prove an ability to supply the merchandise being offered. However, it was also common practice for the Board to look at previous prices for similar contracts with that information used, if appropriate, to force down the price being tendered. Certainly this was the procedure followed in the majority of cases, with rarely a suggestion of favouritism or bribery affecting the final outcome of a bid. However, when it came to some of the larger contracts held over a long period of time, there is every indication of things not being as they ought. One practice described by Knight and Wilcox (2010, p. 44) was to only submit a tender when the box of sealed envelopes had been opened. In November 1810, for instance, Gerald Callaghan, in tendering to the Navy Board, presented his tender only once the 1 p.m. deadline had passed. Presumably it was accompanied by humble apologies, but others had seen him in the vicinity of the Waiting Room set aside for merchant contractors earlier that same morning. For this there can only be one explanation: he was waiting for news of the earlier submitted tenders from a suitably bribed clerk before hastily adjusting his own terms.

The merchants who contracted to the Navy benefited, quite naturally, from the outbreak of war, as this stimulated the demand for the material they supplied. A second group of businessmen who directly benefited from war were the prize agents. A prize was a legitimately captured merchant ship, either owned by the enemy or trading to the advantage of the enemy, which had been taken by a British warship. Once safely brought into port, the vessel and its cargo would be sold and the proceeds distributed between the officers and seamen of all ships involved in the capture. It was the prize agent who undertook the various legal and financial formalities that ensured proper legalisation of the claim, together with subsequent payment of prize money to all those entitled to a share. To this end, the prize agent, or a subagent, immediately took charge of the vessel upon its arrival in a British port, collecting the captured vessel's manifest and copies of the muster lists of all vessels involved in the capture. The manifest was of particular significance in proving the original ownership of the vessel and the port it was sailing for, while the latter was essential for payment of the final prize award, as only those mustered on the day of capture were entitled to money. Any man who deserted immediately forfeited his right to any payment.

Legal formalities for the legitimation of a vessel and its cargo as a prize had to be conducted at an officially designated Admiralty court. A number of Vice-Admiralty courts existed at various ports overseas and in Britain. However, the busiest was the High Court of Admiralty, which sat in Westminster Hall. If nothing else, it was the most convenient court for the majority of prize agents, given that some thirty or more prize agents had their established offices in London. Here, an owner of a captured vessel might make a claim that his vessel was unlawfully seized; particularly a neutral who could provide evidence that the cargo being carried was not destined for an enemy port. Alternatively, a decision might have to be taken as to which vessels were in the area of capture, so leading to an entitlement of further crews to share in the final distribution of prize money. The court had at its head a judge appointed by the Crown with an annual salary that by 1798 had been fixed at £2,500. In addition, there were several other generously rewarded court officials, including the registrar, proctor, marshal and advocate. The existence of so many officials may have been something of a burden on the state, but it also seriously affected the prize sum available, for each was entitled to draw fees out of any awarded prize money in addition to their salary. The prize agents were also entitled to a fee, which was customarily set at 5 per cent of the total prize money allocated. A further tranche from the awarded sum had also to be paid over to the naval hospital at Greenwich.

The fairness of a system that saw men who had risked their lives taking a 'prize' subsequently forfeit so much to those safely ensconced ashore was stridently challenged by Thomas Cochrane in his capacity as an MP for the constituency of Westminster and as a commanding officer while serving in the Mediterranean. In his *Memoirs*, which were first published during the mid-nineteenth century, he went so far as to suggest that the prize agents and court officials entertained just one idea, 'that officers were appointed to ships of war for the sole purpose of enriching them!' In an address to the House of Commons he explained how court officials deliberately inflated the fees they might receive through exaggeration of the work they undertook:

> The most insignificant vessels were condemned [forfeited to the state] at an expense equal to that of the largest, so that the combination of a fishing lugger might be swelled up to the expense of condemning an [East] Indiaman, the labour of capture ending in nothing but putting money into the proctor's pocket. (Cochrane, *Memoirs of a Fighting Captain*, p. 180)

In practical terms, and to ensure that those who benefited from the sale of captured vessels were those most closely involved, he would, while serving in the Mediterranean, arrange to sell any captured vessels himself, often 'to the Spaniards for a trifle'. The sum raised, after Lord Collingwood, his commander-in-chief, had been sent the 'eighth' to which he was entitled, was then divided among the crew. As Cochrane makes clear in his autobiography, had he sent these vessels to the nearest Admiralty court, the heavy bill of costs, mostly in the payment of fees, 'would have greatly exceeded the sums realised by their sale' (Cochrane, 2005, p. 180).

Returning to the prize agents, the profits they made were often quite considerable, with one London firm, Messrs Wills and Waterhouse, in handling work upon 1,400 captured vessels, able to record proceeds of £2.1 million (Green, 1989, p. 103). Apart from the 5 per cent fees that the agents normally charged for their work, they also had numerous additional means by which they could maximise their earnings. A frequent recourse was delaying payment of any awarded prize money. In so doing they took the opportunity of investing it and retaining any accrued profit. Worse still, if the investment failed and the agents actually lost the money, those with entitlements might not be paid at all. In addition, once prize money was released for payment, it was not always satisfactorily advertised, with many seamen and their families unaware of when and where the money could be collected. Of course, any uncollected sums were simply banked by the agents for their own use. Only during the first decade of the nineteenth century were many of these shortcomings corrected, with Parliament introducing laws that required agents to transfer unpaid awards to the Royal Hospital for Seamen at Greenwich and to provide security to the value of £5,000 in the form of bonds lodged with the High Court of Admiralty. A particularly important requirement introduced during this period was that of agents having to make themselves available for the paying of prize money on two days every week with advertisements in the *London Gazette* making it clear which days their offices were open. Only upon the expiration of four months could they close their books, with any unclaimed prize money passed to the Greenwich Hospital. Here, seamen could, for a period of six years, continue to make their claims, it being accepted that some might well have been at sea during the original claim period.

Prize agents, despite their charges and occasional misuse of monies held, were indispensable assets to flag officers, often acting as their bankers and financial advisers. On behalf of those for whom they acted, they would release money in advance in the form of personal loans while offering advice on the investment and use of any prize money. Admiral Collingwood, whose prize agent was Ommaney and Druce and through which his flag 'eighth' for 120 ships taken by captains serving under him had passed, deposited personal items with them including his will (Hilton, 2009, p. 299). Nelson had a particularly close relationship with Alexander Davison, a prize agent whose town house was in St James's Square. It was Davison who Nelson appointed as prize agent for the fleet following the victory at Aboukir Bay, with Davison also taking responsibility for most of Nelson's financial affairs, including purchase of his final home of Merton Place. It was, however, a relationship that extended much further, with the two becoming friends. If nothing else, they met frequently at a social level and, while at sea, Nelson corresponded with Davison, sharing many of his personal thoughts. It was also Davison who served as an intermediary between Nelson and his wife Frances during the highly strained period of Nelson's affair with Lady Hamilton. As with so many prize agents, the handling of money on behalf of naval officers was only one line of work for Davison, as he was also a highly successful government contractor. Whether his transactions with Nelson were fair or otherwise, most certainly his business dealings with the government were not beyond reproach, as Davison was found guilty of fraud in 1809 and sentenced to Newgate Prison for twenty-one months. The potential dangers of a naval officer placing too much trust in a prize agent were demonstrated, albeit in fictional form, by Patrick O'Brian in *Post Captain*. Here, Jack Aubrey falls into serious financial problems due to the misuse of money held by his appointed agent:

Mr. Jackson, his [Captain Aubrey's] prize-agent, one of the most respectable men in the profession had failed. He had bolted, run off to Boulogne with what remained of the firm's cash, and his partner had filed his petition in bankruptcy, with no hope of paying sixpence in the pound.

The outcome was that Aubrey himself had to flee to Boulogne in order to avoid the indignity of being sent to a debtor's prison.

Particularly significant to the City was how merchants who contracted to the Navy were paid. Credit was a long accepted practice in the City and from the outset of the Georgian period it was common for the Navy to meet its debts through the issuing of bills of exchange rather than immediate payments of cash. This was a situation generated by the failure of Parliament to vote sums sufficient to meet the demands of naval expansion but also a product of inadequate levels of taxation. Within Parliament, and ultimately responsible, the elected Members of Parliament neither had an adequate knowledge nor an understanding of the complexities of running a fiscal state, and they seemed unable to match income to expenditure. For the Navy and Victualling boards, bills of exchange effectively bridged the resulting financial shortfall. Indeed, bills of exchange could even be used as money, albeit at a discounted or negotiated rate, for once issued to a merchant who had completed a contractual obligation they could be sold on or exchanged. Of course, the Navy could not continue issuing these bills without some additional money being made available, with large sums intermittently raised by Parliament, either through taxation or secured loans, and credited to the Navy for the purpose of reducing the overall debt.

These naval bills were a considerable boost to the British economy, introducing a negotiable asset that could be quickly turned into cash through onward sale. In this way, and with the Navy's unfunded debt sometimes approaching £10 million, the civil departments of the Navy were pumping quite considerable amounts into the economy, with this in turn encouraging and funding a range of additional entrepreneurial enterprises. Further facilitating the easy exchange of Navy bills was the creation of a separate specialist financial market, consisting of bankers and investors, who were prepared to trade in this commodity, offering discounted rates on purchase.

The need to ensure the financial security of the Navy also gave rise to the Bank of England, a City institution that was first established in 1694. Following a series of naval defeats, it became necessary to rebuild the Navy, a task that required levels of capitalisation that were then simply not available to the government. Instead, and through the establishment of the new bank, a loan of £1.2 million was made available, which was raised by subscription with the subscribers incorporated by the name of the governor and company of the Bank of England (Thornbury, 1878, p. 453). Initially established in the Mercers' Hall, Cheapside, the Bank shortly afterwards moved to Grocers' Hall in Princes Street before a final move to Threadneedle Street in 1734. Here expansion continued throughout the period of the four Georges, with a number of neighbouring properties acquired until the Bank occupied the present-day island site that was provided with a curtain wall in the 1780s.

Through the securing of the national debt by the Bank of England, the Navy was provided with a financial prop that helped overcome an uncertainty as to whether the Navy could meet its debts. City merchants were now more prepared to enter into long-term contracts and accepted payment in the form of navy bills that might otherwise have been rejected as worthless through the likelihood of the government defaulting on payment. With so much additional money flowing into the economy, there was a greater willingness to invest, particularly in areas fulfilling the needs of the military and, in particular, that of the Navy. Once established, these same industries could also meet the needs of other industrial and mercantile enterprises that were expanding to meet newly available trading opportunities resulting from various successful naval exploits.

While some of the new and expanding industries were located within the metropolis, it was the flow of large sums of naval money in and out of the City, often in excess of anything generated by the purely mercantile economy, which was largely driving these changes within the economy. Through much of the infrastructure being already in place, it was simply a matter of ensuring the continuance and efficiency of the system. Among the more essential and previously established institutions that helped facilitate the expansion of trade was the Royal Exchange, on Cornhill, a centre of commerce where finance could be arranged for trading expeditions. However, the coffee house society was a further important venue for discussions, with several of these taking to themselves areas of specialism that facilitated the continuing development of overseas trade. Among them was the Virginia and Baltick Coffee House in Threadneedle Street, the precursor of the Baltic Exchange, which brought together ship owners and those who had cargoes to convey. Those of a naval background also had coffee houses to which they would resort, with clerks and other staff of the Navy Office, when it was located in Crutched Friars, favouring the nearby Mitchell's Coffee House.

It was, however, the Lloyd's Coffee House, which during the early eighteenth century was to be found in Lombard Street, that gained particular fame. Frequented by merchants and ship owners, it was here that reliable shipping news helped financiers determine the risks that might be met in any venture under discussion. In turn, this also attracted underwriters who were interested in insuring ships and the cargoes they carried, a specialist trade that was further expanded when the coffee house, by then managed by a committee of subscribers in 1774, moved into the Royal Exchange. Here, a new coffee house was laid out on the south-east side of the building, having a general room and a more exclusive room that could only be used by the subscribing members. By the end of the eighteenth century Lloyd's had become a major player in the City, handling more than half of the nation's not inconsiderable marine insurance business (Wright and Fayle, 1928, p. 241).

Lloyd's went on to forge a particularly close association with the Navy, supplying the Admiralty with maritime intelligence that included information on ship sailings, developments in foreign ports and the sighting of enemy ships by merchantmen at sea. All of this was possible because many of those who commanded merchant ships would bring either letters from overseas traders or their own observations direct to the coffee house for the attention of the clientele of the coffee house, namely the brokers and underwriters. On one occasion, in February 1740, the coffee house regulars even learned of an important naval victory before the government, with Richard Butler, the then manager of Lloyd's, informing Prime Minister Robert Walpole of Admiral Vernon having taken Porto Bello. *The Gentleman's Magazine* explained:

> This was the first account received thereof, and proving true, Sir Robert was pleased to order him [Richard Baker] a handsome present. Mr. Baker had his letter of advice by the *Titchfield*, Capt. Gardner from Jamaica, who sail'd from thence with the *Triumph*, Capt. Renton, and got to Dover the day before him. (*The Gentleman's Magazine*, March 1740)

The eighteenth century, being dominated by overseas wars, brought mixed blessings for the underwriters at Lloyd's. The loss of large numbers of ships forced numerous subscribers to Lloyd's out of business, although the raising of premiums on those vessels operating in waters commonly frequented by enemy vessels helped offset this particular problem. Indeed, some owners had to pay as much as 20 per cent or more on the amount insured. Conversely, with the potential danger of loss being so great, a large number of ship owners felt forced to take out insurance, so creating a demand for insurance that might not otherwise have existed.

To help mitigate the dangers faced by merchant shipping, the Admiralty introduced the convoy system, collecting together ships bound for similar destinations and providing them with a suitable escort of warships. The Seven Years War in particular saw the development of a finely tuned convoy system for ships crossing the Atlantic to and from North America, Canada and the West Indies, as well as for vessels entering the Baltic, Mediterranean and Indian Ocean. During the Napoleonic Wars, but not until 1798, it became compulsory for all ships to sail in convoy unless specifically declared exempt. In response, Lloyd's would reduce premiums on vessels that sailed under naval protection while naval captains were invited to speak to the subscribing committee about the convoy system and what was expected of those who commanded ships while in convoy. Despite a reduction in insurance premiums and the proven success of the convoy system, some ship owners, prior to it becoming a legal requirement, encouraged those who commanded their ships to break free of the convoy as it approached its destination, with these ships reaping the benefit of being the first to enter port. This was something that underwriters at Lloyd's and the Admiralty attempted to discourage, the possibility of attack being no less when close to port, with a general meeting of the subscribers passing the following resolution in 1794:

> That the committee be requested to take such steps as shall appear to them most effectual for bringing to immediate justice, any captains of merchant vessels who have been, or may hereafter, be represented to them, as having willfully quitted their convoy, or otherwise misconducted themselves while under convoy. (Wright and Fayle, 1928, p. 204)

Without the existence of the Navy, not only would the facilitators of trade have failed to survive but so would the large-scale trading companies that were making a considerable contribution to the wealth of the City. Of these the East India Company was by far the largest and most important. Each year between fifteen to thirty large merchant ships arrived in London carrying on behalf of the Company rich cargoes from the east that included spices, cotton and indigo. However, it was tea from India that the majority of the vessels carried, with this trade alone estimated to be worth somewhere in the region of £1 million per year. The vessels offered rich pickings and consequently were relatively well armed, with many of them carrying, during the late eighteenth century, as many as 30 guns capable of firing 18lb shot. However, despite their size, the Indiamen were at a distinct disadvantage if attacked by an enemy warship of similar size. An attacking warship would carry a great many more guns and a crew greater in number and trained to use those guns to produce a devastating broadside that would quickly force the merchantman into submission. It was therefore imperative that the Navy, during times of war, should escort the East India fleet and so ensure the continuance of this invaluable trade.

While the East India Company had a clear commercial interest, and determined who could and could not trade in Far Eastern waters, this was not the Company's primary task. Instead, the clerks and officials lodged in India House, the Company's administrative centre situated in Leadenhall Street, were primarily involved with the governance of India. Through the collection of taxes and other fees, the Company financed a significant military force that helped ensure its ascendancy over European rivals. Further helping secure the Company's increasing dominance across much of India was it having its own purpose-built warships, primarily quartered in Bombay, from where they could deal with the Red Sea and Indian Ocean pirates. Co-operation with the Royal Navy was, however, essential as the 'Bombay Marine' as it came to be known, was primarily made up of smaller craft that were effective against craft available to the native rulers of India but would be found wanting when coming into conflict with the larger warships of the French, Dutch and Spanish. It was for this reason that the British Navy maintained, for much of the period, an East India Squadron that included a ship of at least 64 guns with additional frigates provided for escorting East India merchantmen convoys. In other circumstances, this might have required the Admiralty to create operational fleet bases, or even overseas dockyards, to support its operations in these waters. However, the East India Company, through its own vast maritime undertakings, possessed maintenance and repair facilities in Bombay and made these available to the Royal Navy.

It was not just the East India Company that came to rely upon the Navy. A large number of trading enterprises were similarly obligated to the Navy, whether their ships were returning with timber, tar and hemp from the Baltic, sugar from the Caribbean or madeira from Portugal. The wars of the eighteenth century put the Navy under considerable strain but one that was bearable through taxation and the raising of loans, to which the increasingly affluent merchant class were able to fully contribute. In this way, the government was able to secure naval expansion and, in so doing, ensured the continued prosperity of British merchant traders wherever they might be operating throughout the world.

Jonas Hanway, a commissioner on the Victualling Board, was one who was fully convinced of the importance of the connection between the increasing prosperity of the City and the strength of the Navy. Addressing himself to Anson, when the latter held the office of First Lord, he noted 'the splendour of this monarchy is supported by commerce and commerce by naval strength' (Lincoln, 2002, p. 78). The Corporation of London also fully realised this connection, choosing to underline the fact in a memorial to the memory of Pitt the Elder, 1st Earl of Chatham. He, as Prime Minister, led Britain during the Seven Years War, a period marked by naval success. Affixed to the wall of the Great Hall within their Guildhall building, the inscription on the memorial makes clear that in this war and as a result of 'decisive victories by sea', the commerce of London was 'made to flourish by war'.

In another way too, the Navy and the merchant marine were totally inseparable and that was with regard to the training of seamen. The Navy looked to the ready-trained merchant seamen to man newly commissioned ships. It was a point often alluded to by merchants when seeking government support or attempting to establish within the mind of the taxpayer the importance of a strong merchant marine. In the words of the affluent London merchant Wyndham Bewes, 'Trade is the nursery of sailors, that sailors are the soul of the Navy, that the Navy is the security of commerce and that these two united produce the riches, power and glory of Great Britain' (Lincoln, 2002, p. 78). However, such sweet talk in peacetime came to nothing upon the actual outbreak of war, the merchant community doing its utmost to hold on to its own trained seamen rather than releasing them to a naval warship or having them taken by the press gang.

The London merchant community, whatever misgivings they might have had about the loss of seamen to the press and the payment of taxes to maintain the strength of the Navy, was nevertheless determined to publicly recognise the sacrifices made by those who served. Lloyd's in particular was noted for its support of naval and military charities, with one of its earliest beneficial subscription lists opened for the widows and children of those who had drowned when the first-rate battleship *Royal George* capsized in 1782. On this occasion over £6,000 was raised from among those who conducted their business within the coffee house. At the outset of the French Revolutionary War, subscriptions were taken at the bar for The United Society for the Relief of Widows and Children of Seamen, Soldiers, Marines and Militiamen, a London-based charity first established in 1792. With the large number of casualties created by the war, the resources available to this Society proved insufficient, leading Lloyd's to establish several independent donation lists, coinciding with news of the larger naval battles that generated particularly large 'butchers' bills' (Wright and Fayle, 1928, p. 226). Following the 'Glorious First of June', Admiral Howe's victory over the French in 1794, £21,282 was raised for the support of the injured and the dependants of those killed while similar well-subscribed subscriptions followed close on the heels of Camperdown (1797), the Nile (1798) and Copenhagen (1801).

It was also Lloyd's that established the Patriotic Fund, a forces' charity that still exists to this day. It differed from the earlier subscription lists created by Lloyd's in that it was not specific to any particular event or battle, with financial support allowed to those either wounded on active service or the wives and children of the men killed. On this occasion, funds accumulated by Lloyd's itself were also transferred into the charity in the form of Consols to the value of £20,000. A further £50,000 was also raised in the first two weeks of the subscription list being opened, with both Charles Flower and John Larking among the recorded subscribers.

The Patriotic Fund, which was managed independently of Lloyd's, was to serve as a magnet drawing in numerous donations from others connected with the City, with merchants, business and professional men taking special pride in the donations they made. Within a few weeks of the Patriotic Fund's announcement, the Bank of England and the East India Company had each given £5,000; the City of London £2,500; the Companies of the Fishmongers, Goldsmiths, Grocers, Merchant Taylors and Skinners £1,000 each; and the Sun Fire Office £2,000, while many theatres also handed over the entire receipts of a night's performance. In granting money to the wounded and giving annuities to the dependants of those killed, the Fund also rewarded those who distinguished themselves through 'exertions of value or merit'. Sometimes this reward came in the form of a piece of plate or a cash sum but a further form of recognition given to naval officers was a presentation sword. These varied in value according to the ornamentation and etchings with which they were adorned, with the swords issued according to rank. Swords valued at £100 were given to commanders and naval captains, those valued at £50 to naval lieutenants and Royal Marine captains, while those of £30 value were awarded to midshipmen, masters' mates and marine lieutenants.

A number of the larger merchant trading companies also erected memorials to naval officers they felt appropriate to commemorate, particularly if they had fought an action in an area of the world in which the company traded. The East India Company raised two statues in Westminster Abbey, one to Admiral Watson, who died in Calcutta after achieving several notable victories in the seas around India, and a second to Captain Edward Cooke who, in 1799, commanded *Sybille* when she captured a French frigate in the Bay of Bengal. Alexander Davison, Nelson's friend and prize agent, was responsible for the creation of a medal commemorating the victory at the Battle of the Nile and the creation of the Nelson Memorial at his estate at Swarland, Northumberland. However, the most famous of all memorials, the monument to Nelson in Trafalgar Square, is post-Georgian, with the complete arrangement not fully completed until 1867 and the unveiling of the Landseer lions. The bronze plinth of the column was supposedly part cast from cannons captured from the French.

10

Cheats and Racketeers

There were other groups of people in London who sought to extract money from sailors, through acts of trickery and deceitfulness. These included the 'bats' or 'ladies of the night', crimps and crimp-house owners, confidence tricksters and organised gangs. In fact, the seaman in returning home to London or remitting money to a dependent had to warily step on a long road that was fraught with many hazards quite as treacherous as anything encountered at sea.

The rolling gait and choice of clothing made a jack tar home from a lengthy voyage easily recognised. Since there was a chance his pockets would brim full with wages following a year or more at sea, he was a target for anyone determined to make a quick buck. The 'bats' of London were especially adept at preying on seamen, aware that a voyage of any length would have denied them the company of a woman. Certainly Bridget King, a barmaid at the Ship and Star in East Smithfield, had little difficulty in taking from Robert Drout, a seaman recently returned to London on the 32-gun frigate *Montreal*, coin to the value of £7. This was on 26 November 1767. Drout had entered the inn hoping to see some of his shipmates, but found no one he knew. Instead, after calling for a pint of ale, he was joined by Bridget King who was already drinking at the bar. Between them they shared some oysters purchased from an oyster woman, with his new female companion going on to enquire of him, 'My dear, will you go with me to my room in the back lane?' In agreeing King asked, 'What will you give me?' To this Drout simply replied, 'I will give you 18*d*.' Having struck an agreement, the two left the Ship and Star and crossed to her nearby room which was lit by a single candle. Taking out his watch, Drout laid it on the table by the bedside but kept his purse and money in his left-hand pocket. With the two now lying next to each other on the bed, Drout felt her hand in his pocket. Carefully removing his purse she pushed herself off the bed while also grabbing the watch on the table and ran out of the door. It was a frequently practised trick and, quite simply, Drout should have known better than to trust such a lady (oldbaileyonline.org t17671209-3).

A not dissimilar experience befell William Michael, an invalided seaman from Yarmouth Hospital, when on 9 October 1800 he entered the Black Dog, in

Drury Lane. Here he was quickly joined by 27-year-old Ann Blake, who invited him back to her nearby lodgings. Here he gave her half a guinea to go out and get something to drink and later a further half guinea to sleep with him. However, due to being in his cups Michael was unable to recall whether she did actually go to bed with him. Sometime around the dead of night he awoke from a deep slumber only to find that not only was the bed empty but that missing from his jacket were 'five half joes, value £8, a bank-note, value £10 and another bank-note, value £5' (oldbaileyonline.org t18001029-5).

Not that these sorry stories always began in a taproom or inn. A drunken seaman on his way home might just as easily be stopped in the street and gently steered in an alternative direction. Such a fate befell James Glass who on the night of 27 June 1765, having just been paid off at Deptford, had round his neck a handkerchief that contained in a carefully tied corner almost 8 guineas. Already he had consumed a great deal of alcohol when he tumbled past Essa Morrison and Barbara Waller seated outside the Red Lion in Bright's Alley (Nightingale Lane). He knew neither of them and was inclined to refuse when they asked him for something to drink. He told them it was rather late but they refused to accept his answer and grabbed hold of his arms. Weakening to their charms (or the effects of his semi-drunken stupor) Glass swore he could get by quite well by himself. Taken by Morrison to her room he asked, 'What should I give you to stay with me all night?' In reply she requested a shilling for herself and a further shilling for her landlady, Barbara Waller, as payment for the bed. 'Yes', he said, 'I will do that.' Lying down on the bed he placed the handkerchief with its money under his head and promptly fell asleep. In the morning, around 4 a.m., he awoke to find his money gone and the handkerchief lying at the foot of the bed (oldbaileyonline.org t17650710-27).

That we know of these three incidents is a result of subsequent arrests and trial at the Old Bailey. In each case, the accused female, together with any accomplices, was sentenced to seven years' transportation. However, these were not isolated cases. The records of the Old Bailey are littered with similar cases that spanned the entire Georgian period. In addition, there were many more seamen who never brought the matter to court. In the incidents described, it had not been too difficult for a charge to be laid as the women concerned used their own lodgings and were locally known. It must be assumed that women more adept in this trade would have created for themselves a degree of anonymity by either working in an area that they were not known or by fleeing to another part of London. Essa Morrison, through her accomplice Barbara Waller, allowed the rumour to spread that she had taken the road to Portsmouth. Her undoing was that she did not leave town and she was shortly after taken while drinking at the Ship in East Smithfield.

Of course, a much simpler way of acquiring the earnings of a newly returned seaman was simply to waylay him on some quiet back street and lay him out cold. Simon Nazaret, a seaman belonging to the naval brig *Friendship*, was robbed of his wages at Deptford in July 1802, having received six £5 notes, three £1 notes and 2 half-guineas. On this occasion no one was brought to justice as it seems that Nazaret, in accusing a waterman and several accomplices of attacking him with sticks and taking his money, may have been mistaken. While there is little doubt that he had been attacked, the waterman was able to produce a good character reference while Nazaret appeared confused as to where he had been attacked, stating it to have been on the north side of the river which he named as Deptford. Given that Deptford is on the south side of the Thames, much of his evidence was considered suspect and a not-guilty verdict saw the waterman set free (oldbaileyonline.org t18020714-49).

Confidence tricksters operating in and around the Navy Pay Office were also adept at getting their hands on money belonging to seamen. Here, methods included the use of forged wills or simple impersonation. In fact, the forging of a will was particularly common. A fairly typical example comes from April 1742, when Robert Rhodes was found guilty of forging the will of John Thompson, a seaman who had died three years earlier on board the 24-gun frigate *Flamborough*. The will, which had been duly proved at the Prerogative Office and apparently signed by Thompson, stated that he gave 'to my Friend, Robert Rhodes, all my Wages, Sum and Sums of Money, Goods, Chattels and Tenements whatsoever as shall be any Way due, owing and belonging to me at the Time of my Decease'. In addition, Thompson apparently declared, 'I give, devise and bequeath the same to my Friend Robert Rhodes aforesaid, and I do hereby nominate and appoint him to be my lawful Executer, revoking all former Wills.'

However, Thompson, who had first joined the Navy in 1737, had made an earlier will naming a certain Mr. Carter as beneficiary, a man to whom he owed a great deal of money. On Carter learning that Thompson had died, he attempted to prove the will in his possession, only to learn that Rhodes had already produced and proved the will made out in his favour. Carter, quite naturally, began a search for Rhodes, soon learning that the Navy Ticket Office had issued tickets to Rhodes on sight of the will, which were delivered to an address in King Street, St Giles. Fearing that they had placed government money in the wrong hands, the Navy Office sanctioned an inquiry. Through questioning a number of individuals who had known Thompson, it became obvious that the signature on the will bore no resemblance to Thompson's real signature, thus helping demonstrate that the will held by Rhodes was a forgery. Following a short appearance at the Old Bailey, Rhodes was sentenced to the 'long drop' (oldbaileyonline.org t17420428-33).

The temptation to forge a seaman's will resulted primarily from those on the lower deck being infrequently paid, with an accumulation of wages mounting up and awaiting collection. Since six months of a wage was always held back until final discharge, there would always be this amount to collect at the very least.

Furthermore, unlike Thompson, very few seamen actually made wills, meaning that a forgery would likely go unchallenged. Although this did not work for him as a defence, Rhodes reminded the court that when seamen did make a will, it was not uncommon for them to make several over time, changing the beneficiary according to the whim of the moment. While Rhodes was brought to justice through a combination of incompetence and ill luck, many similar forgeries went unchallenged, resulting in a great number of wives and children missing out on what rightfully belonged to them.

Impersonation was another frequent trick, often involving a female claiming to be the wife or sister of a deceased seaman. The intention was to collect unclaimed wages from the Navy Pay Office. In December 1743, to provide one example, Christine Squires, although unrelated to Stephen Newen, a midshipman who had died on board *Burford* earlier that same year, claimed not only to be his sister but also his only natural and lawful next of kin. Successfully acquiring letters of administration under the seal of the Prerogative Court of Canterbury she used these to obtain from the Navy Pay Office the sum of £10. However, some months later, the mother of Stephen Newen also appeared at the Pay Office and was surprised to learn that his wages had already been claimed. The resulting inquiry showed that Christine Squires had absolutely no connection with the family and she was therefore arrested. Brought to the Old Bailey, and with no real defence, she was given a relatively light sentence, possibly through being a female and a first-time known offender: she was fined 1s, ordered to serve six months' imprisonment and to stand on the pillory for one hour in the most convenient place near the Navy Office, then in Crutched Friars.

A different form of trickery was employed by Peter Povey, who would approach people coming out of the Navy Pay Office. His favourite targets were elderly women who had just received payment remitted to them by a son or husband serving at sea. With all payments made in cash, it was obvious that a woman leaving the Navy Pay Office might well be carrying something worth stealing. Povey would loiter close to the statue of George III in the forecourt of Somerset House, from where he could see the door leading out of the Pay Office. On seeing a likely victim he would then follow her for a short distance before conducting a simple ruse that would leave the victim with little of their money. We know of at least two such victims, for Povey was brought before the Old Bailey on two separate occasions. He was transported in September 1802 for seven years and then, as a result of committing the same offence upon returning from New South Wales, he was sentenced to be hanged.

Povey's first known victim was Eleanor Coleman, the wife of a seaman serving on board *Excellent*, then in the Mediterranean. She received during the summer of 1798 a remittance letter by which she was to receive at Somerset House £3 1s 6d. William Davis, a clerk in the Bills and Accounts Office, gave her notes to the value of £3. On leaving the office she turned up Exeter Street when Povey tapped her on the shoulder and indicated that Davis had sent him after her as she had £4 more to receive. She said, 'Thank God for it', and went with him to the Baptist Head, Chancery Lane, where he said an agent was to pay her the additional sum. Povey also added that Davis was accustomed to giving out a great many forged bank notes, and as she could not read or write, he would tell her whether the ones she had been given were good or bad. As she took them out of her purse, he snatched them and ran off, confident she would be unable to follow him (oldbaileyonline.org t18020714-49). Eleanor Coleman did catch up with him though, about six months later, in February 1799, when Povey appeared before the magistrates at Bow Street. Eleanor had been alerted to the possibility that the man who had taken her money was appearing on a charge of taking money under false pretenses from Mary Hale, a further victim of his trickery (LMA MJ/SP/1799/02/032).

Depressingly similar was the means by which Povey ensnared his second victim in May 1811, presumably just a few weeks after his return to England from the penal colony of New South Wales. His victim on this occasion was Susannah Mead, an elderly widow who had gone to the Navy Pay Office on 13 May to receive a guinea out of her son's pay. Turning left into the Strand she began to head in the direction of her home in the Broadway, Westminster. Povey, a few steps behind, soon attracted her attention and asked if she had just come from the office of James Lawson, the clerk appointed to pay out money owed to seamen's wives and mothers. On confirming this, he told Mead that he had been sent by Lawson as she was also due for prize money of 30s. He further claimed that Lawson had given him authority to make the payment direct to her then and there. Walking with her as far as Hungerford Market, he asked the widow to wait in the street as he had to get the notes signed. Returning some five minutes later he proffered her two £1 notes. They were, in fact, worthless pieces of paper, but Susannah Mead was unaware of this, not being familiar with the new style paper money. Telling her that he was to exchange the two pound notes given by Lawson for the half-guinea, he snatched it from between her finger and thumb and ran away without even giving her the paper money. Mead quickly returned to Lawson's office where she learnt that she had been duped but was advised to come back the following morning. On doing so, she was surprised to see Povey leaning against the rails, near a statue of King George. 'God bless me,' she said. 'You are the man that robbed me of the half-guinea.' Povey attempted to run but a constable laid hold of him and he was arrested. Charged with grand larceny, a brief trial at the Old Bailey resulted in the Middlesex Jury finding him guilty. With Povey having committed a series of similar offences in 1802, for which he had been sentenced to seven years' transportation, he was sentenced to be hanged (oldbaileyonline.org t18110529-66).

Another risk seamen faced was falling into the hands of a crimp. These were individuals who, through various means, laid hands on experienced seamen in order to sell them to another ship for payment of what was termed 'head money'. A seaman newly discharged from the Navy would be especially prized by a merchant captain in need of extra hands and he would willingly pay the crimp for any men handed over. Of course, crimps did not simply endanger those who had served on the lower deck of a warship; any man thought suitable for sea service was equally endangered. As well as selling men into the merchant service, crimps often had arrangements with lieutenants leading press gangs, with 'head money' also paid. Crimping was technically illegal and certainly despised by the ordinary citizens of London. This was demonstrated by a series of riots that broke out in the mid-1790s. In August 1794 the *Hereford Journal* reported:

> Yesterday [26 August] about one o'clock, in consequence of the unheard-of cruelty exercised by the Crimps on some persons whom they had decoyed, a mob collected opposite a recruiting house, in Stonecutter Street, Fleet Market, and after expressing every mark of indignation against the persons employed in that service, broke open the door which had been locked and bolted on their first appearance and destroyed the windows and part of the furniture. (*Hereford Journal*, 27 August 1794)

Having served justice on one crimping house, the mob attacked several more that same evening, in Bride Lane, Whitcomb Street and Fetter Lane. A year later a further riot broke out, with a mob attacking a crimping house near St George's Field. Some of these rioters also entered Downing Street, breaking windows at No.10; the message being that the Government was not doing enough to close down the numerous London crimping houses.

The normal method used by crimps to lay hold of seamen was to ply them with large amounts of alcohol and then 'encourage' them to sign the necessary papers that would bind them to a particular ship. If alcohol proved ineffective, a captive seaman might be held in chains, with little chance of him gaining his freedom until his signature was acquired. The cause of the riot that broke out in August 1795 was a woman, suspecting that her husband had been taken to a crimping house in Charing Cross, keeping watch on the building:

> Suspecting the crimps had decoyed him, she watched the above house, and by chance, saw her husband chained in the cellar; on endeavouring to alarm the neighbourhood, the Crimps called her in, gave her a guinea and promised to release her husband, she however, doubting the word of wretches of their craft, immediately collected a crowd, who destroyed all the furniture on the premises

and ransacked the cellars where they released two persons who were chained down. (*Hereford Journal*, 27 August 1794)

Numerous examples of crimping appear in the newspapers of the time, including a failed attempt by one crimp to take from a warship in the Nore seven men, some of them Londoners, who were in the process of being transferred to another ship. The crimp claimed to be a lieutenant sent to collect them and he only failed in his mission when the authorised officer appeared. In December 1807, a Greenwich Pensioner was tempted to enter a crimping house in Charing Cross where he remained a few days, being provided with a new coat and watch. Subsequently he was asked to pay a considerable sum to cover the cost of the watch and coat, an indication that crimps, if they could not get money out of seamen through one type of nefarious practice would resort to an alternative (*The Morning Chronicle*, 3 December 1807).

There were a good many ways to dupe a seaman of the lower deck out of his money. As for those of the quarterdeck, they were less susceptible to these dangers, being unlikely to be found in the seedy drinking dens of east London and protected from the crimps around Charing Cross by their 'gentleman' status. If their money was threatened, it was from the horrendous fees and ploys used by the prize agents they employed and the high-class ladies, courtesans and actresses with whom, as with Augustus Hervey, some of them chose to associate. Whatever the cause of a downfall, seamen of any class or background soon learnt that the smile of a well-practised London land shark was likely to place them in as much danger as any meeting they might have with the more toothsome seawater variety.

A Gazetteer and Walking Tour

WESTMINSTER: SIGNIFICANT SITES

Admiralty
Including the three-storey, U-shaped brick building that was completed in 1726 and which I refer to as Wallingford House, this was once the most frequently used term for the building. Nowadays, it is more commonly referred to as the Ripley building, after the architect responsible for its design. Possibly the first purpose-built office building in the country, it accommodated the Board Room, offices and residences. To this was added, in 1788, Admiralty House, a three-storey brick building for exclusive use by the First Lord as his residence. The complex is now part of the Cabinet Office, with Admiralty House, a Grade I listed building, used for various ministerial functions.

Bond Street: 147 New Bond Street
This was the lodgings of Nelson from September 1797 until March 1798. Other lodgings Nelson acquired in the Westminster area include 3 Salisbury Street (1783–84), 3 Lancaster Court, Strand (1784), 10 Marlborough Street (1787), 96 Bond Street (1798), Nerot's Hotel, King Street (1800) and Lothian Hotel (July 1801). Nerot's Hotel in King Street was demolished in the 1830s and replaced by St James' Theatre, which in turn was demolished and replaced in c. 1958 by an office building.

Hanover Lodge, 150 Park Road
A Grade II listed building, the home of Thomas Cochrane, 10th Earl of Dundonald, a significant naval officer and Member of Parliament. Overlooking Regent's Park, Cochrane was in residence here during the years immediately following the Napoleonic Wars but later moved to Queen's Gate, where he died in October 1860.

The Old Palace of Westminster

The meeting place of Lords and Commons up until 1834 when the building was ravaged by fire, with both meeting places destroyed. The naval connection here is quite significant, with matters relating to finance, foreign policy and ultimately the size and function of the Navy debated and agreed. Both chambers had a large sprinkling of naval officers who would contribute. Westminster Hall, the most significant part of the Old Palace to survive the fire, was the home of the Admiralty Court.

Somerset House

A vast quadrangular building that runs alongside the Strand on its north side and Victoria Embankment to the south. A purpose-built office complex, it accommodated, from 1789 until 1832, the officers and clerical staff of the various boards that managed the civil affairs of the Navy. After 1832, the civil affairs of the Navy continued to be centred on Somerset House but under more direct supervision by the Admiralty. On the south side of Somerset House, the now landlocked Watergates once gave direct access to the Thames and Admiralty and Navy board barges passed through them.

Westminster Abbey

Henry Blackwood, who commanded *Euryalus* (74) at Trafalgar, has a wall plaque in the north transept and a further Trafalgar captain, George Johnstone Hope, of *Defence* (74), who died in the Admiralty, is buried in the north-west tower chapel. Others either buried or memorialised in the Abbey are Thomas Cochrane (buried beneath a floor slab in the centre of the nave) and James Cook, the naval captain and explorer (wall plaque in south cloister). In all, the Abbey contains more than thirty memorials to naval officers of the Georgian period while the Abbey Museum has a wax funeral effigy of Nelson.

Whitehall Stairs

Removed on the building of Victoria Embankment, the original location of the Stairs was just south of Pembroke Court and 6 Whitehall Gardens. It was here that members of the Board of Admiralty would board the Admiralty barge.

WESTMINSTER WALK

A number of isolated sites exist in Westminster and these, such as Hanover Lodge, are best looked at independently. However, a compact walk follows the route taken by Nelson's funeral cortege on 9 January 1806, starting at the Admiralty and ending at St Paul's Cathedral. An additional advantage is that this walk takes the same route as the No. 11 bus. Unfortunately, entry into the Admiralty complex is only rarely permitted but the Adam screen and the exterior of Wallingford House and Admiralty House can be readily appreciated from the road. Proceeding north along Whitehall, Trafalgar Square is soon reached. At the time of Nelson's funeral, this was not the open expansive area we see today but a tightly packed intersection of streets emptying out onto what was then Charing Cross. At the time, Whitehall swept neatly round into the Strand but today the route requires a little more care as Northumberland Avenue has to be crossed.

Having entered the Strand, Charing Cross station is soon reached. This was the site of the old Hungerford Market where Susannah Mead was headed when she was tricked into handing over her money to James Povey. A further 600 yards brings us to Somerset House. Feel free to enter the courtyard and explore the building to the south that was once the Navy Office. Entry can be gained through the Seaman's Hall, with some of the small shops (including coffee shops if the mood takes you) and galleries converted from former offices. A stairwell reached through a right-hand corridor (assuming you have entered from the courtyard) leading out of the Seaman's Hall takes you to the elaborate Nelson's staircase, while the opposite corridor connects with the former Pay and Victualling offices. Here are stairs leading to the basement and the barge house. It is possible to exit the building at this point through the old water gate but this now simply brings you on to the Victoria Embankment. Above, and also accessed from the Seaman's Hall, is the terrace that once immediately overlooked the Thames.

Returning to the Strand, while the buildings are mostly of a much later date, it is possible to get a feel for the day of Nelson's funeral. On that occasion, the road was lined with a cordon of soldiers holding back a dense crowd, while wealthier members of society viewed events from either specially erected seating (having purchased tickets) or from windows in the rooms that they had rented for the day. To allow them to attend, the clerks of the naval departments at Somerset House were given a special one-day holiday.

It's about 1 mile from Somerset House to St Paul's Cathedral, but it is served by the No. 11 bus. Further along the Strand a detour can be made at the Aldwych that would take in Covent Garden (a pleasant coffee stop) to view the site of the Theatre Royal (destroyed by fire in 1808 with the site now occupied by the Royal Opera House). This was where, to coincide with Nelson's lying in state at Greenwich, a complimentary interval was inserted into evening performances entitled 'Nelson's Glory'. On reaching Fleet Street, a further short diversion can be taken along Old Bailey to view the courthouse. The present building, dating to 1907, replaced the earlier one on a smaller site. The Old Bailey of Georgian times was where a number of those who attempted to defraud the Navy Pay

Office or those owed money by the Pay Office were sentenced to be executed or transported.

On walking the length of the Strand and Fleet Street into Ludgate Hill, the cathedral becomes readily visible. Although a ticket has to be purchased to view the building, the crypt housing Nelson's coffin and numerous others of the period makes this an interesting final point for this walk.

THE CITY: SIGNIFICANT SITES

Bank of England
Founded in 1694 but moving to its present site in 1734, the Bank of England took responsibility for managing the national debt and proved essential for securing the finances to ensure the continued and remarkable growth of the Navy throughout the Georgian period.

East India House
Situated in Leadenhall Street, East India House was the headquarters of the East India Company, the largest of the Georgian-period trading companies. As completed in 1729, East India House was a five-bayed, three-storey house built on a grand scale.

Guildhall
Situated off Gresham Street, the Guildhall was the administrative centre of the City and where the Corporation met. Built in the fifteenth century, it has a Neo-Gothic grand entrance that was added in 1788. The building contains a memorial to Nelson and an important bust of his likeness that was made after the Battle of the Nile by Anne Seymour Damer. A memorial to William Pitt the Elder (1708–78), who led Britain during the Seven Years War, clearly draws a link between naval successes and the expansion of London's overseas mercantile interest.

Lloyd's Coffee House
Located at 16 Lombard Street from 1691–1785, Lloyd's was the centre of the maritime insurance trade, a role it was able to assume through the specialised provision of shipping information that helped subscribers determine levels of risk.

Mansion House
Completed in 1752 and situated opposite the Bank of England, Mansion House is the official residence of the Lord Mayor of London. Formal banquets to honour leading naval officers were frequently held here, with one of the most

significant taking place soon after the news of Trafalgar, with the room suitably decorated with Nelsonian emblems. The Mansion House was also the City law court and sometimes called upon to force the release of men impressed within the City confines.

Navy Pay Office, Old Broad Street

The Navy Pay Office was apparently created out of three terraced town houses seemingly constructed during the early seventeenth century, of which one was the Falcon Ale House that had been acquired in 1686. The Navy Pay Office moved to Somerset House in 1789.

Old Navy Office

First mentioned in 1649 and rebuilt in 1683, the Old Navy Office stood in Seething Lane, with its main entrance in Crutched Friars. It accommodated the clerical staff and officers of the Navy and the Sick and Hurt boards until the move to Somerset House in 1789.

Royal Exchange

Situated in Cornhill, the central activity of the Royal Exchange was providing a venue for merchants, including those involved in overseas trade, to seek out finance. The success of such ventures was secured by the Navy and its global reach, with the income that flowed into the City allowing further naval expansion. Lloyd's Coffee House was moved into the building from 1774, resulting in the business of mercantile insurance also being centred here. Constructed during the mid-seventeenth century, the Royal Exchange was a large quadrangular building that faced out on to Cornhill.

St Paul's Cathedral

St Paul's Cathedral was the centre for many state occasions, with services frequently held to give thanks for various naval victories. On such occasions the King would also be present. The cathedral is the final resting place of Nelson, with other naval heroes of the age given memorials. Among this latter group are captains who lost their lives in battles conducted by Nelson: Robert Moss, Edward Riou, George Duff, John Cooke and George Blagdon Westcott, together with Richard Burgess (who died at the Battle of Camperdown). In addition, there is a memorial to Edward Codrington and the tomb of William Carnegie, the Earl of Northesk, two Trafalgar captains who went on to achieve further success during the period of the French wars. St Paul's also contains memorials to the most celebrated admirals of the period, namely George Rodney (1st Baron Rodney), Richard Howe (1st Earl Howe), John Jervis (1st Earl of St Vincent) and Adam Duncan (1st Viscount Duncan).

CITY OF LONDON WALK

For purposes of accuracy, this walk should really begin at St Paul's given that the cathedral lies within the City of London. Assuming that this has been included as part of the Westminster walk, then a much better starting point is the Museum of London in the Barbican or (if time does not permit) the Guildhall. The museum has a themed room dedicated to Georgian London while material is also displayed on many of the buildings and structures included in the City of London Walk. The Guildhall, which is in Gresham Street, is only a short distance from the Museum of London and can be approached by turning left out of the street entrance to the museum into St Martin's Le Grand, with Gresham Street the first turning to the left.

Access to the Guildhall Art Gallery is free and several paintings depicting Georgian London are on display but not, alas, the bust of Nelson made for the Corporation by Anne Seymour Damer, which is currently held in store. However, within the medieval Great Hall, which is open to the public when there is no event in progress, the memorial to Nelson by James Smith erected in 1811 is open to view. Despite being subject to much criticism for its over use of symbolism, this particular memorial serves as a useful demonstration of the then current need for the City and its merchants to venerate the British Navy. Depicted on the memorial is a large figure of Neptune who faces Britannia with the diminutive figure of Nelson appearing on a medallion. An additional female figure, representing the City of London and its merchants, is caught in the act of writing 'Nile, Copenhagen, Trafalgar' with a bas relief of the Battle of Trafalgar being watched over by a group of seamen. Also in the Great Hall are memorials to Pitt the Elder and Pitt the Younger, two important wartime Prime Ministers. In addition, a part of the Guildhall approached via Aldermanbury Street houses the Museum of the Worshipful Company of Clockmakers, for which entry is also free. It houses the oldest dedicated selection of clocks and watches in the world, of which the most important are marine time pieces. Included are a silver deck watch by Thomas Earnshaw (used by the British naval officer, George Vancouver, during the expedition of 1791–95 that explored and charted North America's north-western Pacific Coast regions) and a John Harrison timekeeper submitted to the Admiralty in 1770.

Continuing along to the end of Gresham Street and across Princes Street into Lothbury, the next turning on the right is Bartholomew Lane. Since crossing Princes Street, the large building of the right has been the Bank of England. Midway along Bartholomew Lane is the entrance to the Bank of England Museum (open Monday to Friday, 10 a.m. to 5 p.m.). Here the general history of the museum is reviewed with a number of prints and paintings that provide a clear impression of the building and its interior during the Georgian era. Little, however, is made of its connection with the Navy other than a display of four letters of attorney signed by Nelson, one with his right hand and the other three showing his signature written with his left hand following the loss of his right arm in 1797.

Turning right out of the museum and continuing along Bartholomew Lane, it is necessary to turn into Threadneedle Street, with the Royal Exchange immediately opposite. We will return to that building later. In the meantime, the road next left is Old Broad Street, in which was once located the Old Navy Pay Office. This was at the north-west end on the corner with Old Winchester Street, the site now occupied by offices and part of the City of London Club. A return to the Royal Exchange is now useful as the area in front of the building has a helpful orientation board that highlights the position of Mansion House and Lombard Street. Head over to the Mansion House and then into Lombard Street (note that shortly after the beginning of Lombard Street it takes a sharp turn to the left) and follow it as far as Abchurch Street (on the right). Here, was Lloyd's Coffee House, now recorded by a plaque mounted on the wall of a much more recent building that now serves as a supermarket. Returning to the Royal Exchange, it is time to enter this building, the third to be built on this site. The one in existence during the eighteenth century had been built during the late 1660s following the destruction of the earlier building, which was destroyed by fire. However, the second Royal Exchange was itself destroyed by fire in 1838, with the present building, the third Royal Exchange, opened in 1844 and now serving as an up-market shopping centre and so free to enter.

Having walked to the far end of the Royal Exchange, take the exit to the right, which leads into Cornhill, and follow the length of Cornhill until Gracechurch Street at the far end. Turn right into Gracechurch Street and after a very short distance the entrance to Leadenhall Market (on the left) will be reached. This was one of the London meat markets used by the Victualling Board for acquiring fresh meat. It was first established in the fourteenth century, although what you see today is a Victorian reconstruction. Walk through Leadenhall Market and take the exit on the left, which will bring you into Leadenhall Street. Taking a right turn, continue until the Lloyd's building (on the right) is reached. The earliest part of this complex structure (overshadowed by the more recent tower) stands on the former site of East India House with that particular building having been demolished in 1861 when some of its fittings and furnishings were moved to India House (located at Aldwych). Within the tower of the Lloyd's building, and helping maintain the connection with the earlier Coffee House, is a collection of Nelson memorabilia (including silverware, plates, letters and an important painting by Lemuel Abbott). Also within the Lloyd's building is the famous Lutine Bell, which was recovered from the British warship *Lutine* that had sunk in October 1799 while carrying a large cargo of gold insured by Lloyd's. The bell, at one time rung to indicate a ship overdue, is rarely heard today. Tours of the Lloyd's building are possible but are restricted and need to be arranged in advance.

Continue along Leadenhall Street; turn into Fenchurch Street until Mark Lane and upon entering Mark Lane walk as far as Hart Street. Continue for a short distance along Hart Street before turning right into Seething Lane. Here, at the junction of Hart Street and Seething Lane, is St Olave's, the parish church of those who resided in the Navy Office, with Pepys apparently using the churchyard as a short cut to and from the Old Navy Office. Enter the churchyard (which is usually open during week days) and head towards the porch of the church. Immediately next to the porch is a blocked entrance to the church that gave members of the Navy Board direct access to the Navy Office pew that was reserved for their use in the church. If entry can be gained into the church, then take the opportunity to view several fine monuments, including a bewigged bust of Pepys and a monument to Sir Andrew Riccard, a one-time chairman of the East India Company. Further along Seething Lane is a blue plaque and a bust of Samuel Pepys, in Seething Lane Garden, which identifies this as the 'Site of the Navy Office in which Samuel Pepys lived and worked'. Nearby, also, was Mitchell's Coffee House, a frequently used venue by the clerks employed in the Old Navy Office.

To end this walk, the Tower of London is close by, reached by way of Muscovy Street (which is at the opposite end of Seething Lane from Hart Street) and then continuing into Trinity Square, where the Tower is clearly visible. From here, the opportunity might be taken to enter the Tower (used at one time by the Victualling Office) or, as a cheaper option, to view the former site of the Victualling Office (Royal Mint Court) on nearby Tower Hill and explore St Katherine Docks.

Should it be necessary to return to Mansion House or St Paul's Cathedral, a No.15 bus can be taken, or a No.100 from the nearby Minories will return you to the Museum of London.

LONDON TO THE EAST: SIGNIFICANT SITES

Blackwall

An area noted for the construction of merchant ships and warships for the Royal Navy, much of the original Blackwall Yard has seen extensive development, although a dry dock, refurbished in 1991–92, is extant.

Deptford

The naval dockyard, which closed in 1869, retains little of the original Georgian yard above ground other than the early eighteenth-century Master Shipwright's house. Subject to significant future development, an extensive archaeological survey is examining the remains of many of the Georgian features of the yard that have long been buried. Of the victualling yard, now mainly covered by a housing estate, only the gateway and colonnade (1768), Georgian terrace, rum warehouses (1781–89) and superintendent's house survive.

Greenwich

The buildings of the National Maritime Museum formerly served as Greenwich Hospital Schools, with the museum possessing a number of exhibits that directly relate to London and the Georgian Navy. In particular, contemporary models and plans of Deptford and Woolwich dockyards are on display, together with the ship models that were once displayed in the Navy Office museum at Somerset House. In Greenwich Park, looking down over the museum is the Royal Observatory and a fine collection of Harrison clocks, while opposite the main entrance to the museum is the former Royal Hospital for Seamen. This, in outward appearance, has changed little from the reign of George III. The Painted Hall contains modern-day memorials to Nelson and Collingwood and was where Nelson's body was viewed in the days immediately before his state funeral. A bust and memorial to Vice-Admiral Sir Thomas Masterman Hardy, Nelson's former flag captain and a former governor of the hospital, is located in the entrance foyer to the chapel.

Isle of Dogs

While shipyards once existed on the Isle of Dogs, it is the East India Docks that came to dominate the area, with the three original docks and a storehouse range still extant. Here also is the Museum of London Docklands, which highlights a number of the building yards on the east side of London and the growth of London's international trading links during the Georgian era.

Rotherhithe

The riverside area was once home to a number of shipbuilding yards with Greenland Dock a particularly important survivor from the eighteenth century. Nelson House (no connection with the Trafalgar victor), a Grade II listed building, possibly built for one of the owners of a shipbuilding yard, is located on Rotherhithe Street (No.265), while Bermondsey Wall East is the location of The Angel, a public house which, during the Georgian era, was frequented by seamen and therefore a target of the press gangs. Supposedly, Captain Cook drank here while planning his exploratory cruises to the Pacific.

Woolwich

The dockyard, in common with that at Deptford, was closed in 1869 with the Georgian area of the yard now council owned and possessing a mix of housing and community facilities. Several original buildings have been retained but the two dry docks to the east both date to 1843. Outside the area of the Georgian yard, on a site to the immediate west, is the steam yard that had been planned in the late 1820s which retains a number of original buildings. A cast-iron framed smithy, used for the manufacture of anchors and which once existed in the Georgian yard following dismantlement, was taken to the Ironbridge Gorge Museum where it has been re-erected on the Blists Hill site, while at Chatham the covering to a former Woolwich building slip can be found and is to be converted into a shopping mall. Much of the Arsenal complex is open to the public, with orientation boards helping identify the original purpose of many of the buildings. The site also houses two museums, one a local museum that looks at the work of the Arsenal and the dockyard, and the second is Firepower, which tells the story of the Royal Regiment of Artillery and the Arsenal.

LONDON TO THE EAST: WALK

London to the east has a significant number of sites connected with the Georgian Navy, with the Isle of Dogs, Greenwich and Woolwich (all easily reached by rail or river bus) offering a range of museums and sites that are best reserved for a planned series of days rather than a walk. However, Rotherhithe, much of which borders Limehouse Reach, is ideal for perambulation as markers for a riverside walk allow for frequent views across the Thames in an area that was once dominated by a number of shipbuilding yards involved in warship construction. Although this particular walk could extend along the river to Deptford and the few remaining buildings of the victualling yard, the walk here described extends from The Angel on Bermondsey Wall East and follows the riverside walk as far as Greenland Dock.

The easiest way of finding The Angel is from either Canada Water or Rotherhithe stations, following the signs for the Brunel Museum. This will bring you to Rotherhithe Street and a view of the Thames; at this point a left turn to the end of Rotherhithe Street will bring you to The Angel. Although the building itself is quite old, it is not the original Georgian building, having been rebuilt *c.* 1837. Presumably, as well as meeting the needs of numerous thirsty seamen, the inn also served the shipyard artisans and labourers who lived and worked close by. From the adjoining King's Stairs, an excellent view of the Thames is possible. This is the middle section of the route taken in January 1806 by the barge carrying Nelson's coffin. Also to be seen in the distance is St Paul's Cathedral, the ultimate destination of the coffin.

From The Angel, head east into Rotherhithe Street and back towards the Brunel Museum. Here, as with the rest of the route, it is simply a matter of following the riverside walk signs as they follow either the right bank of the Thames or skirt round former warehouses (now mostly converted into fashionable residences). Before reaching the museum, St Mary's church will be passed on the right. Should the building be open, then it is certainly worth a visit, as it contains a memorial to Joseph Wade who was employed during the 1730s at Woolwich and Deptford naval yards as a 'carver'. Quite simply, this meant he was employed on carving the numerous fine figureheads that adorned ships launched in these two yards during that period. In addition, the church also has furnishings made from timbers of the Trafalgar veteran *Temeraire*, a 74-gun warship broken up at Rotherhithe.

The Brunel Museum (open daily 10 a.m. to 4 p.m.), which stands on the site of the Thames Tunnel (opened in 1843), has a connection with the Georgian Navy, as the man who conceived the project was Marc Brunel, a French émigré and father of Isambard Kingdom Brunel. Closely associated with the naval dockyards, Marc Brunel oversaw, during the Napoleonic War period, the construction of machinery of revolutionary importance at Portsmouth and Chatham.

Continuing to follow the river path to the Surrey Lock, we come to John Beatson's shipbreaking yard (where *Temeraire* was taken to pieces) with the lock possibly formed out of the dry dock that was once part of the yard. It is this stretch of the river path, as it leads on to Pageant Stairs, that was particularly dominated by yards engaged in the construction of warships during the Georgian era. Just beyond the Surrey Lock for instance, is the King and Queen Stairs where the Woolcombe and Mestaer yards were located, separated only by a small timber and boat yard. With both yards backing onto Rotherhithe Street, those employed in the two yards were usually to be found living in a number of small, timber houses that lined that thoroughfare and the once close Charlotte Row.

By now the river has turned south to form Limehouse Reach with the Isle of Dogs (once occupied by the East India Docks and several other shipbuilding yards including those of Batson, Hill and Cox) clearly visible on the left bank. Possibly the best way of appreciating the view is by way of taking a tea break at the small riverside restaurant managed by Surrey Docks City Farm which overlooks Limehouse Reach. The wider area once occupied by the Surrey Docks which lies on the landward side of the restaurant once housed the bakery facilities of the Victualling Board. Much of this was destroyed by fire in 1747.

Continuing along the river path, the signs will take you out on to Rotherhithe Street before rounding Nelson House and returning to the river bank through land occupied by the Hilton Hotel. This area was once the domain of Randall and Brent shipbuilding yards.

A 12-pounder gun on a naval carriage will be seen as the Greenland Dock is approached, with the area of the land at the riverside entrance to the lock on the north and south sides having once been occupied by shipbuilding yards owned by Randall and Brent. As for Randall Rents, the passageway traversed immediately before reaching Greenland Dock was, during the eighteenth century, packed with small houses occupied by those who worked in these two yards. Looking further along the right bank of the river, albeit some distance away, can be seen the location of the former Deptford naval dockyard, easily visible by the huge covered sheds, these reshaped in the late nineteenth century and once used to build ships under cover. As for the Greenland Dock, which at one time provided safe moorings for more than 300 merchant ships and which was a frequent target for the press gang, the sheer immensity of trapped water within the dock can best be appreciated from the observation platform at the far end of the lock.

With the walk now complete, the easiest option for a quick return to the centre of London is taking the river bus from the Greenland Dock pier; alternatively the No. 381 bus runs every ten minutes from a stop in nearby Redriff Road.

LONDON: OTHER SIGNIFICANT SITES

Chelsea

Royal Hospital in Royal Hospital Road was a chain in the optical telegraphic line connecting the Admiralty to the outports, with a weather-boarded, timber-framed hut erected on the roof of the east wing. As it was necessary to split the line to Portsmouth and Yarmouth at this point, from 1808 there were two shutter devices erected on the hospital roof and angled differently. The nearby Royal Military Asylum (later the Duke of York's School and now the Saatchi Gallery) formed part of the later semaphore system. Not built until 1801, it had been unavailable for earlier use but was positioned to carry messages to Portsmouth, with the necessary semaphore machinery installed on the roof in 1822.

Lambeth

No. 36 West Square, close to the Imperial War Museum, was the first building in the optical telegraphic system chain between the Admiralty and the outports, using the shutter and the later semaphore. Construction of the house was completed by 1794, with the Admiralty acquiring it shortly after, with the shutter device placed on the roof in 1795. Subsequent construction of the nearby Bethlem Hospital (now the Imperial War Museum), through its height, threatened to break line of sight with the Admiralty, so necessitating the addition of a three-storey, wooden tower on the roof of the house upon which the shutter was placed. In 1816 the shutter system was removed and replaced by the new semaphore, with this continuing in operation until 1846. Durham Place, a group of houses completed in the 1780s, later housed William Bligh, the *Bounty* captain, and is now 100 Lambeth Road. Damaged by bombing during the Second World War, it has since been restored, with the owners claiming it to have a 'quirky ship at sea feeling'. It is now a guesthouse. Bligh and his wife Betsy are buried in a family plot in the church grounds of nearby St Mary's, now the Garden Museum; the tomb is topped by a breadfruit and suitably inscribed.

Author-Led walks

If you would like to take one of these walks with the author, or tailor something to your needs, then contact me through my website: www.philipmacdougallbooks. co.uk.

Bibliography

PRIMARY SOURCES

British Library (BL)

Add Ms 41,368-41,400   Papers of Sir T. Byam Martin

Crace Collection Crace Collection of Maps of London

Kings 43: 'A Survey and Description of the principal Harbours with their accommodations and conveniences for erecting, mooring, securing and refitting the Navy Royall of England ... illustrated by general plans and proper views or prospects of each place ... with an account of the improvements which have been made at each yard since the Revolution 1688', drawn up in 1698. The views are neatly drawn, and many of the plans are on a large scale.

Kings 44: A SUPPLEMENT to the book in His Majesty's. possession which containeth a Survey of all His. Majesty's Dock yards with the buildings &c. therein. taken in the year 1698 illustrated by. plans showing the state of each yard at the three several.

Report, Commissioners on Management of H.M. Dockyards (1847), appendix 16, pp. 485-90

British Library Newspaper Library

Caledonian Mercury
The London Gazette
The Morning Chronicle
The Morning Post
Oxford Journal
The Times

London Metropolitan Archives (LMA)
Bow Street Magistrate Court Records
Trial of Peter Povey, 1799: MJ/SP/1/1799/02/0321

The National Archives (Kew), TNA

ADM1/3462	Internal Admiralty Correspondence, 1822–23
ADM1/3477	Paper relating to the re-organisation of the Navy Board
ADM1/3685	Letters from the Solicitor of the Admiralty and other Crown legal officers
ADM1/5660	Report of a Committee of Enquiry into the Office of Secretary
ADM3/34	Board's minutes, 1722–23
ADM3/61	Board's minutes, 1749–50
ADM3/256	Admiralty, Special Minutes, 1805–08
ADM7/659	Visitation to dockyards, 1771
ADM7/660-2	Visitation to dockyards, 1773–75
ADM7/663	Visitation to dockyards, 1801
ADM7/665	Visitation to dockyards, 1828
ADM106/1185-1300	Navy Board in-letters
ADM106/2622	Navy Board Minutes, 1786
ADM 110/52	Navy Board: Victualling Office: Out-letters, 1804–05
PC2/197	Records of the Privy Council, 1815

National Maritime Museum (NMM)

ADM B series	Letters from Navy Board to Admiralty
NMM POR/F/7	Portsmouth Dockyard Records, 1746

Parliamentary Papers
Report of the Commissioners Appointed to Enquire into the Fees, Gratuities, Perquisites and Emoluments … Admiralty (3rd Report), Treasurer of the Navy (4th), Navy Board (5th), Dockyards (6th), Sick and Hurt Office (7th), Victualling Office (8th and 10th), Transport Board (13th) and Victualling Yards (11th), 1785–1801

Books (Published)
Anon, *The Laws, ordinances, and institutions of the Admiralty of Great* …,Vol. 2 (London, 1746)

Anon, *Memoirs of the Administration of the Board of Admiralty under the Presidency of the Earl St Vincent* (London, 1827) in Smith (1927)

Banbury, Philip, *Shipbuilders of the Thames and Medway* (David & Charles, 1971)

Barrow, John, *An Auto-Biographical Memoir of Sir John Barrow, Bart, Late of the Admiralty: Including Reflections, Observations, and Reminiscences at Home and Abroad, from Early Life to Advanced Age*; Murray, 1847 (reissued by Cambridge University Press, 2009)

Baugh, Daniel, *British Naval Administration in the Age of Walpole* (Princeton University Press, 1965)

Baugh, Daniel, *Naval Administration 1715–50* (Naval Records Society, 1977)

Betts, Jonathan, et al., *Royal Observatory at Greenwich: Souvenir Guide* (NMM Enterprises, 2012)

Bonner-Smith, David, *The Letters of Lord St Vincent*, Vol. II (NRS, 1927)

Brenton, Edward Pelham, *Life and Correspondence of John, Earl of St Vincent, G.C.B., Admiral of the Fleet* (London, 1838)

Briggs, John H., Naval Administrations (London, 1897)

Bromley, J.S. (ed.), *Manning Pamphlets, 1693–1893* (Navy Records Society, 1974)

Burford, Beverley and Watson, Julian (eds), *Aspects of the Arsenal: The Royal Arsenal Woolwich* (Greenwich Borough Museum, 1997)

Cilcennin, Viscount, *Admiralty House* (Country Life, 1960)

Cochrane, Thomas, 10th of Dundonald, *Memoirs of a Fighting Captain: Admiral Lord Cochrane, Admiral of the Red, Rear Admiral of the Fleet* (Folio Book Society, 2004)

Collinge, J.M., *Navy Board Officials 1660–1832* (University of London, 1978)

Colquhoun, Patrick, *Treatise on the Police of the Metropolis*, 6th edn (1800)

Fielding, Henry, *The London and Westminster Guide* (London, 1768)

Gill, Conrad, *The Naval Mutinies of 1797* (Manchester University Press, 1913)

Green, Geoffrey L., *The Royal Navy and Anglo-Jewry 1740–1820* (Geoffrey Green, 1989)

Grainger, Ian and Phillpotts, Christopher, *The Royal Navy Victualling Yard, East Smithfield, London* (Museum of London Archaeology, 2010)

Hamilton, R. Vesey, *Naval Administration* (London, 1896)

Heard, Kieron, *Investigating the Maritime History of Rotherhithe* (Museum of London Archaeology)

Hervey, Augustus John, 3rd Earl of Bristol, *Augustus Hervey's Journal* (William Kimber, 1953)

Humphrey, Stephen, *The Story of Rotherhithe* (London Borough of Southwark, 1997)

Kriegstein, Arnold and Henry, *17th and 18th Century Ship Models from the Kriegstein Collection* (Sea Watch Books, USA, 2010)

Hogg, O.F.G., *The Royal Arsenal: Its Background, Origin and Subsequent History*, Vols 1 and 2 (OUP, 1963)

Jennings, J.L., *The Correspondence and Diaries of John Wilson Croker*, 3 vols (London, 18848–5)

Knight, Roger and Wilcox, Martin, *Sustaining the Fleet, 1793–1815: War, the British Navy and the Contractor State* (Boydell, 2010)

Land, Isaac, *War, Nationalism, and the British Sailor, 1750–1850* (Palgrave Macmillan, 2009)

Lavery, Brian, *The Ship of the Line: Design, Construction, and Fittings* (Naval Institute Press, 1984)

Lincoln, Margarette, *Representing the Royal Navy* (Ashgate Publishing, 2002)

Lincoln, Margarette, *Naval Wives and Mistresses* (The History Press, 2011)

Lloyd, Christopher, *Captain Marryat and the Old Navy* (Longman, 1939)

Lloyd, Christopher, *The Nation and the Navy* (Cresset Press, 1965)

McClean, Alistair, *Captain Cook* (Harper Collins, 1972)

MacDonald, Janet, *Feeding Nelson's Navy* (Chatham Publishing, 2006)

MacDougall, Philip, *Royal Dockyards* (David & Charles, 1982)

Maitland, William, *History of London* (London, 1784)

Marsden, William, *A Brief Memoir of the Life and Writings of the Late William Marsden* (London, 1838)

Masters, Roy, *The Royal Arsenal, Woolwich* (Alan Sutton, 1995)

Moorhouse, E. Hallam, *Nelson in England: A Domestic Chronicle* (E.P. Dutton, 1913)

Pack, A.J., *The Man Who Burned the White House: Admiral of the Fleet Sir George Cockburn 1772–1853* (Maritime, 1987)

Parkinson, C. Northcote, *Trade in the Eastern Seas* (George Allen & Unwin, 1937)

Pocock, Tom, *The Sailor King: Life of William IV* (Sinclair-Stevenson, 1991)

Pope, Dudley, *Life in Nelson's Navy* (George Allen & Unwin, 1981)

Pope, Dudley, *At 12 Mr Byng was Shot* (Secker and Warburg, 1987)

Rennie, John, *Treatise on Harbours* (London, 1851)

Robinson, William, *Jack Nastyface* (Wayland, 1973)

Rodger, N.A.M., *The Admiralty* (Terence Dalton, 1979)

Rodger, N.A.M., *The Insatiable Earl: A Life of John Montagu, 4th Earl of Sandwich* (Norton and Company, 1994)

Rodger, N.A.M., *The Command of the Ocean: A Naval History of Britain 1649–1815* (Penguin, 2006)

Roberts, David H. (ed. and trans.), *18th Century Shipbuilding: Remarks on the Navies of the English and Dutch by Blaise Ollivier* (Jean Boudriot Publications, 1992)

Rogers, Nicholas, *The Press Gang: Naval Impressment and Its Opponents in Georgian Britain* (Continuum, 2007)

Silliman, Benjamin, *A Journal of Travels in England, Holland and Scotland*, Vol. 1 (New York, 1801)

Southey, Robert, *The British Admirals: With an Introductory View of the Naval …*, Vol. 4 (1833)

Tucker, Jedediah Stephens, *Admiral the Right Hon The Earl of St Vincent GCB &C. Memoirs*, Vol. II (London, 1844)

Wade, J., *The Extraordinary Black Book: An Exposition of Abuses in Church and State, Courts of Law* (London, 1832)

Wright, Charles and Fayle, C. Ernest, *A history of Lloyd's from founding Lloyd's Coffee House to Present day* (Macmillan, 1928)

van der Merwe, Pieter, *A Refuge for All* (National Maritime Museum, 1994 and 2010)

Periodicals and Short Articles

Doe, Helen, 'Thames Shipbuilders in the Napoleonic Wars' in Conference Proceedings of 3rd Thames Shipbuilders Conference, Greenwich (August, 2006)

Hilton, J. David, 'An Admiral and his Money: Collingwood' in *Mariner's Mirror*, Vol. 95 (2009), pp. 3, 296–300

Hussey, C., 'The Admiralty Building Whitehall' in *Country Life*, 17 November 1923, p. 687

MacDougall, Philip, 'Royal Dockyards of Woolwich and Deptford' in R.J.M. Carr, *Docklands* (North East London Polytechnic 1986), pp. 111–26

MacDougall, Philip, 'The Woolwich Steamyard' in *Mariner's Mirror*, Vol. 85:2 (1999), pp. 172–81

Morriss, Roger, 'Promise of Power, the British Maritime Economy and the State in the Eighteenth Century' in *Transactions of the Naval Dockyards Society*, Vol. 7 (2011), pp. 49–56

Murray, Sir Oswyn A.R., 'The Admiralty' in *Mariner's Mirror* (1938) XXIV, 333

Thornbury, Walter, 'The Bank of England' in *Old and New London*, Vol. 1 (1878)

Fiction

Forester, C.S., *Hornblower and the Atropos* (1953)

Marryat, Frederick, *Poor Jack* (various dates)

O'Brian, Patrick, *Post Captain* (HarperCollins, 1972)

Pope, Dudley, *Ramage and the Freebooter* (1977)

Smollett, Tobias, *The Expedition of Humphry Clinker* (Oxford World Classics, 2009)

Unpublished

MacDonald, Janet Winifred, *The Victualling Board 1793–1815: A Study of Management Competence* (Kings College, London, PhD thesis 2010)

MacDougall, Philip, *From Somerset House to Whitehall: Reforming the Civil Departments of the Navy 1830–34* (University of Kent, Canterbury, PhD thesis 1995)

Electronic Sources

http://www.british-history.ac.uk/report. Survey of London: Vol. 16: St Martin-in-the-Fields I: Charing Cross (1935)

http://www.british-history.ac.uk/report.aspx?compid=45058 'The Bank of England', Old and New London: Vol. 1 (1878)

www.jjhc.info/marshgeorge1800diary.htm. Diary of George Marsh, Commissioner of the Navy

www.oldbaileyonline.org Proceedings of the Old Bailey: London Central Criminal Court, 1674–1913

Index